Lady
HESTER
STANHOPE

LADY
HESTER
STANHOPE

The Unconventional Life of the
'QUEEN OF THE DESERT'

JOAN HASLIP

SUTTON PUBLISHING

This book was first published by
R. Cobden-Sanderson Ltd, 1934

This edition first published in 2006 by
Sutton Publishing Limited · Phoenix Mill
Thrupp · Stroud · Gloucestershire · GL5 2BU

British Library Cataloguing in Publication Data
A catalogue record for this book is available from the British
Library.

ISBN 0 7509 4337 8

Printed and bound in Great Britain by
J.H. Haynes & Co. Ltd, Sparkford.

CONTENTS

PROLOGUE
(1837)

WAR in the Lebanon! Ibrahim Pasha's army scours the country, tracking down the conscripts hidden in mountain caves, while the fire of revolt spreads from Acre to Damascus, from Tripoli to Jaffa. Druses, Maronites and Metoualys, Ansarys and Ishmaelites, all the different races and religions of the Lebanon have united to throw off the foreign yoke, which for five years has dominated Syria. For five years Mehemet Ali, the Viceroy of Egypt, has enacted the *rôle* of an Eastern Napoleon, threatening the power of the Sublime Porte, while Ibrahim Pasha, ruthless son of a ruthless father, leads his conquering armies from the Arabian deserts to the Taurus mountains.

In the little white villages nestling on the flanks of the Lebanon, in the Maronite monasteries crowning the limestone crags, in the orange orchards and terraced vineyards, soldiers massacre and rape and pillage. One place alone is inviolate – the *dahr el Sytt* – the home of the old Englishwoman who for twenty-five years has been acclaimed as Queen by the Arabs. No soldier of Mehemet Ali dares to cross her threshold, no Druse rebel dares to steal her cattle which pasture in the valley. The sick and the wounded seek refuge in her fortress, where the homeless find shelter and beggars receive alms.

Who is she, this strange old Englishwoman who defies the power of the Egyptian Viceroy and upholds the name of the Sultan in a country where he has lost his power? Mehemet Ali is known to have said "that she had given him more trouble than all the insurgent people of Syria and Palestine," and yet he does not dare touch her. She is now old and ill and in debt to all the merchants of Beyrout and Sidon, so feeble that she can hardly drag herself from her bedroom to the garden, so poor that her bedclothes are tattered, while the ceiling of her room is propped up by the unplaned trunk of a poplar tree.

One sees her through a haze of tobacco smoke, lying back on her untidy bed, sucking the amber mouthpiece of her pipe.

PROLOGUE

The gaunt, emaciated face, with the arrogant nose and broad forehead, is framed in a Bedouin head-dress, and the blue eyes flash dark in anger and impatience. Chatham's granddaughter, a hunch-backed, toothless old crone, lies huddled in a torn pelisse – Lady Hester Stanhope, an aristocrat, whose pride knows no limits, an adventurous pioneer, born in the sophistication of the eighteenth century.

The ghosts of Stanhopes, Pitts and Grenvilles rise behind her: the ancestors from whom she inherited the mad, over-weening pride which drove her out of Europe to realize her dreams of grandeur in the East. Pashas and Emirs paid homage to her; the princes of the desert acclaimed her; black slaves cringed before her. Even now that she is old and penniless, over thirty servants tremble at her call. One old Englishman shares her exile; he has fled from her time after time, only to return faithful and servile to her side. Poor, weak Dr. Meryon, the butt of her sarcastic tongue, the witness of her pathetic, useless rages, the beast of burden on whose shoulders rest all the complicated domestic arrangements of the castle of Djoun. More faithful than any lover, he is never even treated as a friend. Evening after evening he has to sit and listen to her interminable chatter, the last ravings of an egotistical, lonely being.

The superstitious Syrians who live in the village of Djoun under the shadow of her fortress, regard her as holy. To them she is a prophetess and a supernatural being; she reads the future in the stars, and two sacred mares in her stable are destined to bear the Messiah and his bride into Jerusalem. When the story-tellers weave their tales of a thousand Arabian Nights, there are tales even more fantastic to be told of the English *Melika*, tales that are sometimes born in her own over-inventive brain.

The little bourgeois doctor, who knew her in the days when the world still remembered her as the mistress of Downing Street and the petted niece of England's greatest minister, laments the broken teacups, the burnt pelisse, the mattress supported by wooden trestles, and wonders what "the Duchess of Rutland would have said if she had risen from her tomb to have seen her quondam friend, the brilliant ornament of a London drawing-room, clouded in fumes, so that the features were sometimes invisible," sitting in a room more poorly furnished than any servants" hall at Chevening or Dropmore or Stowe.

It is New Year's Eve, but no messenger climbs the steep hill, bearing her letters from England. For years she has not corresponded with her family and they, for their part, are very ready to forget the relation whose eccentricities have been broadcast by every Eastern traveller. Only her spies, whom she still maintains while depriving herself of every ordinary comfort, come to her in the disguise of beggars and water-carriers, bringing her the latest news of Ibrahim's campaign. Then for a few moments she can delude herself that she is still Pitt's niece, directing political intrigues with an inside knowledge as to what is happening at Cairo and Stamboul, until her fits of coughing start again and she collapses into a pathetic, miserable old woman who is slowly dying of consumption.

"Doctor" – her voice, so like her grandfather's, is now scarcely more than a whisper – "to-night in my father's house there used to be a hundred tenants and servants sitting down to a good dinner and dancing and making merry. I see their happy faces now before my eyes, and when I think of that and how I am surrounded here . . ." Her voice breaks and she falls back on her bed and cries from sheer weakness and desperation.

CHAPTER ONE

(1776)

BOOTED and spurred, the messengers stood ready at the gates of Chevening Manor. An air of expectancy hung over the small Kentish village, where every inhabitant, from the Vicar to his Lordship's gamekeeper, waited to hear the news that Viscountess Mahon—Earl Stanhope's daughter-in-law—had given birth to a child.

In the great halls of Chevening, hung with plumaged tapestries presented by Frederick of Prussia to the first Earl, the young husband waited for the doctor to come out of his wife's room. Tall and thin, with nervous, angular movements, his hair unpowdered, his clothes almost aggressive in their simplicity, he might have passed for a poor young student, rather than for the heir of the richest peer in Kent. As a child he had been delicate and his parents, doubly nervous after the death of their eldest son, had sent him to be educated at Geneva, the fermenting ground of those dangerous republican principles which were destined to alter the whole outlook of Europe. The doctrines of Rousseau were not the happiest credo for a young man born to take his seat in the House of Lords, where he would be expected to vote in support of the rigid constitutional government of George III, and, at the age of twenty-three, Charles Stanhope, Viscount Mahon, had already distinguished himself as one of those individual geniuses who form a disconcerting element in polite society. Science was his dominating passion, though his love for his young wife had not yet allowed it to develop into an obsession.

Hester Pitt, the daughter of 'The Great Commoner,' had brought him the glory of the name which had given confidence to the English people and had fired the spirit of patriotism in a country still impregnated with Walpole's slothful corruption. But in the same way as the fall of Chatham's ministry found the public coffers empty, so in his private life his insane extravagance left no provision for his family. At his daughter's

1

marriage in 1774 one finds the young Prince of Wales writing in French to his beloved mentor, Lady Holderness, "Doubtless you know that Lord Mahon has married Lady Hester Pitt. Lord Chatham not being rich enough to give her a dowry, her mother supplied in part by giving her all her jewels, and Lord Temple, her uncle, presented her with a thousand pounds to dress herself."

Luckily there were the Grenvilles, whose cold, crabbed natures formed an odd contrast with their lavish generosity in money matters. The family, who in later years supported the exiled Bourbons, were always ready to help their poor and spendthrift relations from whose glory they had derived so many material benefits, and through her uncle's generosity Hester Pitt arrived at Chevening in a blaze of jewels and finery, while her charming manner and delightful character endeared her to her new family. Many years later her husband's cousin, Lord Haddington, wrote to her daughter, "She was a woman rarely to be met with, wise, temperate and prudent, by nature cheerful without levity, a warm friend and free from all the petty vices that attend little minds."

Now she lay white and inert under the heavy damask hangings of the large four-poster bed, while her mother-in-law crept softly out of the room to announce to her son the birth of a baby daughter. A daughter! The disappointment that Lady Stanhope was too tactful to show was openly voiced in the servants' hall and loudly echoed in the village. But Lord Mahon was only concerned with the fact that his wife was safe and well and the messengers, who all morning had been waiting at the gates, were despatched to bring the joyful tidings to her family.

Through the Kentish lanes, bordered by catkin and willow, across the pale chalk hills and wind-swept commons, they brought the news to the Chathams, now living in retirement at Hayes. They travelled fast to Cambridge, where young William Pitt was studying law at Pembroke College, little guessing what a part he was to play in the life of his sister's

2

child. They carried the tidings to Buckinghamshire, where it was received by polite but indifferent Grenvilles, while that night the mail coach, lumbering north, bore letters from Lady Stanhope to all her Scottish kinsmen.

Four years had passed and Hester Pitt, Viscountess Mahon, lay dying on her great carved bed. As a legacy she was leaving behind her three little girls and it was doubtful whether their father would take any interest in them. Hester, the eldest child, was but four years old, hardly yet the age to realize that in losing her mother she had lost the one person who might have curbed her headstrong nature.

In those four eventful years England's dreams of overseas dominions had received their first crushing blow. Ever since the reins of government had slipped out of Chatham's tired, gouty fingers, ever since North's limp, ineffectual grasp had tried to curb the straining of a brilliant Opposition, disaster had followed upon disaster. America was lost and Chatham was dead, and the country waited, helpless, for the guidance of another Pitt.

Viscountess Mahon, daughter and sister of England's greatest statesmen, was dying at the age of twenty-five. Only two years had passed since her husband and brother had supported her invalid father to make his last great speech in the House of Lords, "when all the peers stood up and made a lane for him to pass," when the words of a dying man echoed in the stillness of a listening House. Out of fear and jealousy of France he protested against the recognition of American independence—he who a few years ago had protested against the nation's right to tax her colonies. His last words were: "Shall this great kingdom now fall prostrate before the house of Bourbon? If we must fall let us fall like men." Prophetic words, for not an hour later he fell back unconscious among the peers, and though for a month he still lingered paralysed and impotent, in the eyes of the country he died that day in the House of Lords.

Such a different death to that of his young daughter, whose life was gently and slowly ebbing out in the large, damask-hung room with the windows overlooking the lake.

At his wife's death Lord Mahon gave way to hysterical grief. Lady Stanhope undertook the care of her grandchildren and, though kindly by nature, her stern Scottish discipline does not seem to have inspired much affection. She must have been generous and open-hearted, for all her Scottish nephews and nieces—Haddingtons and Baillies, Campbells and Hamiltons —were allowed to consider Chevening as their English home; their hunters were kept in the stables and their arrivals and departures seem to have been the chief excitement in the lives of their little cousins.

Lord Mahon did not remain an inconsolable widower for very long. Six months after his wife's death he married her first cousin, Louisa Grenville, a poised, polished young lady of fashion, with that frigid elegance which was characteristic of her house. A picture of her still hangs on the walls at Chevening. Painted by Battoni when she was a child in Rome, it shows her even then to have been sophisticated and charmless.

The new Lady Mahon ignored her stepdaughters and was singularly efficient in producing heirs for the Stanhope family. In spite of her London life of routs and masquerades, alternated by visits to the fashionable watering-places, she spent enough time at Chevening to present her husband with three sons, though Lucy, her youngest stepdaughter, is reported to have said of her that if she had met her in the street she would not have known her.

In Chevening park, with its spreading beeches and dark-shadowed yews, Hester, Griselda and Lucy passed a childhood not quite as monotonous as that which usually fell to the lot of the children belonging to the eighteenth century aristocracy, for they had a father whose vagaries were always diverting. There was the lake with the smoothly gliding swans, where they were never allowed to play, because Lord Mahon was busy perfecting his invention of a model craft propelled by steam, an invention on which he laboured for twenty years, but which, when presented to the Admiralty in 1793, was turned down as impracticable.

Charles Mahon and Louisa Grenville must have been an ill-assorted couple, he with his violence and rhetoric, his amazingly versatile genius and unbalanced judgment; she with her soulless pride and shallow vanity. The local gentry resented her airs and questioned his sanity, for they had never forgotten the famous party held on the upper floor of a wooden house especially constructed by Lord Mahon in order to prove his theory that buildings could be rendered fireproof through the well-known principle that combustion can never take place when all air is excluded. One can imagine the feelings of those ladies and gentlemen who came in their frills and furbelows, their ruffles and buckles, to frivol and eat ices in the grounds of Chevening, when they found themselves entrapped in a wooden box with flames rising on every side, while their host delighted in the success of his experiment.

Perhaps it was reaction and boredom from his worldly, empty-headed wife that led Charles Mahon to seek the company of advanced republicans such as Horne Tooke and Jeremiah Joyce, and that later drove him to adopt the attitude of an aggressive Jacobin. But there was very little of a Jacobin about him in the early eighties, when he received the visit of the French Ambassador. Count D'Adhemar, one of the most polished courtiers of his day, created a sensation at Chevening Manor, and his brilliant retinue, which dazzled the Kentish countryside, made a profound impression on Hester Stanhope. To the child of nine he appeared as a being of a different species. His affectations and mannerisms, his butterfly bows and sweeping feathers, his diamond buttoned waistcoat and cascading laces filled her with a desire to visit the country which could boast of such strange and enthralling inhabitants. This was her first glimpse of the outside world, a world unrestricted by plaguing governesses, who pinched her robust little body between hard boards "in order to reduce her to the size of a puny miss"—a violation which she was to remember all her life—and who committed a still greater sacrilege in trying to flatten the highly arched instep, of which she was inordinately proud; governesses who refused to answer her precocious questions or to satisfy her intense curiosity, and who were utterly incapable of curbing her imperious temper.

She must have been an attractive child with her brilliant colouring and dark blue eyes, reflecting every changing mood, even though her pronounced features dispelled the possibility of her ever developing into a beauty, for the Pitt nose already took its upward, aggressive tilt and her charming mouth was spoilt by the Grenville chin. Her chief charm lay in her intense vitality and she dominated every child with whom she came in contact. She was quick to form attachments, and her friendship with Francis Burdett, the well-known democrat, dated from these early days.

She took none of her companions with her when she embarked on her great adventure to visit the country of which the Count D'Adhemar was such a fascinating representative. It was a summer's morning at Hastings, where the Stanhope children were staying with their governesses. Hester had managed to evade their vigilance and had escaped to the seashore. Once she was on the sands, she was quick to seize her opportunity. A rowing-boat was fastened to the end of a rotting quay, and in a few seconds she had untied it and had set out on her journey. For the first time she gave way to the spirit which in later years impelled her to ride unveiled through the streets of Damascus and to cross the Syrian desert at the head of an Arab tribe. Her triumph, however, was short-lived; a fast boat rowed by determined fishermen, bearing furious and frightened governesses, brought her back to land, where she was soundly punished, though it is doubtful whether on this occasion her father would have treated her with the same severity.

In 1786 old Lord Stanhope died and his son, whose vehemence had become proverbial in the House of Commons, where men spoke of "Mahon outroaring torrents in their course," took his seat in the House of Lords. He had been a supporter of his brother-in-law, William Pitt, ever since the latter had become Prime Minister in 1783. But during the last year he had protested against 'the sinking fund' and now he was to develop into one of his most violent opponents.

Naturally the republican Earl became the favourite butt of the lampoonists and caricaturists of the day, and one hears him described as "the Don Quixote of the Nation who beats his own windmill in gesticulation."

Chevening had fallen into the hands of an erratic and eccentric master and the lovely old house was to suffer through his mania of altering and building according to his fantasy. He ruined the façade by hacking off the stone coignings and window architraves and plastering it with stucco, while he mutilated the architecture of the house by adding a plastered attic storey. He cut down some of the most beautiful trees in his park on the principle that timber should be used for utilitarian purposes, and though he was kind and generous towards his tenants he became a tyrant in his home.

The dowager Countess, who had watched with benevolent firmness over her grandchildren's education, now moved to a house at the edge of the park, and in the tapestry-hung rooms the new Lady Stanhope yawned behind her ivory fan. She always had the vapours during the few months she had to spend at Chevening, for she disliked the rural life, and her maid did not know how to dress her hair; even in London there were only two Frenchmen who did it to her taste. It was difficult to lead a peaceful existence with a husband whose eccentricities became every day more trying. A man who slept without a nightcap, with the window open and twelve covers on his bed, who got up in the morning and put on a thin dressing-gown over the silk breeches he had worn overnight, and then, with slippers and no stockings, would sit on the floor in a part of the room which had no carpet and take his tea with a bit of brown bread—could hardly be considered normal. Poor Lady Stanhope little guessed what was yet in store for her, for while she was in London leading her empty, social life, in Paris the roar of guns announced the fall of the Bastille.

The first breath of the French Revolution swept through the London drawing-rooms, clouding the delicate Chippendale mirrors which reflected the beauties of a mad king's court, for England still trembled on the brink of a regency, and Lady Jersey dispensed the favours of a queen. The King recovered and in Paris the Bastille fell to an insurgent mob, but London society was chiefly interested in Warren Hastings' trial, and though liberty became a popular word in the Devonshire House set, where the lovely Duchess echoed the principles of Fox, the majority of Englishmen were still uninterested in their neighbour's doings.

Lady Stanhope was not allowed to ignore the news that couriers brought from across the Channel, for in a few months she found that she was married to a rabid Jacobin. Her husband sympathized and corresponded with the leaders of the revolution, who welcomed him as another Condorcet. He styled himself Citizen Stanhope and erased the armorial bearings from his plate. The tapestries were taken down from the walls and put away as being "too damned aristocratical," and for a short while he suspended his horses and carriages, considering it healthier for his family to walk. His children's education suffered most, for he appointed a dissenting teacher, Jeremiah Joyce, as tutor to his sons, while the governesses were despatched and Hester, a tall, healthy girl of fourteen, was sent to tend turkeys on the common.

From now on she received little education except an occasional lecture on logic from her father with whom she seems to have been a favourite, for he would send her sisters out of the room and turn to her, saying, "Now we must talk a little philosophy," and he would invariably interrupt her arguments by saying, "The reasoning is good, but the basis is bad." From him she inherited her violence and humour, her brilliant horsemanship and unflinching courage, and he appreciated the fact that she was the only one of his family who dared to stand up against him. He bullied and tyrannized her by forcing her to wear coarse and hideous clothes and to perform manual labours, but in spite of her republican schooling she grew up into an aristocrat. She was kind and thoughtful to her family, as long as she could feel that she was indispensable to them, and on many occasions she acted as an intermediary between them and her father. She was fond of her sisters, but she had very little use for women, and though she admired Lucy's beauty, she resented Griselda being cleverer than her; not that Griselda's cleverness availed her much, for she was always being pushed into the background by her brilliant and domineering sister. Very little is known of Griselda, except that she was jealous and assertive, and disliked both by her father and uncle. Lucy was sweet and gentle with a beautiful Madonna face, which won her the love of her cousin Binning, Lord Haddington's heir, who meant to propose to her as soon as she had left the schoolroom, if the unfortunate Stanhope temperament had not induced her, at the age of sixteen, to elope with the local apothecary.

Hester's real interest centred in her little half-brothers. She showered on them that warm, possessive love which their frigid mother had never given them, but in return she expected blind adoration and explicit obedience. Lord Stanhope, following the example of the *sansculottes* who had appointed a shoe-maker as guardian to the Dauphin, had his sons apprenticed to the smithy and the forge. It is strange that a man whose mordant wit and penetrating mind have been praised by both Lady Bessborough and Lady Holland should have committed such grotesque and unbalanced actions. And it needed all Hester's invincible self-confidence and cheerfulness to keep her from falling into the state of depression which overcame the rest of the family.

Still, there were compensations. There was the memorable visit to Warren Hastings' trial, where she first captured the attention of a young man, pale and elegant in his corbeau coat with steel buttons, his white satin breeches and buckled shoes. It was the future Lord Grey, and though she was only a child of fifteen, she already had romantic leanings. Their friendship was founded on what was for her a humiliating incident. She dropped her garter and, confused with shyness, she watched him pick it up and hand it unobtrusively to the attendant who was serving coffee. Many years later she quoted this example of his perfect manners.

Even life at Chevening could be quite amusing, for Lord Stanhope's Jacobin fervour did not prevent his daughter from hunting, and Lady Hester's wonderful horsemanship won the admiration of all the officers stationed in the district. Her tall, rather largely proportioned figure was at its best in a riding habit, and her brilliant complexion withstood the onslaughts of rain and sun. She had friends in Sevenoaks where she could go and eat the good homely rounds of beef and pork pies, which she never got in her own home. In spite of her pride she had a very human streak in her and she liked kind, simple people. In an age when servants were but rarely treated as human beings she found the time to take an interest in every dependent who came under her care, and she was as quick to notice the good looks of a groom as those of a peer. Her weakness lay in the fact that she made little difference between her dependents and her friends. They all had to look up to her and follow her advice unquestioningly.

In 1794 her half-brothers' desultory education was interrupted, for their tutor, Joyce, the author of *Scientific Dialogues*, was arrested on the charge of high treason. Tom Paine's *Rights of Man*, written in answer to Burke's *Thoughts on the French Revolution*, had roused sedition throughout the country and the English government, at war with the French republic, with London crowded with *emigrés*, many of them disguised revolutionary spies, hunted down with severity all those who were accused of Jacobin tendencies. Even peers were not exempt from suspicion, for Lord Thanet was thrown into jail, and Lord Stanhope's London house was attacked by the mob, he himself being obliged to make his escape by the leads. Two warrant officers arrived at Chevening and arrested Jeremiah Joyce on the charge of high treason, but owing to lack of evidence he was set free without a trial, and Hester Stanhope's 'coming out' party was the banquet given by her father to celebrate his secretary's acquittal.

CHAPTER TWO

IN 1796 Hester Stanhope made her first public appearance at
Lord Romney's review, where all the gentry of Kent assembled
to pay homage to their sovereigns. Her father had forbidden
her to go, for he disapproved of any militaristic display after
having withdrawn his presence from the House of Lords on
account of their refusing to consider his motion against interfering with the internal policy of France. But she managed to
evade his vigilance, and she drove over alone to Lord Romney's
castle without even a maid to chaperon her. In similar
circumstances most young girls of twenty would have been
overcome with nervousness, but her brazen self-confidence and
pride helped her to make a brilliant entry into the society
where her birth and talents entitled her to play a leading
rôle. She saw her uncle, William Pitt, being courted and flattered as the greatest man in England, while her other uncle,
Lord Chatham, rode handsome and debonair at the head of his
troops. She was intoxicated by the pomp and pageantry of the
review, the fluttering banners and beating drums, the brave
display of red coats and gold lace. What a contrast to the dour
scholars who gathered in her father's library were these
powdered and perfumed courtiers, these fine ladies in their
rustling taffetas and gold-sprigged muslins, their gossamer caps
and fantastic hats bearing baskets of flowers and forests of
plumes!

Officers and courtiers flocked around her, delighted at her
lively sallies, while she ignored their wives with a magnificent
impertinence. She was a mixture of an irrepressible hoyden and
a great lady, and her outspoken and unguarded tongue was apt
to cause offence where none was intended. But a good deal of
latitude was allowed to one who was the great Chatham's granddaughter and Pitt's niece, and duchesses and countesses were
only too anxious to act as her chaperon in order to curry favour
with the 'spotless Minister.' Uncle and niece were strangely

alike, so tall and straight, with their contemptuous, uplifted noses and proudly poised heads. But his eyes were cold and grey, disdaining the ground and searching the heavens for ideas, while hers were wild and blue, reflecting Chatham's fire.

George III, accompanied by his ministers, surrounded by his bored and sophisticated courtiers, his handsome and somewhat bovine sons, heard her fresh childish laughter, and asked Pitt to present her. Why hadn't he seen her before? She was far too attractive to be imprisoned in 'Democracy Hall,' as he called her father's house, and at dinner he insisted on her having a place of honour at an adjoining table, which was served by the local gentry, while Lord and Lady Romney waited on their Majesties. The courtiers took up their quizzing-glasses to scan the girl who had taken the old King's fancy. She was not strictly beautiful, but there was a radiance and magnetism about her which was indefinable. The ladies shrugged their white shoulders and sneered at her height. "These Pitts are a race of giants, and how badly brought up—no veneer—no manners; but what can one expect from a Jacobin father?"

Even at twenty Hester was impervious to criticism, just as Lord Stanhope was impervious to the opposition of the peers. She snatched at life greedily and avidly and she had no time to consider the bruised and battered feelings of those she pushed aside. As he watched the success of his young niece, Pitt's cold face was lit by a charming smile, but he would have been horrified if someone had told him that in a few years this highly-spirited, unmanageable child would be living under his roof. These were the days of his only romance; Eleanor Eden, Lord Auckland's lovely daughter, had inspired him with a passion, which almost involved him in marriage, and though he finally decided to sacrifice her to his career, in later years he is suspected of having borne an unreasonable grudge to her husband, the Earl of Buckinghamshire.

Lady Hester's triumph was complete when, on leaving the castle, the old King remarked jocularly that she should ride bodkin between him and the Queen, who said in her prim, humourless way "that Lady Hester had not got her maid with her and that it would be inconvenient for her to come at such a short notice."

George III, whom so many have accused of ingratitude, always proved a good friend to Pitt's niece and, at the statesman's death, it was his wish that the highest pension should be granted to her; but in the last years of the eighteenth century it was hard to visualize her as a pensioned spinster with fading prospects.

In 1796 Lady Lucy eloped with her young apothecary and Lord Stanhope's republican sentiments suffered their first reverse. His resentful attitude was caricatured by James Gillray in a drawing called *Democratic Levelling* or *Alliance à la Francaise*, for though he had quarrelled with all his relations except the Grenvilles, as a son-in-law he would have preferred a future Earl of Haddington to a Mr. Taylor of Sevenoaks. It was all very well to tear down the coronets from the iron gates of Chevening, to exchange friendly greetings penned in exquisite French with the rebels who had guillotined their king, but that his youngest and prettiest daughter should disgrace her family by putting his theories into practice was a lamentable misfortune. His rage vented itself on Lady Griselda who had always been miserable at home and now accepted Pitt's offer of a cottage near Walmer Castle. It was an offer made more out of compassion than affection and the minister's sense of duty towards his nieces prompted him to better Mr. Taylor's position by finding him a post in the Customs.

Hester remained at Chevening, watching over her little half-brothers whose education was being sadly neglected, but her life was now less monotonous, for her father, still smarting from Lucy's *mésalliance*, relaxed his severity and allowed her occasional visits to London.

The society in which she found herself was divided into a few great strongholds, ruled by beautiful and ambitious women. Pitt and Dundas and the Tory ministers patronized the parties of the lively and eccentric Duchess of Gordon, whose daughters were offered on a gilded platter to all the eligible young men in town. The Royal Dukes found there the gaiety and warmth which was lacking at their mother's court, and young Scottish peers, such as Aberdeen, made their first appearance in her drawing-room. At the Duchess of Rutland's, it was all very formal and stiff, and not even the presence of the Prince and his friends could dissipate the high-bred gloom; but her parties were fashionable and even the King of the Dandies condescended to dance with her flower-like sisters.

All London flocked to Devonshire House to praise or criticize according to their natures, yet few young men came away with their hearts intact, for even if they were able to withstand the effusive charms of the beautiful Georgiana, there was the subtler fascination of her inseparable friend, Lady Elizabeth Foster, one of those exquisite Hervey sisters of whom was said "There are men, women, and the Herveys." And lastly there was the Duchess's sister, Lady Bessborough, feminine and enchanting with her dark vivacious beauty. How could anyone resist women who had men like Fox and Gibbon and Sheridan at their feet? Many mothers sighed when they saw their sons caught up in the toils of the Devonshire House circle, where morals were easy and play was high. The political sentiments of the Duchess who had showered cherished kisses on the butchers of Westminster in order to secure votes for Fox, did not prevent her from inviting Canning and Hawkesbury and Castlereagh, the young hopes of the Tory party. Members quarrelled in the House of Commons and became reconciled at her suppers, for these were the days when women were subtle shadows against the political background.

There was Holland House, the great Whig fortress where the brilliant young hostess forced many to forget that she was a *divorcée*, and there were dull, pompous parties given by Lady Salisbury and Lady Sunderland, and uproarious drunken debauches at Carlton House, where Lady Jersey and George Brummel ruled a misguided prince.

Lady Hester made her *début* under the chaperonage of the

Harringtons and Grenvilles, whose houses were crowded with French *emigrés*, and it is in the memoirs of a French woman that one finds a description of her first appearance in society. The Duchess of Gontaut met her at a masquerade given by Lady Stafford in her gardens looking out on the Thames, where, in a *mêlée* of Dresden shepherdesses and classical goddesses, she stood out tall and slim in "a costume which had nothing feminine about it except the mask." Mrs. Wilmot, who was one of the beautiful Ogle sisters, Lady Clarendon and the Duchess formed a picturesque group of fortune-tellers, but they had the unfortunate idea of introducing a live donkey into the decorous gardens of Stafford House. The continual braying of this animal excited a good deal of unpleasant comment, and in a loud, clear voice Lady Hester was heard to assert that "whoever had brought it was still more stupid than the ass." A little later in the evening Pitt came and asked Lady Clarendon to chaperon his young niece and the girl, whom the Duchess had already labelled as a mannerless hoyden, displayed a rudeness that no one would have tolerated if she had not been related to the Prime Minister.

It was hardly likely that a woman brought up in the court of Marie Antoinette would have appreciated someone so far removed from a *jeune fille bien elevée*, but London society, always tolerant to those in power, pretended to be amused by Hester's outspoken opinions and ruthless laughter. "And after all," as the Comtesse de Boigne, another Frenchwoman, said a few years later, "for a Stanhope, she was prudence itself." She made great friends with the Royal Dukes but she never liked the Prince of Wales, though she rode and danced with his friends regardless of her reputation. Her vitality and spontaneity attracted the spoilt debauchees, tired of the demi-reps and harlots who frequented Carlton House. It was natural that she should appeal to men like Bouverie, but it is difficult to understand her friendship with George Brummel. The King of the Dandies was at the very height of his fame. He could affront with impunity the greatest peers in the realm, who waited in his dressing-room while he brushed his teeth. Even Pitt's niece could be proud when he singled her out at a party by admiring the contours of her cheeks, saying in his cool, familiar way, "For God's sake do take off those ear-rings and let us see what is beneath them." One day they met while riding in Bond Street, she strong and vital in a scarlet amazon and plumed hat, gaily tilted on her chestnut curls; he indolent and foppish, "riding with his bridle between his forefinger and his thumb as if he held a pinch of snuff." He greeted her with, "Dear creature! Who is that man you were talking to just now?" "Why," she answered, "that is Colonel ——" "Colonel ——?" he said in his peculiar manner. "Whoever heard of his father?" She replied, "And whoever heard of George Brummel's father?" "Ah, Lady Hester," he rejoined, half seriously, "and who would have ever heard of George Brummel if he had been anything but what he is? But you know, my dear Lady Hester, it is my folly that is the making of me. If I did not impertinently stare duchesses out of countenance and nod over my shoulder at a prince, I would be forgotten in a week, and if the world is so silly as to admire my absurdities, you and I may know better, but what does that signify?"

Faced by Lady Hester's calm impertinence the beau dropped his mask of a snobbish fop. A curious friendship developed between them of which very little is known, though one of his biographers goes so far as to hint that on her part it might have grown into something more. It is a surmise based on the very scanty evidence of a few intimate letters, which she was as ready to write to any subaltern who took her passing fancy. He admired her superb carriage and lithe grace in the crowded drawing-rooms, where women like over-plumaged birds minced or strutted, fluttering their painted fans; he admired her cruel mimicry, so quick to ridicule the affectations and pretensions of the toasted beauties, and chiefly he admired her as an aristocrat, who was so proud and self-willed that she put herself on a pedestal above the criticism of the world. Many years later in Syria, when she was a warped, bitter old woman who had thrown off the civilization of the West, one of the few whom she remembered with kindness was the over-civilized dandy, George Brummel.

Lady Hester was indiscriminating in her friendships. It was a trait which might have had disastrous results if she had not been saved by an extraordinary insight into people's characters. Gossip gathered thick around her, but as Lady Suffolk said in her defence, "She will never let anybody do a bit more than she intends; what she does is with *connaissance de cause.*" She might ride in the Park with Bouverie, absent herself at a party with Sir Gilbert Heathcote, have intimate friendships with young diplomats such as Francis Jackson and Noel Hill, and flirt with Sir Sidney Smith, fresh from his triumphs at Acre; but during her first seasons she was never seriously compromised. After a few gay weeks she would return to Chevening, to the life which, according to Bouverie, suited her best. There was something very courageous about the way in which she tried to remain loyal to her father, deserted by her sisters, alienated from his class. She loathed what she called 'a pack of dirty Jacobins,' but she was broad-minded enough to admit the cleverness of Payne and Horne Tooke, at the same time as doing her best to prevent her father from getting embroiled in their seditious politics.

Mutinies and riots, dissatisfaction caused by an unsuccessful and costly war, marked the closing of the century. Ireland, still flaming with revolt, was added as a wreath of thorns to King George's overburdened crown, and the hated words 'Catholic Emancipation' hung ominously over the House of Commons.

Lord Stanhope had retired to Chevening, where he kept a jealous watch over his eldest son, denying him any decent education in the hopes of getting him completely under his influence, so that on attaining his majority he would allow him to dispose of the estate. Mahon bitterly deplored finding himself "in a situation of all others the most odious and oppressive." But when he asked to be sent to college and, following Pitt's advice, made proposals regarding the entail, Lord Stanhope refused to consider them. In despair he turned to his step-sister, who was powerless to help him as long as she remained at Chevening. And when in the spring of 1800 she accepted her grandmother Chatham's offer of a home at Burton Pynsent, it was not of herself alone that she was thinking, but of the future of her young step-brothers. At home she had suffered far less than them, for her Pitt blood had helped her to withstand the tyranny of a father who had succeeded in crushing his wife and sons; and it must have entailed some sacrifice on the part of a vain, spoilt young girl to settle down in the depths of Somersetshire with an old lady living in retirement with a companion and another granddaughter. Chevening was comparatively near to London; there were amusing neighbours, and the London dandies made occasional excursions into Kent to do some unofficial horse-dealing by buying chestnuts from the farmers, smartening them up and selling them in town at a handsome profit. This helped them to get a little spare cash to repair the ravages the Prince had made into their stock of claret.

Hester left her home with regret, but she certainly did not have time to get bored in Somersetshire, for all that year she schemed and plotted for her brother's welfare. She had always been fond of him, but now he became doubly dear to her for he gave her the first chance to indulge her passion for mystery and intrigue. She pulled strings in influential quarters, and Pitt, who was always ready to help his young relations, gave her valuable advice. She went to London and solicited the aid of her Grenville cousins, who approved of the idea that Mahon should escape to the Continent, where under an assumed name he could be enrolled as a student of a foreign university; yet, though they were encouraging and kind, none of them wanted to commit themselves by interfering with Lord Stanhope's education of his son, and it was from young men, not so careful about jeopardizing their reputations, that Lady Hester managed to obtain everything that was necessary for her brother's successful escape. Francis Burdett, her childhood's friend, procured her the money, for it was easy to procure money when one was married to a Coutts, and Francis Jackson, the charming young diplomat who had amused her during a London season, proved to be a faithful and loyal friend by furnishing passports and letters of credit as well as introductions to the Professors of Erlangen University and the Margravine of Brandenburg-Bayreuth. Her brother's miserable letters spurred her on, and by the end of the year all the plans were laid. With the help of a faithful servant, Mahon escaped from Chevening during the winter months of 1801. His flight was discovered a few hours later and messengers were sent in hot pursuit, but by the time they reached the coast he was already on his way to France and by the end of March he was enrolled as a student at the University of Erlangen.

Hester jubilated over the safety of her "charming and incomparable Mahon" whose grateful and adoring letters were shown with pride round the Chatham family. For once the tactless and inconsiderate girl seems to have behaved with unusual thoughtfulness and discretion. She communicated with her father's lawyer in order to reassure her step-mother and 'Grandmama Stanhope.' She wrote that Mahon was safe and well and that letters would be forwarded by her as long as they did not try to find out his whereabouts. It is surprising that she should have borne no grudge to the step-mother who had systematically neglected her, nor to the grandmother whose blind adoration for her son had prevented her from ever lifting a finger to help her grandchildren.

Frantic with fury, Lord Stanhope sent expresses to Pitt and Burdett, to Lucy, now living at Bromley, and to Griselda who was married to an officer stationed at Dover. Luckily, Hester had been careful not to incriminate the younger boys who were still living at Chevening, for their father would have been capable of flogging them to death if he had suspected them of having helped their brother. Tired and nervous after her months of anxiety, she expected him to come storming and raging to Burton Pynsent. She dreaded a repetition of some of the scenes she had witnessed at Chevening, where in moments of uncontrollable fury Lord Stanhope had been liable to threaten her, holding a knife to her throat, but even then she had known no fear and had "felt only pity for the hand that held the knife." She never seems to have disliked her father; perhaps there was too much similarity between their strange, wild natures, and even now she worried that his behaviour towards his family might expose him to public criticism and disapproval.

Lord Stanhope never came to Burton Pynsent, and Hester triumphed in the knowledge that her brother had secured happiness through her intervention. She was congratulated by her handsome and indolent uncle, Chatham, by Buckingham and Glastonbury, her powerful Grenville cousins who promised to protect Mahon in the future, and she received warm and affectionate letters from her father's cousin, Lord Haddington; letters full of good advice, which for once she was ready to take. The one man to whom she turned with real love and gratitude was her uncle, William Pitt. The suspended sword of Catholic Emancipation had fallen on his head and he was now but a dethroned minister with duns clamouring at his door.

CHAPTER THREE

BURTON PYNSENT stands on the ridge of a hill overlooking Sedgemoor and the lonely survivors of Chatham's hundred cedars throw dark shadows along the sharp crest which drops so abruptly into the plain. Nothing remains of the great rambling house, which Sir William Pynsent left in gratitude to Chatham and his heirs, nothing except the library wing added by the statesman himself, which was connected by a gallery to the main building. Here he could read and study, undisturbed by his family and the constant clamour and bustle of a large country house. And when his tired and irascible nerves needed soothing, he could wander into the *volière*, which led out of his study, and listen to the myriad songs of strange, exotic birds, which, according to the fashion of the time, were brought by traders from England's new-found colonies to wilt and moult in damp, cold country mansions and help some gouty nobleman to forget his pain.

What used to comprise Chatham's library and servants' quarters has now become a delightful country house. Built of mellow red bricks and Somersetshire stone, it is surrounded by a wide, sweeping terrace, whose proud, carved balustrades date from the days when the imposing façade of Burton Pynsent dominated the countryside. The garden with its trellised arbours bound in vine, its scented lime walk and enclosed orchard, still breathes the pressed, faint essence of the eighteenth century. And when the present owners came there thirty years ago, there were old women living in the village whose fathers had told them stories of Lady Hester riding across the country on her black mare. Her name conjured up strange Arabian legends and West Country housewives treasured flacons of attar of roses and strings of amber, which their old friend had sent them from the East. Was 'friend' the right word to use in connection with Lady Hester? At times she condescended graciously, choosing to give them as much of her attention as

22

if they were royalties, who showered compliments on her arrogant little head. At other times she domineered and commanded, and her temper was as terrible as had been that of her grandfather "who cowed the tumultuous Commons with a frown." But one of those quiet Somersetshire women never forgot her and to a child at her knee she told tales of the wild, adventurous girl who had become a queen in the East—tales that fired the imagination that gave birth to *Eothen*.

Hester found life at Burton Pynsent very calm and peaceful after the restless, nerve-racking atmosphere of Chevening, yet peace never dwelt for long in the neighbourhood of a Stanhope and every inmate of the house was made to share her excitement over Mahon's escape. It is small wonder that on the death of the dowager Lady Chatham her son should have chosen to adopt his other niece, the sweet and gentle Harriet Elliot, in preference to the stormy, brilliant creature, who ruined the calm of his home.

Hester queened it in her new surroundings where her adoring grandmother indulged her every whim, but there seems to have been little sympathy between her and her uncle's wife, whose covetous money-greed made her resent and fear the niece who might become a dangerous rival with regard to family inheritances. Lord Chatham, charming and indolent, slightly over-burdened by the weight of his illustrious name, took very little interest in his family. An incompetent general and a wretched administrator, he yet possessed a judgment so shrewd and balanced that Lord Eldon, who can hardly be accused of partiality, considered him the ablest man in the Cabinet. It is not surprising that his faded little wife should have been avaricious and mean, when his Lordship carried out the Pitt tradition of scattering gold with insane liberality. He never travelled without a mistress, and *aides-de-camp* waited for their orders, while he dallied in bed with his latest love. It was always, "To-morrow I shall see to this and to-morrow I shall see to that." And to-morrow found him tired and vague, and averse to anything which might mean a little work.

Worry and anxiety over her brother had told on Lady Hester's health. Her glowing colouring faded and her face, with its large, prominent features, looked heavy and pasty. She, who usually thought nothing of riding twenty to thirty miles a day, was now exhausted by the slightest exertion, and in February of 1801 she was sent to recuperate at Bath. It was not her first visit; she had come there as a young girl of twenty in the full flush of her London triumphs, when the dandies had first begun to notice the debutante, whose effrontery more than equalled their own. The fresh, mannerless hoyden had developed into a mature and fascinating woman of twenty-five, but though men sought her company, confided in her and let her believe that they were her willing slaves, they rarely fell in love with her. As a young French horsebreeder, who visited her twenty years later in Syria, said of her, *"Quoique douée d'une beauté remarquable, les sentiments tendres n'ont rien d'analogue à ce qu'on éprouve à sa vue. C'est une créature à part qu'étonne, mais ne peut charmer; elle subjuge et n'attache pas."*

Flirtation succeeded flirtation and women no longer chose to defend her with the ardour of Lady Suffolk, for the way in which she flaunted her love affairs made it hard for the best-intentioned friends to believe in her virtue. She herself wrote to Francis Jackson when he congratulated her on a rumoured engagement: "Thanks for your news. I have been going to be married fifty times in my life, said to have been married half as often and run away with once. But, provided I have my own way, the world may have theirs and welcome." The world refused to believe the truth, which was that Hester, though unconventional and temperamental, was neither sensual nor voluptuous. Her critical and exacting nature made it difficult for her to fall in love and her admirers turned with relief to clinging, feminine women, whose tongues had never learned to wound. During the winter of 1801 she was suffering from her first serious attachment, for love is not the right term to describe the mingled hero-worship and admiration which she felt towards her cousin, Lord Camelford, and how could the world believe in the chastity of a girl whose name was coupled with one whose morals were such that even the vices of Carlton House paled in comparison.

A society, only too ready to smile at the eccentricities of a rich young peer, hinted at his insanity; many who invited him to their parties dismissed him in private as a murderer. When the young giant with the pale, bony face and mad eyes entered into a drawing-room, men moved silently away and women stared at him with the fascinated gaze of frightened rabbits.

Thomas Pitt, second and last Lord Camelford, was descended from the older branch of the family and inherited the fortune and estates of his ancestor, 'Diamond' Pitt, the ruthless East India trader, whose daughter, Lucy, had married the first Earl Stanhope, thus making Lady Hester doubly related to the Pitts. Camelford's father was a cultured, erudite pedant, who made no attempt to play any part in public life. The correspondence between him and his uncle, Lord Chatham, is more devoted to discussing the arts than politics, but by some strange irony of fate, the mild and gentle æsthete, who translated Horace and worried over the niceties of a Latin verse, became the father of a man whose wild, notorious deeds were the scandal of London. Camelford's choice of a naval career was singularly unfortunate, and, even as a midshipman, he picked quarrels with his contemporaries and challenged his superiors to duels. Yet, though one of the captains whom he accused of ill-treatment towards his juniors threatened to have him court-martialled, no open scandal came to light till 1798, when Camelford, then a lieutenant stationed at St. Kitts, shot a brother officer dead in the middle of the dockyards. He and Peterson had quarrelled over a question of precedence, for the captain had gone on shore and Camelford had unrightfully assumed the post of commanding officer. When Peterson refused to obey him, he repeated his orders three times and at the third refusal he fired. It was plain murder committed in a moment of insane fury, but the coroner, out of consideration for the defendant's rank, decreed that the dead man had lost his life in a mutiny, and the court-martial, which took place on board the *Invincible* at Port Royal, Martinique, passed the same verdict. Camelford was acquitted and put in command of the *Charon*. And though in future the more prudent minded avoided his society, many, including Hester Stanhope, considered him as a hero in having quelled insubordination by taking the law into his own hands. When mutiny broke out at the Nore, they regretted "that there were not more officers like Camelford."

Scandal followed scandal, and in what must have been little short of a fit of insanity, Camelford, regardless of the fact that a European war was going on, planned a secret journey to Paris in order to obtain some French charts. He hired a boat at Dover, but when he attempted to embark he was immediately arrested. A letter to Barras was found hidden among his clothes and he was taken to the office of the Duke of Portland, who was extremely embarrassed at having in his custody the well-known young peer who was Pitt's cousin. He was examined before the Privy Council and set free, but the Admiralty, disapproving of his conduct, suspended his command. Enraged, he asked for his name to be struck off the list of commanders and retired from the Navy. From then onwards he was a familiar figure in the London streets, and night-watchmen knew and feared the gaunt giant with the plain lieutenant's coat, the shaven head "and monstrous large gold-laced cocked hat, which from its appearance one would think had seen service with Sir Walter Raleigh." And the veterans among them noticed the frightening resemblance he bore to Lord George Gordon, who half a century earlier had fanned the famous riots. Though the watchmen feared his mad, drunken bouts, there were many sailors and vagrants who had cause to bless the stranger, who treated them to drinks in the humblest taverns of the city, encouraging them to recount their tales of hard luck and poverty and then pressed fifty or a hundred guineas in their hands, warning them with a terrible frown never to try to discover his identity. A trained wrestler and boxer, he was always ready to champion the poor and the oppressed against swindlers and extortioners, and even Pitt, who avoided his disreputable young cousin, had the greatest admiration for his character. Only his sense of propriety forbade him to take much notice of a man whose boon companions were drunken sea captains and bawdy prostitutes.

The Chathams were only too anxious to be intimate with the cousin whose estates they hoped to inherit, for though Lord Camelford was only twenty-six, no one gave him many years to live. His passion for provoking fights and duels was bound to lead him to an untimely end, even if his physique could stand the strain of continual dissipation. He was a favoured guest at Burton Pynsent, but Lady Chatham's smile turned acid when she noticed that the young rake (who had never been known to take any interest in a woman of his own class) was paying court to her niece, for she thought of Boconnoc and the acres of rich Cornish country, which her husband would never inherit if Lord Camelford suddenly took it in his head to marry. With a sore heart she had watched him squandering his money in true Pitt fashion, but at least she had been secure in the knowledge that he could not touch the entailed estates. It was intolerable to visualize Hester Stanhope as a possible mistress of Boconnoc, and Lady Chatham suddenly took a maternal interest in her niece and pointed out to her brother-in-law that it would be disastrous for a young girl to compromise herself with a man whose eccentricities were definitely mental.

Hester disregarded the warnings of her family and brazenly coupled herself with her cousin. She recognized in him those latent qualities which the world ignored, his generosity, his hatred of injustice, his revolt against the hypocritical society of their day, and she took pleasure in defying public opinion by behaving in a manner which allowed everyone to question the nature of their relationship. Hardly anyone suspected that she seriously thought of marrying him, but Hester was romantic enough at heart to consider marriage as the ultimate aim to a serious attachment. She who had refused so many proposals now waited for Camelford's declaration. Here was a man different from the dandified diplomats and courtiers with their mincing affectations and extravagant compliments; with their "For God's sake, Lady Hester, don't quiz me so: I shall die, I vow and protest—I shall expire from laughing. Now pray, Lady Hester, be kind."

Camelford's speech was rude and to the point and his jokes belonged to the fo'c'sle, but he was a good mathematician as well as being interested in chemistry and theology. And Hester, too proud to be married to a mediocrity and too independent to submit to a personality superior to her own, was ready to consider him as a perfect husband. The Chathams firmly opposed the marriage, and William Pitt, self-appointed guardian to the young Stanhopes, refused to consider the affair in a serious light, for Lord Camelford's temporary fits of insanity were too well known to be ignored by the most indulgent of relations. Every one of his actions were inconsistent. In 1800, on the occasion of Lord Stanhope's return to the House of Lords, Camelford was his only supporter in a motion for peace with Napoleon, but not a year later the same man fought an angry mob for refusing to illuminate his house in honour of the Peace of Amiens. He allowed Horne Tooke to be elected for the rotten borough of Old Sarum, not because he sympathized with his principles, but because he despised the whole parliamentary system; in fact, "he had half a mind to put up his negro servant for election."

People began to talk in whispers of 'poor Lord Camelford,' for it was no longer possible to hush up his scandals, which reflected on the young girl, who pretended she was engaged to him. In the Pump Room and coffee-houses of Bath she was constantly hearing rumours of his London duels, for the fashionable resort with its graceful colonnaded crescents and elegant parks seethed with gossip. There was nothing to do but gossip. As they floated in unbecoming shifts on the tide of the health-giving waters, the beaux and belles exchanged the latest items of London news, and as they breakfasted off dishes of tea and 'Sally Lunns,' painted old harridans supplemented the news with pithy extracts of local scandal. Yet no one dared to slander the girl who was the inseparable friend of the Duke and Duchess of York, and few unmarried women of her class were allowed as much freedom as Lady Hester. She had set her own standards and the world was forced to accept them. Her letters to Francis Jackson, full of affectionate gratitude for his share in her brother's escape, mention projected visits to race meetings and house parties, though she was not yet well enough to stand the strain of a full London season.

After a visit to the comparatively humble home of her sister Lucy, she returned to town and shocked her greatest friends by appearing publicly at parties accompanied by her cousin. She went about with him unchaperoned, and on one occasion she found herself involved in an unpleasant street brawl. They were driving out into the country and Camelford had paid the man at the turnpike gate, who had given him some halfpennies in exchange. Hester, knowing his careless extravagance, was surprised to see him turning over the dirty coppers in his ungloved hand. Her fastidious Ladyship raised her eyebrows and thought what strange tastes her cousin had to finger a few greasy pennies. Her surprise was still greater when he jumped out of the curricle, threw her the reins, and seized the turnpike man by the throat. A crowd collected immediately and their cries startled the nervous thoroughbreds, so that she had the greatest difficulty in keeping them under control. Passing travellers stopped for a moment, but hurried on when they saw that Lord Camelford was involved in a fight, for no one cared to embroil themselves in the quarrels of one who was considered the most accomplished duellist of the day. The row was soon over. Camelford resumed his seat and condescended to give an explanation of his conduct. "I daresay you thought," he said very quietly, "that I was going to put myself in a passion. But the fact is, these rascals have barrels of bad half-pennies and they pass them in change to the people who go through the gate. Some poor carter perhaps has nothing but his change to pay for his supper and, when he gets to his journey's end, finds he can't get his bread and cheese. The law, 'tis true, will fine them, but how is a poor devil to go to law? To you and me it would not signify, but to the poor it does, and I merely wanted to teach these blackguards a lesson by showing them that they cannot always play such tricks with impunity."

No wonder Hester admired her cousin, for, like him, her blood fired at any fraud or injustice, and in old age she would draw herself up proudly, flashing defiance at Syrian tyrants and English ministers, saying, "Let anyone attack me and they will find that I am a proper cousin to Lord Camelford."

Lady Chatham trembled at the thought of the marriage which Hester contemplated, but which probably never for one moment entered into Lord Camelford's head. He looked upon his cousin as a generous friend and a good companion; her masculine courage and fearlessness appealed to him, but her colossal egotism and inordinate vanity must have repelled one who was used to the warm, simple affection of the lower classes. He never dreamed of giving up his coarse, voluptuous mistresses for a spoilt, pampered aristocrat, whose brilliant exterior covered an exacting and domineering nature, and he alone was in a position to judge the limitations of Hester's emotional capacities. She never loved him with the passionate, devouring love which later she bestowed on the beautiful and effeminate Granville Leveson-Gower. Yet when she had forgotten the heartache and humiliation and when Granville Leveson-Gower was merely a name linked on the string of her London reminiscences, Camelford's memory was always vivid in her mind. That disturbed, overheated mind, hovering so near to the brink of insanity, found a certain pleasure in copying her cousin's most curious eccentricities. Horses and cattle were shot the moment she discovered they had been used for purposes contrary to her orders. Herds of goats were killed when the goatherd was found making profits out of the milk, and her frightened doctor was surprised to hear that what he thought were the crazy whims of a cruel old woman were complete imitations of Lord Camelford's unusual methods.

They drifted apart, and one reads of Lady Hester making nervous inquiries from one of her friends in London. "If I may ask a question of you, how is Lord Camelford? I like him better than people do in general and am anxious about him after the strange reports I have heard, but do not answer if you do not like it." Soon her passion for hero-worship found a worthier object in her uncle, William Pitt, and as she saw Pitt more she saw Camelford less. Even a dethroned minister had certain obligations with regard to his position, for the 'Doctor' and his friends (as Addington's party was called) would be only too ready to rejoice at the thought of Pitt extricating his young cousin out of the guard-rooms, where he had been locked up for drunken and disorderly behaviour.

Lady Chatham sighed with relief when Camelford returned to his old haunts, but she was disappointed in her expectations, for Camelford paid off the entail on his estates and made his sister Anne his sole heiress. Anne Pitt had married Lord Grenville, the stiffest and most uncompromising of politicians. The fiery, impetuous Pitts seemed destined to marry the frigid, heartless Grenvilles. And when, in 1804, Camelford was fatally shot in the fields of Kensington, which had witnessed so many dramatic episodes in his career, William Wyndham, Lord Grenville, that proud, fastidious statesman, had to hurry down from the House of Lords to be present at his brother-in-law's death-bed. It was such a sordid, unnecessary death, for Camelford had challenged his opponent on the scanty evidence of some backstair gossip repeated to him by one of his cast-off mistresses. Few mourned for him; even Hester was too immersed in her social and political triumphs to be seriously affected by his death. Her world centred round William Pitt and in a letter full of light, social gossip, in between describing a visit to the Princess of Wales and a house party at Mr. Canning's, she mentions somewhat casually, "Lord Camelford has been shot in duel, and there is no chance of his recovering. You know my opinion of him, I believe, therefore can judge if I am not likely to mourn his untimely end. He had vices but also great virtues, but these were not known to the world at large." She does not seem to have wasted many tears on his 'untimely end.'

CHAPTER FOUR

Two years of peace brought little contentment to the country. While English countesses gratified their curiosity by rushing over to Paris in order to have a glimpse of Bonaparte, and great ladies like the Duchess of Gordon paid homage to an obscure Creole, yeomanry had to be called in to quell the riots which had now broken out all over England. The people's rage was directed chiefly against the farmers, who were selling wheat at an exorbitant price, and starving viragoes threatened to hang and burn those who had defrauded them out of their daily bread. Insurgent mobs passed outside the gates of Burton Pynsent, where Lady Hester, following the fashionable trend, was busy planning a journey abroad.

It was a journey which took a year to materialize and she deliberately chose as her travelling companions a rather obscure couple called Egerton. All she wanted was a nominal chaperon and she knew that her humble and admiring friends would be only too anxious to gratify her caprices. As Pitt's niece she would bear credentials to every ambassador and every court, and shy, sensible people like the Egertons would never mind being left at home, when she found more congenial company, for they were bound to approve her conduct, however selfish or inconsiderate it might be. She admitted this in a letter to Francis Jackson. "You will perhaps wonder at my not having fixed upon more dashing persons for companions. In that case we must all have dashed away together; in the present case I shall have perfect liberty to act in all respects as is most pleasing to myself and in so doing be certain of pleasing them." It is small wonder that a woman, who so frankly labelled herself as an egotist, should have commanded more admiration than affection, and even the devoted Francis Jackson (though he always remained a loyal friend) piqued her vanity by becoming engaged to a German girl shortly after his appointment as minister to Berlin.

Old Lady Chatham's health was failing fast, and during the year which elapsed before she set out on her travels, Hester had many qualms about leaving the adoring grandmother, whom she might not see on her return. Lady Chatham possessed a charming nature, which was rarely found in a Grenville, and her sweetness and patience (a patience tried by over twenty years of marriage to a suffering invalid) made her beloved by the most unruly and refractory of grandchildren. She alone was able to understand a character which reflected so many of Chatham's moods; she alone made allowance for the blood of Diamond Pitt, which, according to Lord Rosebery, "came all aflame from the East and flowed like burning lava to his remotest descendants with the exception of Chatham's children, but even then it blazed up again in Hester Stanhope."

Her other grand-daughter, the charming, gentle orphan, Harriet Elliot, inherited none of her grandfather's fire, and Hester dominated her in the same way as she had dominated her sisters. She was always ready to give her advice, to praise her looks and disposition and talk of her as "a dear, sweet girl," but she had no real interest in her. She was bored with her company and preferred the rowdy dissipation of military camps, where her uncle, Lord Chatham, reigned supreme and where admiring officers saluted her with martial honours. "Such charming, charming men!" Hester regarded them with none of the indifference with which she looked upon her own sex. Every kind of masculine admiration was tolerable; she was even amused when during a stay at Ramsgate some drunken officers followed her to her house, but when one of them became too bold, she remembered her father's republican upbringing and dealt him a formidable blow on the jaw, which sent him reeling down the steps. She indulged in none of the over-charged sensibility and delicate languishments affected by the Devonshire House set and she could be a formidable opponent, whether to a drunken officer or a presumptuous peer. 'Little Bulldog' was the name given to her by the Duke of Cumberland, the only one of the Royal Princes whose name was not coupled with that of a woman. All London hinted discreetly at his strange morals and even the Regency rakes looked askance at the beautiful youths who formed his suite at Brighton; yet Lady Hester, who, in spite of her brazen worldliness preserved an extraordinary moral *naïveté*, looked upon him as one of those jolly, healthy princes, who were so different to their debauched eldest brother. Perhaps it was her masculinity which appealed to him, for he singled her out at parties, so that cynics wondered whether Pitt's niece was going to redeem His Royal Highness.

If Lady Hester was severe towards the heir-presumptive, she was equally severe towards his slattern of a wife. Caroline of Brunswick, friendless and ignorant, would have liked to have made a confidante of the proud young woman who was intimate with the whole Royal Family, but Hester Stanhope wrinkled her contemptuous nose at the coarse, vulgar creature, who gartered below the knee and whose clothes smelt of perspiration. A dinner at Blackheath was an ordeal to be endured rather than an act of royal condescension, and she blushed for 'the divine right of kings' when the sea captains averted their eyes from the indecent antics of the clockwork doll which the Princess delighted in. Canning and Brougham were amused by her Royal Highness's hilarious parties, but Pitt looked cold and disgusted when her adopted child, the pampered little Austin, was dangled over the table to snatch at his favourite fruits and sweets. Hester followed her uncle's example and openly criticized the Princess for over-indulging the boy.

Hester's ideas about disciplining children were unusually severe. When she was staying at Bromley with her sister Lucy, her little nephew was noticed to be remarkably docile in her presence. She explained it by saying that once when he was naughty she had taken him in her arms and had held him out of the window, threatening to drop him the next time he was disobedient. This was a mild foretaste of the disciplinary methods which were to fertilize on Syrian soil. Yet there was nothing cold and heartless about her. Now that her eldest brother had obtained freedom through her intervention, she enlisted Pitt's protection in order to secure commissions for the younger Stanhopes, whose education had been so neglected that Charles, the elder of the two, was hardly able to write or spell. They were brought by stealth to London and Charles obtained a commission in the twenty-fifth Foot Regiment, while his brother James was enrolled as a midshipman. Lord Stanhope seems to have been exceptionally mild about the flight of his younger sons, but he revenged himself by making a new will in which all his children's names were eliminated. Hester fussed and fluttered over her charges; Charles's fate was put in the hands of the Duke of York, the most beloved of the Royal Princes, and even indolent Lord Chatham offered to take him into his house, "probably in the hopes," as his niece somewhat cattily remarked, "of having an honourable *aide-de-camp*." Charles was her favourite, for his shy, sensitive nature had suffered from the treatment he had received at Chevening, and he was ready to give her an un-questioning, adoring love, which never changed. He was neither as brilliant nor as handsome as his little brother, whose engaging charm endeared him to the toughest sea captains; but his sister's prayer that he would make a fine soldier was realized, for Charles Stanhope's name became immortalized as one of the heroes of Corunna.

At twenty-six Hester possessed a strong maternal instinct, and even the incense of masculine admiration was not as pleasurable as hearing her brother's praises sung, while she softened towards the wildest young naval officers if they were kind to her little midshipman. There was something slightly absurd about the possessive mother-love which she bestowed on her brothers, who were only a few years younger than herself, and soon she was to have her first disappointment, for her 'charming, incomparable Mahon,' whom she had planned to meet on her travels, would no longer be the docile, admiring boy who took her words for gospel truth.

On an autumn day in 1802, one of Leader's most comfortable travelling carriages waited at the gate of a Cheshire manor house, and Mr. and Mrs. Egerton, full of nervous trepidation at the dreadful tales they had been recounted of foreign brigands and disbanded French soldiers, bid good-bye to their beloved home and set out for Dover, where Lady Hester was joining them.

She had gone there a few days previously to visit Pitt at Walmer Castle. On her arrival she found him suffering from a bad attack of gout, but he recovered almost immediately, and she had no opportunity of showing her capacity as a nurse. It is hard to imagine anyone appreciating a nurse as domineering as Hester, but there was no talent she was so proud of, and perhaps her methods with her favourite uncle might have been different to those which in later life she employed in Syria, where her black doses were famous throughout the length and breadth of the country.

William Pitt, depressed and harassed by the turmoil of party intrigues, was cheered by her gaiety and vitality, and he wrote to his mother's companion, Mrs. Stapleton, "Hester arrived here yesterday on her way to join her travelling friends at Dover. I hope to enjoy the pleasure of her society at all events till Monday, and perhaps, if the winds are contrary, a few days longer."

Hester was in her element at Walmer, for she delighted in the fact that she was surrounded by nothing but delightful men and that she had not seen a single woman's face. Her sister Griselda, now married to a Captain Tekell, was living there at the time, but an obscure, unattractive sister was of no consequence, and it is not surprising that Griselda was jealous when she saw Hester being courted by all Pitt's friends, while she and her husband were tolerated as poor dependents. She harboured this jealousy all her life and, as an old lady, she told her niece, the Duchess of Cleveland, disparaging tales of her sister's superficial brilliance. She had every right to criticize, for the cultured and erudite must have been horrified by

Hester's blatant ignorance, which was accentuated by the fact that she had no wish to learn. She pitted herself against the best brains in England, and when they gave way to her out of politeness or deference to her sex, so colossal was her conceit that she fondly imagined that she had had the best of the argument. She was not content to remain silent, listening to the conversation of her uncle and his friends, for she always had to assert her own opinions, and Pitt, the gentlest and most unassuming of men, rarely bothered to contradict her.

The woman who became the greatest traveller of her day and who even as a child had shown a bold and adventurous spirit, set out on her first journey, just as ignorant and as insular as hundreds of other fashionable young ladies. Paris was her ultimate goal, and it was reserved till the last because every other place was bound to pale before the capital of Bonaparte, where English hostesses gave nightly balls. Like most of her compatriots she deliberately sought out the travellers of her own class and nationality and she, who in later years preferred the company of a Mahomedan sheik to that of an English duke, was frankly pleased to find the Continent crowded with young 'milords.'

Mahon joined the party at Lyons, and Hester found him grown into a polished, finished man of the world. At the court of the Margravine of Brandenburg-Bayreuth there had been charming women, only too ready to listen to his opinions, and it was hardly likely that he was going to allow himself to be bullied by his dogmatic sister. At first they got on very well together. When they crossed the Mont Cenis they calmly left their party to 'their own frights and fears,' and hired mules and muleteers to lead them over the mountains. This ride seems to have made more impression on Hester than all the wonders of Turin and Florence, and while Mr. and Mrs. Egerton trembled for their carriage springs on the bad roads, brother and sister enjoyed the wild and dangerous pass and their lunch of fresh trout in the inn on top of the mountain.

This idyllic relationship did not last long. In Italy they

began to get on each other's nerves, for Hester was more interested in people than in churches and museums and her brother was horrified at her lack of culture. Her merciless teasing irritated him, for a young man who prided himself on his knowledge of European politics and remarkable conversational powers could not have enjoyed being told that he talked like a Frenchman out of humour. He must have got tired of having his uncle quoted to him in every sentence, even though he had every reason to be grateful to Pitt, who on his return to England had promised him the post of Lieutenant-Governor of Dover Castle. Hester quizzed her brother on his foppish dress and on his hurried manner of speech, and was furious when he attempted to contradict her. She inveighed against his conceit, not realizing that her own was still more formidable, and neither was sorry to say good-bye to the other in Florence, for Mahon and his black poodle had not been a happy addition to the party. Hester certainly did not deserve the charming, modest letter which he wrote her from Leghorn, begging her without reserve to give him her opinion of his conduct and to send him any instructions she might think necessary. These pretty phrases only partially appeased her, for he had shown her too definitely that he was able to get on very well without her advice.

Still harbouring her grievance, she proceeded to Naples, where a bevy of young milords helped her to forget an 'ungrateful brother,' and where William Drummond, the scholar diplomat, gave her royal entertainment at the English Legation. There must have been very little affinity between her and the young minister, who wrote classical plays and translated from the Greek, but they became great friends and he allowed her to tease him about his pedantry, while occasionally he lectured her on her unconventional behaviour. Neapolitan morals were lax and the Queen, who had befriended Emma Hamilton, was hardly likely to disapprove of Hester Stanhope's harmless though injudicious flirtations. Her chaperons faded into the background, for, surrounded by those dashing young peers,

Grantham and Brooke and Montague, she had very little use for a couple whom she labelled as "a fidget married to a fool."

The spread wings of the Napoleonic eagle cast but a faint shadow on the gay and licentious town, where, guarded by English gunboats, the last surviving daughter of Maria Theresa ruled over a fantastic and baroque court.

The niece of Pitt was flattered and fêted to her heart's content and she felt perfectly at home in a place where there were enough sensible men to converse with and enough handsome ones for an escort. Mr. and Mrs. Egerton were left to their own resources, to admire Vesuvius and buy strings of amber and Roman pearl, while her Ladyship frivolled in the gardens of Caserta.

The whole winter was spent in Italy and the following May found Hester in Venice, where she heard the news of the outbreak of hostilities. Paris, the final goal of their journey, was now the enemy's headquarters, and plans had to be remade involving a long and tedious route through Germany. The Egertons, who had been ignored all through the winter, suddenly asserted themselves by insisting on travelling through Stuttgart, the reason being that they had once met the Electress and hoped to be able to impress Hester with their grand connections. It was a stupid plan, and Hester, who looked forward to visiting Vienna and Berlin, was justly irritated at their ridiculous snobbery. How humiliated they must have been when the Electress could not even remember their name and lavished all her attentions on Hester because she was the niece of her old friend, Harriet Elliot! However, the compliments and homage paid her at the court of Stuttgart could not compensate her for missing Jackson's company and the military glories of Potsdam, while she bitterly bewailed the fact that through not going to Berlin she would not be able to buy the perfect poodle which she hoped to bring back as a present for her uncle.

Her chance was gone; Bonaparte's soldiers occupied every

frontier, and her frightened companions hurried to the coast, where they took sail for England.

Lady Hester's homecoming was a sad one. Her beloved grandmother was dead and Burton Pynsent could no longer be called her home. On the continent she had been treated as a queen, but in her own country she had not a single anchorage; the gates of Chevening were closed to her; her uncle, Lord Chatham, had adopted his orphaned niece; and her brother, Lord Mahon, had already profited by his few months in England by becoming engaged to one of Lord Carrington's daughters. In despair she turned to William Pitt, the one person who had never refused her help.

CHAPTER FIVE

"How amiable it is of Pitt to take compassion on poor Lady Hester Stanhope, and that in a way which must break in upon his habits of life. He is as good as he is great." So wrote Lord Mulgrave to the Honourable Major-General Phipps, and these sentiments were echoed by all Pitt's friends when they heard that the reserved middle-aged bachelor had offered a permanent home to his exuberant, tempestuous niece. Only his high sense of duty prompted him to make such a quixotically generous offer, for he must have dreaded the responsibility of chaperoning a young woman whose headstrong nature might involve her in every kind of scrape. They had never been on terms of great intimacy, and though she might amuse him for a few days, it did not mean that she would prove a satisfactory element in his essentially male society. All his intimates were men, with the exception of a few women friends of that susceptible Scotsman, Henry Dundas.

William Pitt was unique in an age when men re-married a few months after their wife's death, when lovers and *cicisbeos* formed the necessary retinue of every lady of fashion, when a general's mistress accompanied him on parade and when Eton schoolboys were granted a holiday in honour of Lord Nelson, with Lady Hamilton on his arm. All London smiled when 'the spotless minister' took his niece into his house, and in their smiles there was a touch of commiseration. But from the moment that Hester entered Walmer Castle she became a different person. She had only one thought, and that was to please her uncle, and his biographer, the fifth Earl Stanhope, writes: "His kind act as by a propitious order of things is often the case with such acts, brought, after all, its own reward. Lady Hester quickly formed for him a strong and devoted attachment which she extended to his memory, so long as her own life endured. On his part he came to regard her with almost a father's affection."

However inconsiderate or selfish she might be to others, with him she was always charming and attentive. She watched over his health and protected him from the tedious solicitations of aspiring politicians, she acted as his secretary during the time he was out of office, and the 'Doctor's' party found that she had a sharp eye for noticing and a biting tongue with which to point out their blunders. The officers who came to pay their respects to the guardian of the Cinque Ports were received by a delightful hostess, who was not above flirting with the obscurest lieutenant, for though her pride might forbid her to marry any but the highest in the land, there was no reason why she should not amuse herself with the attractive military. Under her rule Pitt's somewhat bleak domain was transformed into a flowering park. Yews and evergreen oaks sprang from the barren soil and the Channel winds swept over the delicate shrubs she had transplanted from Lord Guildford's nurseries. Chatham's passion for landscape gardening was revived in his granddaughter and the woman who made a blossoming paradise rise out of the rocks of the Lebanon, learned her lesson on the chalk hills of the Kentish coast. The lovely garden which one sees to-day was Lady Hester's creation. The rose arbours and carved yew hedges were planted under her directions. Nothing was too much trouble if it was rewarded by a smile from the 'great man.' And while the guns in front of the castle pointed menacingly towards France, the volunteers for the coastal defence acted as Lady Hester's gardeners. No one was more fitted to give orders and when two regiments were placed under her nominal command, she took her duties seriously and exhausted herself by taking part in the most strenuous parades, riding for twenty miles and then remaining immovable on horseback for hours on end. The honours she received were worth the fatigue, for how she must have enjoyed having an orderly at her beck and call and the military band at her disposal!

Every day there were rumoured reports of a threatened invasion of England and the country people jubilated whenever a captured French gunboat was brought into the harbour. At Walmer one realized the proximity of the war, for the castle was little more than a base camp for the active hostilities across the Channel; but in London the fashionable world was tired of discussing Bonaparte, and the name of young Roscius, the child actor, was on everybody's lips.

In the spring of 1804, Addington's party fell and William Pitt was once more Prime Minister. All eyes turned to the young unmarried woman who sat at the head of his table at Putney and Downing Street. No modesty or misgivings were noticeable in her demeanour. Mocking and intolerant, her deep blue eyes looked out at the world from under heavy, shadowed lids, so dark in contrast to her dazzling white skin. The draperies of Indian muslin, which Pitt with his discerning eye was always ready to approve or criticize, revealed the form of a Roman statue. Tall and graceful and exquisitely dressed, she made many beauties pale beside her, and the established queens of fashion tightened their lips in envy, for there was nothing gracious or conciliating in her manner towards them. She openly mimicked the Devonshire House lisp and yawned in front of ministers' wives, and even Pitt's remonstrances could not curb her unbridled tongue.

No one was more eager to further the cause of a *protégé*, but no one was more vehement in assaulting an enemy, and her uncle's colleagues learned to tremble at her merciless sarcasm. The well-meaning, punctilious Castlereagh was dismissed as his 'monotonous Lordship.' Lord Abercorn roused her vindictive spirit for having solicited from Addington the favours refused by Pitt. When she saw him come into a drawing-room flaunting the cherished Garter, she humiliated him in public by alluding to his infirmity, asking if he used the order to tie up his broken leg. She could not even resist teasing her uncle. When Addington's wounded vanity was being soothed by the offer of a peerage, Pitt contemplated conferring on him the title of Lord Raleigh. But Hester was indignant that a man who was nothing more than the son of her grandfather's

44

physician should bear such an historic name. She came one morning to her uncle, telling him that she had seen such an amusing caricature, which depicted him as Queen Elizabeth with George III dressed as a Royal jester, and Addington prostrating himself in the *rôle* of the gallant courtier. Pitt believed her story and told Addington, who had all London searched for the malicious caricature, which existed only in Hester's imagination. The poisoned shaft went home and Addington now chose the more unassuming title of Lord Sidmouth.

She made fun of the 'broad-bottomed' Grenvilles and then was surprised when none of them left her a penny in their wills. She allowed herself to be rude to the Prince of Wales, yet felt insulted when he cut her after her uncle's death. Her head was turned, and during two triumphant years she never stopped to think that she might reap what she sowed. Politicians sought her advice, princes and ambassadors begged to be introduced to her. In a humble and almost cringing letter Canning assured her that through her he came to Pitt with more confidence of not being misunderstood. He told her, "You stand instead of pages of preface and apology, and as a voucher for us to each other that we mean each other kindly and fairly."

With Canning her feelings vacillated between passionate assurances of friendship and cold distrust for the 'fiery Irish politician.' In later years she attributed her dislike on account of his disloyalty to her uncle. But no one was more responsible than she for making mischief between them. Both Canning and Pitt possessed a strong love for the classics, and Hester resented the fact that through her lack of culture she was unable to take part in their conversations. She made fun of Canning's brilliant, erudite speeches, which were gibberish to the simple country squires, and though he sent her dedicated copies of his finest poems it is doubtful whether they were appreciated by her in the same way as they were appreciated by her uncle. Pitt was genuinely fond of his handsome disciple, and Hester, like a jealous watch-dog guarding his interests, was over-zealous in reporting the slightest signs of defection— Canning had been seen too often dining at Devonshire House. They had not even asked his wife, for no hostess was more avid than the beautiful Duchess for having unattached young men at her parties. Canning had been asked for the week-end to Stowe, for now that the Grenvilles had joined the Opposition, they were trying to corrupt Pitt's friends. There was enough gossip carried to and fro to foster uneasy suspicions, and Hester gave Canning little consolation when his frustrated ambition lamented Lord Mulgrave's appointment as Minister for Foreign Affairs. His Lordship's somewhat mediocre ability hardly entitled him to such an important post, and though Hester might not sympathize with Canning's justifiable resentment, she was ready to sneer at him herself. Her jokes were invariably in the worst of taste. One day when Lord Mulgrave was break-fasting at Putney, he remarked on the fact that he was served with a broken egg-spoon. Quick as lightning she answered, "Haven't you noticed that Mr. Pitt uses very often slight and weak instruments to effect his ends?" Perhaps she disliked the implication that she was not a *soignée* housewife, but even so her answer was unnecessarily cruel.

Lord Hawkesbury, the scheming time-server with his melancholy gait, was often held up to ridicule, though his wife, the youngest of the lovely Hervey sisters, was one of the few women whom Hester really admired. One cannot blame her for laughing at her uncle's colleagues, for, with the exception of Dundas, Pitt treated them all with disdain.

Her relationship with her younger brothers and their friends shows one a far pleasanter side to her character. Mahon, since he was married and independent, had fallen into disgrace, for she accused him of laziness and ingratitude towards his benefactor. It was a purely imaginary grievance on her part, for Pitt always seems to have remained on excellent terms with him; but Mahon had inherited his father's philosophic tastes without any of his father's energy, and to his sister's disgust he preferred studying by his own fireside to fulfilling his official duties as Lieutenant-Governor of Dover Castle. The officers gave orders without bothering to consult him, a circumstance so mortifying that Hester assured him "that she would shoot herself were she in his situation." Luckily, her younger brothers possessed her military spirit; her little midshipman had left the Navy for the Army, and in these days of patronage and protection, was immediately given a commission in a regiment of the Guards, stationed at Dover Castle. Charles had gained rapid promotion and still remained his sister's favourite. Any friend of his was sure to find a welcome at Putney, a welcome often warmer than that which was accorded to the most important minister.

No wonder young William Napier, whom Charles Stanhope brought to the house in 1804, forgot his loyalty to Whig principles and succumbed to the graciousness of Pitt and the fascination of his niece. He found "that it was quite impossible not to fall at once into her direction and become her slave, whether for laughter or seriousness." He did not consider her beautiful, for the son of the lovely Sarah Lennox must have had a high standard in looks, but she made so great an impression on him that over thirty years later, when her name aroused nothing but mockery and derision, he was the only one of her old friends who was chivalrous enough to take up arms in her defence. His letter to *The Times* vindicating her honour and purity of motive was one of the few tributes of devotion and gratitude which she received in her loveless old age, for he never forgot that the brilliant, spoilt young woman, the idol of the London drawing-rooms, had found time to exert her powerful influence in order to obtain a pension for his mother.

These were happy days at Putney, when the young Stanhopes transformed the minister's sober villa into a romping beargarden, and no one enjoyed romping as much as Pitt. There were wild scrambles when Hester and her brothers threatened to cork their uncle's face, and delirious pillow-fights, suddenly interrupted by importunate ministers craving audience.

William Napier gives an account of Castlereagh and Hawkesbury entering the room, 'bending like spaniels,' while Pitt, who a minute before had been belabouring his young relations with cushions in order to revenge his blackened face, now assumed a completely different manner.

"His tall, ungainly, bony figure seemed to grow to the ceiling. His head was thrown back, his eyes fixed immovable in one position, as if reading the heavens and totally regardless of the bending figures near him. For some time they spoke; he made now and then some short observation and finally, with an abrupt, stiff inclination of the body, but without casting his eyes down, dismissed them. Then turning to us with a laugh, caught up the cushions and resumed our fight." And this was the statesman whom the world considered dour and proud.

Both William Napier and Charles Stanhope served under General Moore, whose strategic talents Pitt was one of the first to appreciate. What Pitt praised, Lady Hester was ready to adore, and Charles Stanhope's enthusiastic hero-worship for his general was echoed by his sister. In 1804, Moore's gentle, quiet manner and noble character had not yet captured her heart; she was indulging in a far more dangerous passion, a passion which gave her her first heartache, her first humiliation.

CHAPTER SIX

AMONG all the aspiring politicians, the dandies and the beaux, who formed the entourage of Devonshire House, none was more fêted and none was more spoilt than Lord Granville Leveson-Gower. The youngest child of the Marquess of Stafford, he was brought up in the strictest Tory circles. His greatest friend was Canning and his god was William Pitt; but during the 'grand tour,' which the decree of fashion deemed necessary for all young men of his class, he passed through Naples where he fell a victim to the spell of the fascinating Lady Bessborough, whom the sacrilegious dared to acclaim as the cleverer of the lovely Spencer sisters. She was twelve years older than he and she gave him the love which she had denied to Sheridan. By that love she bound him with the subtlest of chains; chains no more irksome than skeins of silk, so delicate that he never tried to break them.

He came home and stood for Parliament as a supporter of Pitt, but from now on his evenings were spent at Devonshire House and Cavendish Square, and Lady Stafford, the most doting of mothers, lamented the pernicious influence that the notorious sirens might have over her darling Granville. It was hardly desirable for a younger son to play at faro with the friends of Fox, and it was not long before the members of White's raised their eyebrows at the stupendous figures of Lord Granville's gambling debts. As a diplomat it was imperative that he should marry a rich wife, but how could he be expected to settle down when he was coupled with the mother of a grown-up daughter? There was the beautiful Sarah Jane who flirted with him, but then, probably realizing that his affections were centred in another quarter, very wisely went and married Lord Villiers. Both Lord Granville and his Dulcinea were strangely piqued at her behaviour, "for nothing," said Lady Bessborough, "could have pleased her better than to see dear Granville well and happily married." Only by some odd

49

coincidence, whenever marriage happened to be on the *tapis*, she always found something slightly derogatory to say about the young lady in question. Naturally her beautiful 'Antinous' was not faithful to her. How could he be when all London begged for his smiles? He was painted by Lawrence but the face, which caused so much suffering and heartache, now strikes one as insipid and effeminate. One no longer admires the man with a full mouth and limpid eyes, while the curling, chestnut hair and Roman nose belong to past standards of beauty.

Lord Granville may have been a distinguished diplomat and a reckless gambler, but around him there hangs the faint aroma of a petticoat hero. He was always pursued and never pursuing. Nevertheless he graciously allowed himself to be loved, and when his victims became too importunate he complained to Lady Bessborough. He was ambitious, and ambition must have played a large part in his relations with Hester Stanhope. His sister-in-law, Lady Stafford, the beautiful Elizabeth Sunderland, heiress and peeress in her own right, was her most frequent chaperon; Canning, his best friend, treated her as a political oracle; she was an intimate of his sister, Lady Harrowby, and even Henrietta Bessborough professed the warmest affection for her 'dearest Hetty.' It was flattering to dine in intimacy with William Pitt, but it was dangerous to flirt with his niece, for Hester, in spite of all her worldliness, was not able to withstand the amorous tactics of London's most accomplished Don Juan. He never deliberately courted her, for he certainly had no intention of involving himself in a compromising situation, but he was not a man to content himself with the bantering sallies and light-hearted quizzing which were part of Hester's stock in trade. He expected to rouse passion and he succeeded, but twenty-eight is a dangerous age in which to fall in love for the first time and soon the whole town was talking of the mad way in which Lady Hester flaunted her infatuation.

The bitterest gossip is usually started by unsuccessful rivals and no one was more malicious than Noel Hill, the well-known wit, who had sunned himself in Hester's favour before Lord Granville's inopportune appearance. Noel Hill was an *habitué* of Devonshire House and delighted in scaring Lady Bessborough with tales of her lover's defection, and even the Duchess was annoyed when Lord Granville excused himself from her suppers on the plea that he was detained at Putney or Downing Street. The young diplomat forgot his wise resolutions and, regardless of the complications that might arise from the Stanhope temperament, set himself out to gratify Lady Hester's ardour. He forgot that she was the niece of the Prime Minister and considered her merely as an attractive, full-blooded young woman, who might with a little discreet encouragement be persuaded to carry the flirtation beyond the established limits. Never for one moment did he dream of marrying her and in spite of her odd and unconventional behaviour, Hester still looked upon marriage as the only possible solution to a love affair. She still cherished the ideals of a well-brought-up young girl; these ideals were only thrown to the winds six years later when she became the mistress of Michael Bruce. There was hardly a woman in London who would vouch for her virtue and Henrietta Bessborough, instead of making jealous scenes with her young lover, counselled and warned him as gently as a mother. "Think," she writes, "how many unpleasant things anything like a scrape with her might entail on you. You are a pretty gentleman to be sure." And later on, in a more serious tone she repeats these warnings. "Is it quite honourable, dear Granville, to encourage a passion you do not mean seriously to return, and which if you do not, must make the owner of it miserable? And how can you be certain of what lengths you or she may be drawn into? We know she has strong passions and indulges them with great latitude. May you not both of you be hurried further than you intend? If Mr. Pitt knew even what had passed already do you think he would like it?"

She was right. Pitt did not enjoy his niece making a public exhibition of her feelings, and in the autumn of 1804 Lord

Granville was offered the post of Ambassador to Petersburg, which he was wise enough to accept.

Before he left England, he told Hester quite clearly that he would never marry her. It was her first knock, and she reacted to it in a childish and primitive manner. The poised edifice of her pride crumbled and she allowed the whole world to see her misery. In a cynical, sophisticated society no one believed that she would be so miserable if the affair had not entailed some considerable sacrifice on her part. Henrietta Bessborough, feline and insincere, sought her company, received her confidences and constituted herself as a somewhat half-hearted defender of her morals, at the same time as lending an eager ear to the scurrilous gossip circulating round London. She was having ample revenge for the proud little notes in which Hester used to inform her that Lord Granville was spending the night at Putney.

The dowager Lady Stafford met Hester Stanhope for the first time at her daughter Susan Harrowby's, and wrote to her son that she was sadly disappointed in her appearance. "I had pictured her to myself as very pretty, in place of which she looked like a middle-aged married woman with a dingy complexion, no rouge, a broad face and an unbecoming fur cap." The fashionable world could not forgive Hester for refusing to mask her sorrow. Such an exaggerated display of one's feelings was considered indecent and Pitt raised no opposition when she suggested retiring to Walmer. All during the days of misery and hysteria he had treated her with the greatest patience and indulgence, for it must have been incredibly irritating for a proud, reserved man to be faced by the uncontrolled emotions of a jilted young woman. He had taken a fatherly pride in her metallic brilliance, which had attracted a constant bevy of young men whom he used to call her 'adoring slaves,' but it is doubtful if she ever appealed to him as a woman. The man who had loved the gentle Eleanor Eden must have been slightly repelled by the brazen determination with which Hester pursued the handsome young dandy.

He never bore Lord Granville any grudge for refusing to marry her, but it was humiliating for the Prime Minister to have the whole of London discussing his niece's thwarted love affair.

According to her own words Pitt used to say that "Hester would never marry because she would never find anyone as clever as herself." But it was not Lord Granville's brain which had primarily attracted her. It was his dream-like classic beauty; his mad recklessness, which many years later when he was Ambassador in Paris won him the title of "*le Wellington des joueurs*"; his diffident, appealing charm; his sudden fits of melancholy alternating with outbursts of irresponsible gaiety; a sensitive, somewhat effeminate streak in his character which endeared him to her masculine, decided nature. If she had been more subtle and more patient she might have wrested him from Lady Bessborough's silken chains, but she was possessive and direct. Her love-making was stormy and exhausting and her demands were exacting. Lord Granville took fright. The spoilt Don Juan of thirty was not going to allow himself to be entrapped by a domineering young woman, who would take it upon herself to rule his life and dictate his career. When the time came for him to marry he could take his choice among the charming young ladies of Devonshire House, delicate, elf-like creatures, frail little shadows of their exuberant mothers, lisping poetry in the affected accents which were characteristic of their family. Lord Granville was tired of his six-foot amazon with the blue, flashing eyes, and he was slightly shocked by the lack of decorum with which she waylaid him at every party. Even the prospect of a Russian winter was preferable to her tantrums and scenes of jealousy. The offer of the Petersburg Embassy was accepted and elegantly, tactfully he decamped.

At first when Hester realized that he would never marry her, she was so stunned with grief that she was even grateful for Lady Bessborough's shallow sympathy, but soon her friends dissuaded her from seeing the woman, whom the whole town knew to be Lord Granville's mistress. Both the old Queen and the Princess of Wales advised her to avoid her and Lady Bessborough's finely-tuned sensibilities received an unpleasant shock when Hester visited her for the last time. There were tears and kisses and Hester was naïve enough to blurt out that she had been warned against her, while Lady Bessborough pretended to be deeply hurt at her ingratitude. The next courier bound for Petersburg contained a vivid account of this interview, in which her Ladyship took care to show herself in the kindest of lights. She assured her dearest Granville that, in spite of everything, she would always protect and help the girl who had been foolish enough to fall in love with him. She told him, "I shall always be kind to her for a strange reason. She belongs in some way to you."

Letters sped to Petersburg, charming, tactful letters with only the discreetest innuendoes, the most delicate allusions to poor Hetty; warm, loving letters which made the lonely young Ambassador, bored by the gloom and grandeur of the Russian court, feel as if he were within a stone's throw of the lighted portals of Devonshire House. Hester only wrote once, a noble, courageous little note in which she blamed herself for everything that had passed. Then she retired to Walmer and allowed scandal to do its worst. People wondered and conjectured and soon there were whispered rumours of an 'accouchement.' She aggravated matters by writing strange and mysterious letters to his colleagues and neither Canning (whom the wits accused of playing base to his friend by seeking Lady Hester's attentions) nor Noel Hill nor Lord Boringdon were the acme of discretion. They were responsible for spreading the story of Lady Hester having made an unsuccessful attempt to poison herself, and Noel Hill even committed the unpardonable action of showing one of her letters to Lady Bessborough. All Granville's friends knew that he had jilted her and her pride no longer prompted her to keep up any pretences.

Only the faithful Francis Jackson never betrayed her confidences. Many months previously he had jocularly accused her of neglecting her old friends and she answered him with brave and rather pathetic words:

"It is not my enviable situation (as the world calls it) to which I owe my head being turned and my neglecting my friends. For many months after I received your last kind letter I believe this was the case and now my heart (however devoted it will always be to those who have served me) points like the compass to the north. Now perhaps you understand, and also understand I am not happy; indeed, how can I be when I have shown my taste more than my prudence in admiring an object which fills more hearts than one? You know me too well, I believe, to accuse me of being fond of idle confidences, and I esteem you too much to give you any false reason for an apparent neglect which even the cause will hardly justify to myself. Last spring and part of this summer I bore in the great world much more than my value for talents, looks, etc.; everything was overrated, and although I was perfectly aware of it at the time, then I own, I enjoyed it, now if I could command it, it would be indifferent to me. But my looks are gone (as they always do with the absence of health) and I have been recommended to come into the country to regain them, and here I have been three weeks. To be near my sister-in-law was a good excuse to leave town; they (Mahon and her) see I am not well or as gay as usual, but do not understand why. As we have been quite in different society Mahon and her Ladyship are as ignorant as you would have been had I not written what I have. Indeed, *il n'est pas permis* to write such stuff, but I have been too much in habits of confidence with you to recede from them without a cause. My sincerity will, I hope, procure me a pardon for apparent ingratitude and not draw upon me the ridicule of a member of a corps I am now more attached to than ever. I think there is a sort of sympathy in my preference as they all flock about me, and seldom a day passes in town, but one or two constantly spend hours with me. . . .

"I often wish I was a bird—you might then see me at Berlin, but only in my flight; there might be some danger in this season of my wings being frozen, but the warmth of my heart would, I think, overcome it. . . ."

There was something very dignified in these broken-hearted confessions. Sorrow had softened her and she was even grateful for the kindness of the brother, whom only a few months ago she had so bitterly criticized. She was strong-minded enough not to give way to the inertia of grief, and while at Walmer she resumed her hobby of landscape gardening. She even made an effort to entertain some of her old army friends, but she was hardly in the right mood to enjoy their heavy mess-room jokes.

Towards the end of the spring she plucked up the courage to return to London and to show herself at the season's balls. But though the country air had done her good, she still looked pale and listless, and her blue eyes were dark and lustreless. The Duchess of Devonshire pursued her sister's rival with a vindictiveness strange to find in a woman who was famous for her good nature. At one party Hester was unfortunate enough to faint; at another party she was unfortunate enough to appear without any rouge, and these two incidents were sufficient for the Duchess to insist that she *affichéd* the fact that she was with child. Even Lady Bessborough half believed the story and took great care to tell everyone that it was not dear Lord Granville's fault.

Soon people lost interest in Hester Stanhope and her beautiful Ambassador. Lord Melville's threatened impeachment and young Roscius's interpretation of Hamlet were the two topics of absorbing interest. Tory peers like Aberdeen were seen no more at Devonshire House, for they refused to meet Lord Melville's prosecutors, and in spite of the fact that England was in the throes of the Napoleonic wars, parliament was adjourned, so that Pitt and his colleagues could witness the performance that had taken London by storm.

Lady Bessborough still cherished a marble cast of Antinous in her front hall and wrote to Petersburg by every courier. But as the summer ripened into autumn old flames pressed their claims on Lady Hester and one heard of Sidney Smith as a constant guest at Putney and of Noel Hill once more escorting her to parties. Yet gaiety and laughter had deserted Pitt's house. The guns fired at Woolwich in honour of the Victory of Trafalgar announced the death of his greatest admiral; the *grande armée* marched in triumph across the plains of Central Europe, and at home the impeachment of his best friend and most valuable colleague dealt a crushing blow to the immaculate honesty of Pitt's Cabinet. His health gave way, and worry and anxiety over her uncle's illness cured Lady Hester's broken heart. Her love for Lord Granville had been little more than a physical infatuation, which temporarily had succeeded in destroying her pride and self-respect. But her love for Pitt was the one dominating emotion of her life, and now her only thought was to make herself indispensable to him. The news of Lord Granville's return to England was of no interest to the woman who watched over the Prime Minister's sick-bed.

CHAPTER SEVEN

"ROLL up that map. It will not be wanted these ten years."
Pitt spoke with the voice of a dying man. The map of Europe
hanging on the wall reminded him too vividly of Ulm and
Austerlitz.

He had returned from Bath, but the waters, which so often
had proved beneficial, could no longer help him. Worry and
depression had made him lose the calm, equable temperament
and sanguine disposition which for years had enabled him to
fight against his terrible disease. Painfully he dragged himself
up the stairs of his home and as he spoke in a cracked, hollow
voice, so unlike his usual mellow tones, Lady Hester realized
that there was no longer any hope. It was useless for his
physician, Sir Walter Farquhar, to persist in his unconvincing
optimism, useless for Pitt to plan country visits in order to
delude her as to the state of his health. Adams, his faithful
secretary, Rose and Long, his most loyal friends, knew
that he was dying, and in London people already named his
possible successors.

It must have needed all Lady Hester's courage to keep up a
brave appearance during the last month. The rigid etiquette of
the day forced her to go to town to attend the Queen's birthday
party, where she appeared in a gorgeous creation of black and
green velvet, heavily embossed with gold and studded with rubies.
It was her last public appearance as a leader of society, and
though the old Queen and royal Princesses singled her out with
marked attention everyone knew that her day was over. There
was no longer any need for those who were jealous to simulate
their smiles, or for those she had offended to hide their rancour. For the last time she was courted and flattered by a cold
and hypocritical society. With what heartache she must have
returned to Putney to the uncle who would never more hear
the cheering of the London mobs as they dragged his carriage
from the Guildhall; who would never again stand on the

terrace of Walmer Castle, while the gunboats saluted him from the harbour. Pitt was dying, and with him went the glory and the grandeur which his niece claimed as her birthright.

He had been more than a father to her and to her brothers and his loss would be irretrievable. Even on his death-bed he still worried about their futures, begging her to keep a strict eye on James, "who was a young man to be kept under, otherwise he would always be trying to be a *joli garcon* and any day he might fall into the hands of men who would gain him over and unsettle his political principles." With Charles there was no need to worry. He was safe under the tutelage of General Moore, but both brothers had considerable financial difficulties, though Mahon occasionally helped them by raising money on the entail. Neither they nor their sister had learned thrift and economy in their uncle's house. They were hardened to the importunities of clamouring tradesmen, for Pitt had a curious manner of settling his debts. When he was presented with a bill, instead of paying, he immediately gave another large order, and no one cared to dun the Prime Minister. His niece and nephews followed his example, and though Hester occasionally played at being a careful housewife, it is doubtful if she ever managed to cut down the weekly bills. The fantastic extravagance of the castle of Djoun can be traced back to these days. Both at Putney and at Downing Street there was a constant come-and-go of visitors, constant dinner parties and entertainments. Servants were magnificently pensioned and lavishly rewarded and gifts from foreign potentates mouldered in the Customs, because the Prime Minister followed the rigid rule of never accepting presents. His niece was known to be one of the best dressed women in London, and it was a matter of course that she should have her own carriage with footmen waiting at the door. No one worried about the unpaid bills, and the tradesmen were only waiting to settle their accounts with Pitt's executors.

Hester Stanhope had only a small income of her own. Her father, whose eccentricities had driven his own wife out of the

house, would not give a farthing to the daughter who had preferred her uncle's protection to his own. But the Minister,
who had never asked for any remunerative benefice, uttered a
dying wish. "If the nation should think fit to reward my
services, let them take charge of my niece," and Parliament,
whose outraged respectability allowed Emma Hamilton to starve,
granted a pension to the daughter of one of England's richest peers.

On the 24th January the country went into mourning for
the statesman who had guided her safely through some of the
most turbulent years of European history, and who for her
sake had sacrificed health and the amenities of family life.
Even on his death-bed he sighed, "Oh, what times, oh, my
country." Honourable, selfless and incorruptible, he died as
poor as when he started his career as a young law student living
on Lord Temple's allowance. His scrupulous honesty in public
affairs was balanced by the stupendous figures of his private
debts. Party feuds were forgotten and Whigs and Tories voted
unanimously the sum necessary to discharge these bills, while
the Crown granted twelve hundred pounds a year to Lady Hester
Stanhope, and six hundred to each of her sisters. It was a noble
gesture, but twelve hundred pounds was but a trifling sum for a
woman, who during the thirty years of her life had been accus-
tomed to live in a profligate, extravagant society, and Fox, whose
traditional principles had forced him to oppose the motion that
Pitt should be honoured by a public funeral, showed the warmth
and generosity of his nature by offering the niece of his late
opponent a royal grant, which would entail an annual revenue
of several thousand pounds. There was nothing small and petty
about the man, who after opposing the vote of homage as a
mere matter of form, stood up and delivered a eulogistic
tribute to the memory of his bitterest political foe. But though
Lady Hester bore him no personal rancour, her pride, that
fantastic, unbalanced pride which dominated every action of
her life, forced her to refuse the offer. The world only knew
Fox as Pitt's opponent and her political principles would
never permit her to accept favours from a Whig.

It was her pride which bore her up during those dark winter months of 1806. With her violent and passionate nature she had allowed her whole being to become obsessed by her adoration of her uncle. He had supplied the place of father, lover, guardian, and her maternal instincts had received an outlet in nursing and watching over his health. In his house her restless, feverish energy had found constant employment and excitement. She had shared his friends and enemies, his tastes and interests; for once her vain and egotistical nature had become submerged in a dominating and genuine affection. He had been grateful for her love. On the night before he died, while Sir Walter Farquhar was at dinner, she went into his room, where he immediately recognized her and wished her future happiness and gave her his blessing. Then he bade her farewell. On her leaving the room, her brother James entered, and for some time afterwards Pitt continued to speak of her, and several times repeated, "Dear soul, I know she loves me! Where is Hester? Is Hester gone?"

Now her grief was too deep for tears and she clung pathetically to his friends. The one occasion on which she gave way was when Lord Melville called to see her and she found that the robust, handsome Scotsman had turned into a grey old man. Lord Melville, who as Henry Dundas had supported Pitt through the most difficult years of his administration, who had participated in his triumphs and failures, was now forced to stand the shame and obloquy of a public inquiry into his financial transactions at the Admiralty. His best friend had died at the moment when he really needed his help. His presence at Putney roused too many happy memories in Hester's mind; memories of the Duchess of Gordon's balls, when she was little more than a debutante chaperoned by Lady Jean Dundas, that worthy, colourless creature whom Pitt used to refer to laughingly as 'the sickly sea nymph.' She and her uncle had many private little jokes between them, apt nicknames and coined words, witty, trenchant nonsense, only understood by those who formed their small, intimate circle.

Dear, kind-hearted Dundas, who had always been ready to find a place for one of her favourite *protégés*, how low he had fallen; and Hester wept over the sight of her uncle's colleague.

Pitt's friends were his greatest legacy; Canning, with warm Irish hospitality, offered Lady Hester and her brother James a temporary home at South Hill. It was an invitation gratefully accepted, for Lord Chatham, though he appeared as the central figure in the magnificent pageant of his brother's funeral, made no attempt to offer his niece one room in St. James's Square. Emotional and highly-strung, George Canning and Hester Stanhope had forgotten their differences and quarrels and had made friends during her unfortunate episode with Lord Granville Leveson-Gower. It was a precarious friendship and was destined not to last, yet while it lived it was both exaggerated and imprudent. Confidences are a dangerous basis for any attachment, and Pitt's death, which unsettled both their mental equilibriums, intensified an hysterical and unnatural relationship.

From South Hill Hester came to town to attend her uncle's funeral and saw his bier conducted to Westminster with all the pomp and grandeur he had never sought for during his lifetime. Royal Princes, Dukes and Peers took part in the impressive *cortège*. Lord Grenville, the new Prime Minister, and Mr. Taylor, the apothecary's son, were two of the family mourners. Castlereagh and Hawkesbury, Sidmouth and George Canning were among those who acted as pall-bearers, but no place was found for the disgraced Lord Melville who had been Pitt's greatest friend.

Lord Grenville moved to Downing Street and sat in the place of the cousin to whom he had so often been disloyal, and Hester Stanhope moved to Montagu Square and tried to keep up a brave appearance before the world, a world only too ready to criticize and find fault with the behaviour of a pensioned spinster living on public bounty. She still called the Prime Minister 'cousin.' The Dukes of Cumberland and York still sought her advice and listened to her opinions. The warm-hearted Princess of Wales sent her expensive presents for her new house and Pitt's friends formed a loyal little court around her. But people now talked of 'Poor Hester Stanhope' and wondered why she had never married. Her eccentricities were no longer considered amusing and her pride was condemned. Society worshipped at new altars. The appealing charm of Caroline Lamb, the exquisite poise of Emily Cooper and the beauty of Elizabeth Oxford fired the enthusiasm of the beaux and dandies of the day. She was no longer the fashion, but young politicians still thought it worth their while to ask her advice, and every night while she was in town she received the latest news from the House of Commons.

She spent part of the summer of 1806 at Bognor, trying to recover her health, trying to find some new interest and occupation. Her chief correspondent during this period was Mr. Adams, for she felt that the world was beginning to forget her uncle and that his devoted secretary was the one person who really remained loyal to his memory. She still adopted Pitt's point of view and echoed his opinions and ideas. In one of her letters to Adams she writes, "I feel I am like dear Mr. Pitt, when I am in the country, for I recollect hearing him say he never saw a house or cottage or garden he liked but he immediately struck out improvements in his own mind."

Both the Stanhopes and the Pitts had a mania for building and planning. Chevening was a crying example of how one man's fantasy could succeed in spoiling a house built on the plans of Inigo Jones. Only the kitchen and servants' quarters had profited by Lord Stanhope's passion for utilitarian house-planning. Lady Hester's grandfather, Lord Chatham, could not remain six months in a simple country manor without converting it into a superb mansion, and Pitt made his greatest sacrifice when on retirement from office he was forced to sell Holwood and the gardens he had created. They all had active, nervous minds which had to organize and construct, imaginative minds with wide horizons and extraordinary accuracy for detail. The blood of Diamond Pitt had become infused in two families. The ruthless old pioneer had left a dangerous heritage which sometimes flared into genius or smouldered into insanity. With the Stanhopes, the creative genius took a scientific turn, while under the rule of the two Pitts unchartered lands and unknown islands received new political significance; yet neither Lord Camelford nor Lord Stanhope nor even the great Lord Chatham had escaped suffering from the abnormal exaltations and insane passions which were liable to dominate them at any time. The two streams of blood diverging from Diamond Pitt met again in Hester Stanhope. Qualities and defects were alike intensified and she was too proud and virile to live the decorous life of a respectable high-born spinster.

She returned to London and, together with her two younger brothers, set up house in Montagu Square. Charles and James had each a luxurious suite of their own, where they could entertain their fellow-officers, and now and then she gave a dinner for some of Pitt's particular friends. But soon the young Stanhopes discovered that the tradesmen who had been so obliging during their uncle's life-time were no longer willing to take credit, and Hester, who expected to lead the same life as when she had been chaperoned by a Prime Minister, found that all her actions were being spied on by malicious gossips. She had not been back in London a month before there were new rumours of her engagement to Noel Hill, and it was a sign of the turning of the tide that she was now considered lucky to be able to secure such a suitable *parti*.

Soon the rumour was contradicted by more pungent scandal. Fox died. The ministry 'of all the Talents' crumbled and, in the Duke of Portland's Cabinet, George Canning was awarded the post of Foreign Secretary. It did not take people long to discover that when he left the Foreign Office or the House of Commons he directed his steps towards Montagu Square. Lady Bessborough, with whom he had quarrelled, asserted "he was there not only all day but all night," whereas in reality Hester used him chiefly as a means of obtaining inside

LADY HESTER STANHOPE

information. She could not bear the feeling that she was now
merely a private individual and it was not Canning's Irish
charm which attracted her so much as the fact that he could
give her the latest news of the advance of Napoleon's armies.
Canning, enthusiastic and new to power, still talked of Pitt's
'glorious system' and Lady Hester received an affection which
was but a reflection of the former hero-worship he had felt
for her uncle. There was no sensual bond between them. It
was a case of two selfish, ambitious natures seeing themselves
mirrored in one another. Hester, whose fresh, radiant looks had
fascinated fastidious connoisseurs like George Brummel, whom
Sidney Smith recalled as "exciting everyone's admiration by
her magnificent and majestic figure, while the roses and lilies
blended in her face and the ineffable smiles of her countenance
diffused happiness around her," was now an experienced and
disillusioned woman. Aspiring lovers and flattering courtiers were
on the wane. George Canning, who had an adoring young wife
at home, was hardly likely to land himself with a dangerous
and unsatisfactory liaison, and unconsciously Hester resented
the fact that he never attempted to be her lover. She had a
craving for emotional excitement, and a suitor could be as
importunate as he liked so long as it amused her.

Sir John Moore returned from his campaign in Sicily, where
England had made a last attempt to preserve the throne of the
useless Bourbons from the grasp of Napoleon. The treaty of
Tilsit had shaken the morale of Europe. Baroque princi-
palities and kingdoms, with their rulers playing traditional
eighteenth century politics, were being wiped off the map.
English warships were kept busy in the Mediterranean, giving
free trips to dethroned monarchs, and English armies were
despatched from Sicily to Scandinavia, from Germany to
Spain. Sir John Moore, tired from a wearisome and unsatisfactory campaign, disappointed in his love for Caroline Fox,
the daughter of the general who had served with him in
Sicily, came to pay his respects at Montagu Square. All he
had received at the War Office had been a tepid reception from

65

Lord Castlereagh and a few words of grudging praise, but at Montagu Square he was given a warm and effusive welcome. Charles Stanhope fêted his heroic general and his sister revived a friendship which had started three years before on the downs of Shorncliffe.

During an arduous life spent in camps and small military towns, Moore had never met anyone as overwhelming and as enthralling as Hester Stanhope. Her scintillating conversation, a mixture of sophistication and simple common sense, of wit and sympathy, of flippant mimicry and intense seriousness, bewildered yet fascinated him. Day after day he found himself at her house, and before she had realized that she was in love with him, his leave was over. A protracted intimacy would have ruined their relationship, for no two temperaments could have been more incompatible, no two natures more alien. But he went to Sweden, and Hester's affections, fanned by her brother's enthusiasm, developed into a grand passion. She had to have one absorbing interest, and usually that interest was centred in one person. There was a quixotic streak in her character which was always inspiring her to fight other people's battles, however uncomfortable she might make them with her misplaced ardour. Already in Pitt's days, she had been a warm advocate of Moore's talents, and once, when an infirm old general dared to say a word against him, she had turned on him in cold rage, denouncing him as 'a paralytic old kangaroo.' When Moore returned from Sweden, embittered by the way in which he had been treated by his Government, she immediately took up arms against the Cabinet, which consisted of some of her oldest friends. Her resentment was chiefly directed against Canning for failing to appreciate her general's talents. Luckily the King realized Moore's strategic genius, and by his express wish he was appointed in command of the forces in Spain. Lord Castlereagh somewhat half-heartedly supported the King, but Canning strongly opposed the appointment, and it did not take long for the news of his opposition to reach Lady Hester's ears. From now onwards she inveighed against the Government and the Foreign Secretary was seen no more at Montagu Square.

In the summer of 1808, Sir John Moore embarked for Portugal, taking Charles Stanhope as his *aide-de-camp*. Before leaving, he bade a tender and respectful farewell to Lady Hester, but no word was said of marriage.

CHAPTER EIGHT

THE battle was raging outside the house where General
Moore lay dying and a small group of bare-headed men waited
for his last commands. The tallest and finest of them all was
James Stanhope, who had arrived from England a few days
previously, bearing dispatches from the Duke of York. As
he took his orders from his general, he did not know that his
brother Charles lay mortally wounded on the battlefield.

Charles Stanhope, Moore's youngest major, had shown himself worthy of his rank; he and William Napier, the two
nephews of Pitt and Fox, had fought side by side, and in the
heat of battle their intrepid bravery had wrested from Moore
the spontaneous cry of "Well done, my majors!" Hester's
prayer that her brothers would make fine soldiers had been
fully realized, for now James, the youngest of them all, had
been sent out to face for the first time the horrors of active
warfare. He had kept up a brave front under the fire of Soult's
musketry, but it was hard to be brave now that his general and
best friend lay bleeding to death on a rude mattress. Moore
turned his glazed eyes towards him and his last words re-echoed
above the distant cannon roar. "Stanhope, remember me to
your sister." To the small group of young officers those words
evoked memories of a gay, animating presence, a lithe figure in
a scarlet habit, galloping over the downs of Shorncliffe. They
all knew her, and for a second her vision hovered in the fug
and smoke of the tiny room, where the windows were tightly
shut to keep out the sleet and hail of a Spanish winter.

Then Moore fell back dead, and James Stanhope, his eyes
blinded with tears, stumbled out into the cold January night.
He went back to his post, burning to revenge his general's
death, and when he reached the firing-line he heard the news
that his brother had been shot. They led him to where he lay
among the snow-covered vineyards of 'La Coruna,' and the
tears that James Stanhope had not dared to shed in front of

Moore's *aides-de-camp* now flowed unchecked over his brother's corpse.

No victory was more dearly bought than the victory of Corunna, for England lost the one general whom Napoleon had considered a worthy opponent. In those days the news of a general's death travelled quicker than the news of the death of a young *aide-de-camp*, and Hester Stanhope mourned for Moore long before she heard that her brother had been killed. She mourned for him as one mourns for a lover, and she told her friends that they were going to have become engaged at the end of the campaign.

When one glances to-day at the terse, short notes which she treasured as his love-letters, one wonders how she could ever have misinterpreted what on his part must have been nothing more than a sincere friendship. The correspondence which passed between them was formal and respectful. He was heart and soul in his work and he hardly ever allowed himself to discuss any personal matters. Poor Hester had to content herself with trite phrases and shy assurances of devotion. Once, in a letter written from Lisbon, he went so far as to say, "I wish you were with us. The climate now is charming, and in your red habit *à l'amazone* you would animate and do us all much good," and the last words he ever wrote to her were "Farewell, my dear Lady Hester. If I extricate myself and these with me from our present difficulties, and if I can beat the French, I shall return to you with satisfaction, but if not, it will be better I shall never quit Spain." There is not a loving phrase, not a hint of passion in these letters—but he died with her name on his lips.

Hester Stanhope was more capable of inspiring soldiers than poets. Byron met her and she did not inspire one line from his facile pen; Lamartine met her and his poetry hardened into prose; but Moore's last words recorded in English history gave her immortal fame. She mourned for 'Charles's general' in the large, silent house in Montagu Square, in the rooms which usually re-echoed with the laughter of her brothers and their friends. During the last two years all her thoughts had been concentrated on them and their careers, and her romantic attachment for Moore had grown out of the heroic legends which Charles wove around his chief. When he first came to Montagu Square he came to worship at a shrine sacred to Pitt's memory, for every corner contained some bust or picture of the Stanhope's famous uncle, and at the beginning Hester loved him as her uncle's friend and brother's general, but the latent passions roused by Lord Granville Leveson-Gower were still hungry and unsatisfied. Lady Hester was a spinster at a dangerous age and the very barrenness of her romance with Moore, the very fact that he refused to treat her with anything more than respectful tenderness, accentuated the hysterical quality of her love. Unconsciously Charles used to encourage her physical cravings. In his naïve, childish way he would ask her if she did not consider Moore to be the perfect example of manly beauty, and on her answering in the affirmative he would add, laughing, "But, Hester, you should see him in his bath. He is like a god."

According to Colonel Anderson, the general's greatest friend, the only woman he ever thought of marrying was Caroline Fox. Two years before he had given her up on account of the disparity in their ages, and after his death she became the wife of William Napier, one of his junior officers. There is no doubt that if Moore had returned from Spain, and if Lady Hester had persevered, in the end she would have succeeded in marrying him. Now that she had no longer many opportunities she wanted to marry desperately, for it was galling and humiliating to live in London as a single woman on an inadequate income. When her brothers went off to fight she remained quite alone. She had never indulged in many women friends, and even when she heard the news of Charles's death she was too proud to allow her own kinsmen to console her. Why should she now be grateful for Lord Chatham's sympathy? He had never even offered them a home after Pitt's death, he had never lifted a hand to help Charles in his career;

though in the old days at Burton Pynsent he used to assure them of his protection. Moore's praise of her brother's bravery had been worth all her uncle's grand condescension, and her own personal friendship with the Duke of York had secured him the patronage so indispensable in the army. She was proud of Charles. His career had been due to her and she had helped and advised him at every turn. Now he was dead, shot through the heart as he led his regiment into battle, and when they saw him fall, his men had rushed forward like lions, shouting, "They shall pay for it. We will be revenged." Even in death he had imitated the heroism of his general.

There were still many days of misery and anxiety to go through before she knew that at least 'little James' had been spared her; black hours when she felt that it was impossible for him to have escaped from the carnage of Corunna. At last she heard that he was safe, and together with Colonel Anderson he arrived at Montagu Square. She gave him a pathetic and touching welcome. He was all that she had left to care for, and she wrote to one of her friends, "Heaven be praised that he has been spared me. I often consider him with astonishment and wonder how it is possible that he is alive."

James Stanhope, who had left London as a gay, dashing young Guards' officer, was now sadly changed. Emotional and unbalanced, like all his family, the horrors of the last few weeks had affected his nervous system, and his grief over his brother's death had brought out an underlying melancholy streak in his nature. He was too volatile and unstable to offer Hester the steady support which Charles had provided during the last two years, and in their loneliness both brother and sister turned to Colonel Anderson. It was Colonel Anderson who gave Hester accounts of the general's death, who handed her the last blood-stained relics he had worn on the battlefield. All her life she preserved one of Moore's stained gauntlets; it survived shipwrecks and plagues and desert journeys; and towards the end of her days it could be found hidden away in some dusty, mildewed corner of her Syrian castle.

Time after time Colonel Anderson was asked to reconstruct the details of the battle, and the famous retreat was the chief topic of conversation. Francis Jackson, who had just returned from Berlin, was one of the few guests at Montagu Square, and when he came to dinner, a part of the Spanish campaign, both military and political, was fought over again for his benefit. In spite of Lady Hester's grief he found that she took an intense interest in every current event, for she was determined not to get into a rut, not to degenerate into a misinformed old spinster. She had one sacred duty, to defend her general's memory against the virulent attacks of Canning and his party. Canning had even dared to condole with her, had even dared to address her as 'Dearest Lady Hester,' but she answered him with the curtest and coldest of notes. The Secretary of War, whose only care had been to defend his own conduct in the House of Commons, was dismissed as that 'vile Castlereagh,' and she made no allowances for the difficulties of a Cabinet minister faced by an angry Parliament. She was at odds with the world and ready to take offence where none was intended. She had definitely quarrelléd with her eldest brother owing to her believing a false report that, only a few weeks after Pitt's death, he had dined at Holland House in order to meet the leaders of the Opposition. Tom Grenville, the most human member of his family, was one of the few relations whom she would condescend to receive.

The winter and spring of 1809 dragged slowly on. Hester and her brother went to Bath accompanied by Colonel Anderson, but even the healing waters could do little to help her, for the state of her health depended on her nerves, and apart from all her sorrows and disappointments she was now sorely worried over money matters, for as yet she was unable to lay hands on the ten thousand pounds which Charles had left her in his will. Her London establishment was too expensive for her to keep up and she felt the ignominy of being a poor gentlewoman who was unable to afford a carriage. During the French revolution Princesses of the House of Orleans had been seen driving through London streets in hackney coaches, but if Lady Hester dared to follow their example she would be immediately criticized. If she walked abroad accompanied by a footman she was liable to be mistaken for a lady of the town; on the other hand, if any gentleman of her acquaintance met her by chance alone in the street, he would remonstrate in horror that a woman in her position should be obliged to walk by herself and would immediately offer to accompany her. Then some kind friend would come across them by chance and say, "How monstrous foolish that poor man looked helping Lady Hester across the road!" Lord Temple offered to lend her some of his horses but she stubbornly refused to accept any favour, at the same time complaining that none of the Grenvilles gave her any financial assistance. It was not very pleasant for her to realize that the grand and powerful members of her family whom she had slighted and made fun of during Pitt's life-time, were now being magnanimously kind merely out of pity and condescension.

In the old days she had taken pleasure in parading her friendship with obscure subalterns, introducing them to spoilt Dukes and dandies with that tremendous assurance of "I am Hester Stanhope and I can afford to be friends with whom I like." Now she avoided the red-faced officers whom James invited to Montagu Square and who, according to her butler, very often made a good dinner out of her brother's late breakfasts. It was not from snobbery that she avoided them; only she could no longer afford to be sitting at a theatre with some of her smart friends and to be greeted by a lumbering major claiming acquaintance with her. Women like Elizabeth Sunderland would lift their delicate, arched eyebrows in astonishment at a voice which dared to be blunt and loud, at a laugh which dared to be hearty, and at clothes which had not been cut by a Bond Street tailor. By virtue of her birth and position Lady Hester had been allowed to break many mirrors in a fragile, artificial world, but now she was only tolerated as long as she moved gently and circumspectly.

For many years she had exploited her friendship with the Royal Family, but royalty was under a cloud. The marital disputes of the Prince and Princess of Wales were common property, their *secrets d'alcove* were known to the London mob, and the friendship of a lampooned, abused Princess offered no kind of protection. The strange tastes of the Duke of Cumberland caused him to be ostracized by the more strait-laced members of society, and Lady Hester's personal friend, the Duke of York, who up till now had been the most popular of the royal Princes, was involved in the greatest scandal of the day. Never had the Army been so corrupt as under his rule; his mistress, pretty, common little Mrs. Clarke, made a practice of selling commissions at a handsome price, and she was not fussy as to who became an officer in His Majesty's Army. Any of her ex-lovers with a few thousand pounds of ready cash were admitted, and when Mrs. Clarke suggested a captaincy for one of her *protégés*, the Prince was unable to refuse her. There was more public washing of purple linen, and Parliament insisted on an inquiry into the administration of the Army. His Royal Highness was divested of his command, and Lady Hester, who still possessed an indomitable fighting spirit, took up arms at once in defence of the fallen Duke. But the opinions of a belligerent spinster were not taken into much account.

People were still kind; the Duchess of Richmond invited her to Ireland, the Duchess of Rutland invited her to Belvoir, her cousins, the Haddingtons, invited her to Scotland, and had she wanted it, she could have been a welcome guest at Wooton or Dropmore or Stowe. Somewhat perversely she chose to bury herself in the depths of Wales, in a tiny cottage which she had discovered during the previous summer. James had gone abroad on a mission with General Clinton. There was nothing to keep her in London and she was disgusted with the cold, ungrateful 'hypocrites' who no longer venerated the memory of the two men whom she had really loved. Time-servers like Castlereagh and Liverpool received credit for the schemes

which had been organized by Pitt. Moore's name was forgotten, while Arthur Wellesley was acclaimed as the hero
of the Peninsular War. Lady Hester was sick in mind
and body; she was bitter and disappointed and she knew
that she had few chances to re-start her life at the age of
thirty-three.

Glen Irfon, a little farmhouse situated in one of the lovely
valleys of the river Wye, had taken Lady Hester's fancy during
a short journey she had made in Wales, and with a coach and
country carriage, a pair of thoroughbreds and a vast amount of
trunks, including full-size portraits of Mr. Pitt and the Duke
of York, two serving maids and a couple of grooms, she set out
to lead the simple life. For a few months she amused herself in
playing Lady Bountiful to the villagers and in entertaining the
vicar's family. She dabbled in dairy produce and skimmed
milk and churned the cream, and affected a somewhat rural
air. She had a favourite cow called 'Pretty Face,' and encouraged the artistic pretensions of Thomas Price, the vicar's son.
His account of Lady Hester is the one redeeming spot in the
musty dreariness of his literary remains. He described her as
"neither handsome nor beautiful in any degree, for her visage
was long, very full and fat about the lower part and quite pale,
bearing altogether a strong resemblance to the portraits and
busts of Mr. Pitt." The Prices had made her acquaintance the
previous summer and had been much impressed by her
gracious condescension, for no one could be more charming and
more affable than she towards people in a more humble station
of life, and now that she was settled at Glen Irfon the Prices
became her intimates. They discussed crops and gardens and
she took a genuine interest in the local homespun industries.
It was during this period that she seriously took up the study of
medicine, and her first victims were the Welsh villagers. But
acting before a gallery of yokels did not satisfy Lady Hester for
very long. News from London still reached her by slow stages:
the latest charge against the Duke of York, the disaster of
Walcheren, for which Lord Chatham was mainly responsible,

and the engagement of Harriet Cavendish to Lord Granville Leveson-Gower.

The news of Lord Granville's *fiancailles* must have roused somewhat bitter memories; even now Lady Bessborough triumphed in marrying her lover to her plain, unassuming niece, for the beauty of Georgiana Devonshire had not been inherited by her younger daughter. After the Duchess's death in 1806, Elizabeth Foster had ruled supreme at Chatsworth and Piccadilly, until finally she had slipped unobtrusively into the *rôle* of the second Duchess. Lord Granville started his courtship at the right moment, for Harriet resented her stepmother and was only too ready to respond to the attentions of her aunt's *cicisbeo*. Everything happened just as it had been planned four years ago, and many times Lord Granville must have congratulated himself on the lucky escape he had had from Hester Stanhope.

During the summer Lady Hester realized that her marrying days were over. James returned from his mission and came down to Wales, accompanied by Mr. Nassau Sutton, and for lack of something better to do she set herself out to captivate and fascinate her brother's friend. During the last years she had not had a single proposal, and she knew that if she remained in England she would have to settle down to a life of good work and studious pastimes. It was not a cheerful prospect for a woman of her temperament and she was too tired and nervous to look out for new interests. Sir Walter Farquhar ordered her a complete change of surroundings. James offered to accompany her abroad, and Nassau Sutton, who was recovering from a severe illness, was only too anxious to join them. As an *aide-de-camp* he suited Hester admirably and the first vague plans of a journey which was to extend beyond the limits of her imagination hovered in the air.

CHAPTER NINE

DR. CHARLES LEWIS MERYON was in bed suffering from a
severe nasal catarrh. It was a raw December day and the small
wood fire gave little warmth to his damp and dingy lodgings.
In this weather London was not a very desirable place for a
delicate, impecunious young man, who had only just taken
his degree and who had no rich patrons and no prospective
patients.

Charles Meryon had ambitions beyond his station. At
Oxford he had studied hard in order to possess that veneer of
culture which he admired so much in the æsthetic young
aristocrats who frequented the exclusive circles where he had
never gained admittance. He was a snob, and his friend, Henry
Cline, had only to mention the name of Lady Hester Stanhope
for him to prick up his ears in excitement. Her Ladyship was
going abroad for the sake of her health, and she had asked
Cline's father, the celebrated surgeon, to recommend to her a
young doctor who would accompany her on her travels.
Meryon was fully qualified for the post; the salary would be
small, but if his services proved satisfactory, they would be
handsomely rewarded at the end of the journey and there were
many social advantages to be gained from travelling with a
woman of position. Dr. Meryon blew his nose, wiped his rather
watery eyes and accepted the heaven-sent offer. Marble palaces
surrounded by orange groves would take the place of his
humble lodgings, and ambassadorial banquets would supplant
unappetizing meals at cheap eating-houses. Not for nothing
had he studied his Classics; as they wandered through Italy
and Greece he would have a chance of impressing Pitt's niece
with his erudition.

When he rose from his sick-bed his first duty was to call on
her Ladyship, whom he found charming and affable. He was
engaged on the spot, and though Lady Hester's character
would have benefited by a doctor with a more determined

personality, she could not have found a more faithful or a more loyal friend.

The house in Montagu Square was let, and as in those days no one crossed the Channel without putting their affairs in order, Lady Hester spent most of the last month in London in visiting her lawyer, Mr. Murray, and her banker, Mr. Coutts. A codicil was added to her will, leaving the whole of her estate to her brother James, and in the case of his death, to Colonel Anderson. She indulged in no sentimental regrets, and had no tender farewells to make before leaving town. London had merely been a background for her triumphs. Heart and soul she was attached to the Kentish countryside, and the happiest days of her youth had been spent at Chevening and Walmer, but the doors of her home were now closed to her. Lord Stanhope had no use for his children 'who had chosen to be saddled on the public purse.' As a matter of fact he had very little use for any of his relations; even his long-suffering wife had returned to the wealth and comfort of her own family after having been half starved and forced to submit to the bullying of the cook-housekeeper who had obtained complete domination over his Lordship. This woman lined her pockets while Lord Stanhope laboured under the illusion that the parsimonious fare at his table enabled him to have enough money to carry out his valuable scientific experiments. Only his aged mother still persisted in admiring his conduct, and when she died in 1811, she left him all her money 'out of approbation of his private and public conduct.'

Curiously enough, Hester never bore her father any of the bitter rancour with which she vituperated against her inoffensive eldest brother. In later years she even took a certain pleasure in expatiating on Lord Stanhope's curious eccentricities, and Dr. Meryon was fated to hear long, wearisome stories of the grandeur of the early days at Chevening. The fact that she was homeless and had not enough money to keep her place in society was mainly responsible for driving her out of England. Her plans were vague, though necessarily restricted on account of there being hardly any countries on the Continent open to English visitors. Finally she decided to go to Sicily, which was one of the few pleasant places under British rule, for though Murat reigned at Naples, the Hapsburg Queen, protected by the Union Jack, still intrigued across the Straits of Messina.

On the 10th February, 1810, Lady Hester and her party embarked at Portsmouth on the frigate *Jason*, which was conducting a convoy of merchant vessels bound for Gibraltar. The journey which had been planned so casually and calmly was doomed to difficulties from the very beginning. Owing to contrary winds a dreary fortnight had to be spent at Portsmouth, where Dr. Meryon had joined the party, and they had hardly been a few hours at sea before the ship ran into a calm, so that it took seven days to reach Land's End. Dr. Meryon sunned himself in his new surroundings. Her Ladyship was gracious and condescending, though she rarely discussed with him any subject except that of her health—in those days the family physician did not expect to be regarded as an equal. Nassau Sutton was too busy fetching and carrying for Lady Hester to pay much attention to him, but James Stanhope, who always made himself beloved by his boyish simplicity, treated him as a friend.

The ship had barely passed Land's End before they ran into a severe Atlantic storm, and Dr. Meryon had only just got his sea-legs when he had to take to his bunk. Nassau Sutton followed his example, but Hester and her brother, who prided themselves on being good sailors, remained on deck. James had gathered enough experience as a midshipman to exchange technical seafaring gossip with the Honourable James King, who commanded the frigate, while Hester had always evinced a partiality for sailors, whom she considered to be 'good, fine fellows,' and her spirits rose as the storm augmented. Owing to alternate calms and gales it took a month for the *Jason* to navigate between Portsmouth and Gibraltar, and the party narrowly escaped shipwreck on the shoals of Trafalgar. Finally, on the 7th March, weathering a tremendous sea,

the frigate managed to cast anchor in the Bay of Tetuan, and
Dr. Meryon's classical knowledge received its first shock when
he saw that the Atlas was a chain of mountains and not a
single peak.

Lady Hester landed at Gibraltar, and took an intense dislike
to that crowded garrison town. She and her brother were guests
at the Convent, the Governor's residence, and to her horror she
found that she was expected to take part in the gaieties of
military life. She was too old and tired to enjoy the kind of
parties which she had so often organized at Walmer, and she
disliked the feeling that she was marooned on a barren rock,
for the whole of Spain was overrun by French soldiers and the
orange grove of Algeciras was the only neutral ground. The
hospitality of the Governor, General Campbell, was sorely
tried by the number of Spanish grandees who sought refuge on
the rock, and prices soared owing to the difficulties in obtaining
provisions from the mainland.

One day there was a great commotion in the harbour. Lord
Sligo's brig had put into port, and in those days of war it was
not often that one saw a brig adapted as a private yacht. The
extravagance of the young Irish Marquis had gained him fame
throughout the Mediterranean, and every loafer, porter and
interpreter, thief, swindler and vendor of native goods rushed
to the harbour as soon as his Lordship's arrival was announced.

Howe Peter Browne, Marquis of Sligo, was a charming and
irresponsible young man; his irresponsibility had gone so far
as to allow his servants to seduce two able-bodied seamen off
His Majesty's ships in order to man his yacht. In time of war
this was a criminal offence, and when a naval captain at Malta
made inquiries into the matter, his Lordship denied that they
were on his brig. He considered this a vastly funny story, not
realizing the trouble in which it was going to involve him, and
he and his friend, Michael Bruce, laughed at the practical
joke they had played on the British navy. At the age of twenty-
two they both looked upon the world as though it were created
exclusively for their amusement, for they were both so hand-

some and rich that few men or women were able to withstand their charms.

Lady Hester, who for several days had stifled her yawns at wearisome official banquets, was delighted to find two new and attractive faces at the Governor's table. Nassau Sutton was beginning to bore her; her pride would not allow her to become too friendly with her doctor, though she was considerate enough to insist on his being included in all her invitations, and soon she was to lose her brother's companionship owing to his regiment being called to Cadiz. Both Lord Sligo and Mr. Bruce were old acquaintances of James, and it was only natural that they should attach themselves to Lady Hester's party. They were both young enough to be impressed by her biting wit and arrogant manner, but Lord Sligo was too busy posing as a patron of the arts and amateur archæologist to take much interest in her as a woman, whereas Michael Bruce, the scion of a rich business family, was fascinated by her charms as well as being thrilled by the position she had occupied in London society. He was a pale prototype of Lord Granville Leveson-Gower and there was the same curious effeminate streak in his character which appealed so strongly to a woman of Lady Hester's calibre.

Their friendship quickly blossomed into intimacy, and among the shadowed walks of the Convent garden Hester Stanhope could be found flirting with a boy fourteen years younger than herself. Nassau Sutton was utterly neglected and, deeply offended, he went off to Minorca. She had never taken him seriously and from now onwards she did not give him a single thought. Once when she was lamenting James's departure Michael Bruce casually but gallantly suggested himself as an escort, and no one was probably more surprised than he when the offer was accepted.

Brother and sister bade an affectionate farewell to one another, and Dr. Meryon had to pay for his friendship with the great, by parting with a much-prized saddle which he had had the forethought to buy before leaving Portsmouth. James Stanhope had forgotten to procure one in England, and in his casual, airy way he thought nothing of depriving the doctor of his most treasured possession.

The clouds which already at Malta were gathering over Lord Sligo's head, were beginning to darken the Mediterranean, and his Lordship left the ominous shadow of the British flag for the more friendly precincts of Ottoman waters. Lady Hester and Mr. Bruce remained behind, waiting for the arrival of the frigate bound for Malta, and on the 7th April they embarked on the *Cerberus*, which landed them at La Valetta on the twenty-first.

It was Easter Day as they sailed into the harbour and all the bells were ringing in the town. Guns were being fired and multi-coloured flags fluttered from the ships anchored in the port, while the steep, narrow streets with their overhanging balconies were seething with life and animation. It was spring and the air was heavy with the scent of incense and orange-blossom. As she drove through the streets with Michael Bruce, Hester no longer looked gaunt and haggard. There was something young, almost shy about her expression, and even Dr. Meryon noticed that she was beginning to look rather winning; not that Dr. Meryon had much time to spare for admiring his patient's appearance; he was far too excited by the seductive little Maltese ladies with their swaying hips and full bosoms. The doctor fancied himself as a connoisseur of female charms, and in later years his vulnerable heart and appraising eye were doomed to involve him in a lot of trouble and expense.

The Governor of Malta, General Hildebrand Oakes, was one of those charming, chivalrous Englishmen who help towards raising their country's prestige abroad, but, though Lady Hester was eager for his friendship, she had a very definite reason for refusing his hospitality and for contenting herself with a humble lodging in the house of Mr. Fernandez, the deputy Commissary General, who had married her companion's sister. The two Miss Williams's had owed their education to the generosity of Mr. Pitt, and when the elder one had married, the Prime Minister's protection had been extended to the husband, while the younger one had remained in Lady Hester's service.

The Fernandez family lived in the palace which had formerly belonged to the French knights, and Dr. Meryon retained enough of his middle-class insularity to grumble at the gloomy bedchambers, with their stone walls and floors; but Lady Hester was regardless of discomfort. In the company of Michael Bruce she re-found her youth and health. His buoyant spirits acted as a tonic to her frayed and suffering nerves and for the first time in her life she forgot her pride and rank and allowed herself to fall genuinely in love with a charming, good-looking young man, whose only claim to social position was that he had a fat bank balance. She did not even take his wealth into account, for the woman who had been used to the wild extravagance of a Camelford or a Granville Leveson-Gower, was hardly likely to be impressed by an obscure civilian who had two thousand a year for pocket money. His childish ostentation amused her, and in forgetting the disparity of their ages, she sympathized when she should have condemned and laughed when she should have frowned. The arrogant masculinity which had repelled so many of her suitors attracted a certain perverted streak in his nature, and at the age of thirty-four Hester Stanhope finally inspired both passion and love.

Michael Bruce was a very passive lover, and he was far too deferential to take the initiative, while Hester possessed all the sexual self-consciousness of an elderly virgin. Gradually he became necessary to her, and their intimacy, though pure, was of such a nature as to have given rise to malicious gossip had they been staying at the Governor's palace. The Fernandez were not in a position to criticize the behaviour of their generous benefactress, and the doctor had to limit his remarks to private circulation in letters to his family. At first he was so enchanted with Maltese society that he took very little interest in his patient's private life. He could only write of the brilliant parties given by General Oakes, the splendid banquets of sixty covers, where English lords rubbed shoulders with Neapolitan dukes, and how once he had sat at the high table with only the breadth of the wood separating him from the Governor, with the Duchess of Pienne on his right and Lady Hester on his left.

These were glorious days for the doctor, for his patient took up so little of his time that he was able to lead the life of a gentleman of leisure. Excursions on horseback, race meetings, and picnics to La Boschetta, Malta's wooded park, were part of the delightful routine. But soon Dr. Meryon found that there were thorns among the roses. Michael Bruce deliberately ignored his diffident overtures of friendship and seemed bent on excluding him from Lady Hester's intimacy, till finally there arrived the bitter moment when the two dined at Government House and left him behind.

Malta was crowded with English; Lord Ebrington, a cousin of Lady Hester, Tom Sheridan, and Mr. Drummond, the wealthy banker's son, were all guests at the Governor's palace, while his country villa of Sant Antonio was lent to Lord and Lady Bute. Her Ladyship, who was a daughter of Mr. Coutts, never included the doctor in her effusive invitations to Lady Hester. Meryon chiefly resented these slights as they damaged his position in the eyes of the local society, the colonels and officials at whose parties he felt far more at ease than at those grand aristocratic dinners where no one deigned to treat him as an equal.

Lady Bute was one of the few women to whom Lady Hester was devoted, and she was sincerely distressed when one evening she gave mortal offence through her unbridled tongue. In the middle of a large dinner party, Lord Bute asked her what she thought of Drummond, the banker's son. "Oh!" she said, "I think of him as I do of all bankers' sons I see skipping about the Continent, that they had much better be behind the counter; for if they are intended to follow their father's trade, this skipping about only unfits them for it and they never after can be brought to sit in some dark room in a narrow street in the city, and if they are intended to be fine gentlemen, it is ten to one that they ruin themselves, or, if they do not that, their house gets a bad name—am I not right, my Lord?" "Why, you know, Lady Hester," answered Lord Bute, "I generally agree with you, but on this point I am not quite sure. Then you don't like bankers, Lady Hester?" "Not particularly, my Lord," she answered, but, as she looked up, she saw Lord Ebrington screwing up his mouth, and Lady Bute looking very odd, whilst Lord Bute looked very cunning, the butler all the while standing first on one leg and then the other in a state of the strangest uneasiness. All of a sudden her old friend Mr. Coutts came into her head and she saw what a blunder she had made.

In going out of the room, Lady Bute said, "Hester, you are always wild as you have been, but I know you never mean any harm in what you say," and there, as she thought, the matter ended. But though she and Lady Bute corresponded for over fifteen years the insult was never forgotten, and when in 1827 Lady Hester was hard pressed for money and wrote to Lady Bute asking for a loan of three hundred pounds, the reply was a cold and polite refusal.

The Butes left Malta at the end of May, and General Oakes strongly dissuaded Lady Hester from carrying out her plan of going to Sicily, for there was bad news from the island. By his marriage to Marie Louise, Napoleon had become a cousin of the Queen of Palermo. Murat was plotting in Calabria, and the English, who were still protecting the Straits, were never sure that the intriguing Queen might not suddenly join forces with the Bonapartes. As an alternative, the Governor offered his summer villa as a residence for Lady Hester, and at Sant Antonio began the most idyllic period of her crowded, restless life. In the cool loggias and formal gardens, strolling along the avenues of orange trees past carved myrtle hedges, could be seen the tall, imposing figure of a handsome, mature woman leaning on the arm of a slim, lithe young man, whose face still retained the dreaming charm of adolescence.

Michael Bruce allowed the prelude of the love affair to play itself out through long summer nights in moonlit gardens, heavy with the hot, dusty scent of oleander, and though in the streets of La Valetta one whispered of Lady Hester Stanhope and her young lover, that title was premature. What did her Ladyship care about gossip! During the last two years her restless spirit had been broken by sorrow and ill-health, but now once more she lifted her head high and defied all the accepted conventions of society. She refused to accept any invitations except those of the Governor, and Dr. Meryon regretted that her dislike of her own sex excluded him from becoming acquainted with many delightful Maltese ladies.

Her antipathy to female society was almost abnormal. She met John Cam Hobhouse at dinner and told him bluntly that she would as soon live with pack-horses as women. In his letter to Byron, in which he mentioned their meeting, he had very little to say in her favour. She did not improve on a closer acquaintance, for after spending an evening with her at the Opera, Hobhouse described her as a violent, peremptory person with whom he had a long and tiresome argument.

Love had not softened her, though temporarily it blinded her to Michael Bruce's obvious deficiencies. The superficial culture of a young Cambridge æsthete passed for brilliant originality. "No one was ever so handsome nor so clever and no one was destined to a greater future than he." In her infatuation she even allowed him to influence her in her behaviour towards the doctor, who soon found that conversation was so strained in his presence as to impel him to suggest taking his meals at a separate table. Relations between him and his patient improved when the excessive heat caused boils to erupt on her Ladyship's finely modelled cheeks. She showed exemplary courage in the face of an unpleasant and painful complaint, and the poetical doctor compared her to all his favourite heroines—to Elvira, Portia and Semiramis, while in her turn she rewarded his services by asking Bruce to be more civil towards him.

Four months of Malta had been enough for Lady Hester. The heat was now insufferable and even the fountains of Sant Antonio could not cool the stifling air. She needed a change; the Ottoman Empire was the only friendly territory left to British visitors, and Lord Sligo's effusive letters, giving a glowing account of the Aegean islands and Turkish hospitality, decided her plans. On the 2nd August, 1810, Lady Hester's party embarked on the *Belle Poule*, a frigate bound for Zante.

CHAPTER TEN

THE rugged outline of the coast of Greece was veiled in the blue mists of the early morning. Not a breeze stirred the orange sails of the caiques, which hung like listless leaves over the metal surface of the sea, while the red flag of the crescent fell in limp folds over the crenellated fortress of Patras. Burnt and bare, the hills trailed their dusty feet in the warm Ionian foam. Then the sun rose high and struck hard at the metallic rocks, splintering in shafts of merciless white light, while the whole town shimmered in a haze of dust and heat. In the filthy streets, with their miserable mud hovels, pariah dogs sniffed among rotting refuse, and beggars sat huddled on the quays waiting to gather alms from the English *kyrios*.

There was great excitement in the harbour, for Lord Sligo had arrived from the interior of Arcadia, where he had been paying a visit to the *Veli* of Tripolitza, and his yacht, which aroused the admiration of the townspeople, had been remanded to Malta. Every Greek captain hoped that his Lordship would hire his vessel and there was considerable disappointment when he announced that he was embarking on the *felucca* of the English 'Princess' and the young 'milord,' who had arrived a few days previously on a British transport. Every foreigner who was lavish with his piastres was entitled to be called 'milord,' and Michael lived up to the popular conception of an English peer. But even 'that learned thane Athenian Aberdeen' and 'Childe Harold' himself could not vie with the spectacular reputation of the young Irish Marquis who now arrived from the wilds of Arcadia with a fantastic retinue of armed Albanians, dragomans and Turkish cooks, European valets and Tartar couriers, not to mention an English artist who had been engaged to paint the varied scenes of travel. Lord Sligo was the bearer of Turkish *firmans*, which assured him and his party the hospitality of every town through which they passed, and he presented Lady Hester Stanhope with a letter from the

Veli of Tripolitza, the Pasha of Morea, regretting that he would be unable to receive her as he had been summoned to the Porte.

Lady Hester had made a triumphant progress across the Ionian sea; British Governors, consuls and naval captains had been only too anxious to pay homage to the niece of Pitt, and Michael Bruce sunned himself in her reflected glory. But however much he adored and admired Lady Hester, travelling with her was somewhat of a strain. She suffered from the heat and the restricted quarters made her often irritable and peevish. There was little privacy on board ship and she was too fastidious to indulge in public love-making. As she lay under a striped awning with her maid fanning her head, while her valet prepared her cooling drinks, Michael Bruce was left to spend the day with the doctor, who was not very amusing company for a spoilt young æsthete. Lady Hester's virtue was bounded by walls of inviolable pride, a pride that dominated those unruly passions that had so often threatened to change the whole course of her life. On board a British transport, surrounded by a crew of English sailors, she maintained a cold and rigid *hauteur*. Curiously enough her capriciousness and tiresome whims never alienated Michael Bruce's affection, for though she might choose to play the *rôle* of an exacting spinster, he remembered the half-promises she had made him during those long summer nights in the gardens of Sant Antonio and he was content to wait his time and continue in his part of a passive lover.

In spite of his newly roused emotions he missed Lord Sligo's company. He was slightly shocked to find that Hester cared nothing about the treasures of ancient Greece and that she was more interested in the manœuvring of a battleship than in any ruined temple, and at the same time he was bored to death by Dr. Meryon's self-conscious pedantry. Sligo and he had both studied under the famous archæologist, Dr. Gell, and the former spent vast sums on excavating in Athens and the Peloponnesus. Marble torsos of gods and goddesses were carried over the seas to decorate his Lordship's Irish mansion, and for many years the great gates of the treasury of Atreus, wreathed in moss and ivy, served as a garden arbour under whose shadow Irish ladies could entertain their friends to tea.

Bruce wrote to Lord Sligo from Zante persuading him to join their party. Like most young Englishmen he required male support. Lady Hester was older and more experienced than he. Her actions were often unaccountable and mystifying, and though she petted and indulged him, there were moments when, in her colossal egotism, her own figure occupied the whole stage; moments when he and the doctor were ranked indiscriminately together as her 'travelling staff.'

Sligo was delighted to hear that his friend was in Grecian waters, for not only was he attached to Michael Bruce, but he was also extremely sociable, and life with formal Turkish pashas was not particularly exciting. At Tripolitza he and the *Veli* had partaken of solemn *tête-à-tête* dinners, consisting of eighty courses, and for several weeks he had not come across any of his own countrymen. He hurried to Patras and arrived on the very day when Lady Hester and her party were about to embark for Corinth, and he received an enthusiastic welcome from both her and Bruce, while Meryon was only too happy to renew his acquaintance with one whom he regarded as the beau-ideal of a great noble.

On the night of the 27th August, they set sail in a Greek *felucca*, a primitive open boat, where it was impossible to keep up any pretence of etiquette. Lady Hester slept under a tilted awning while the rest of the party had their mattresses spread all over the deck. There was no spotlessly dressed British captain waiting for her Ladyship's orders and there was no longer any need for appearances to be maintained in front of respectful British sailors.

The little *felucca* slowly sailed past the old Venetian fortresses of the Gulf of Corinth, under the heights of Parnassus, which rose pale and insubstantial in the glistening sunlight, by groves of myrtle and arbutus clambering up the slopes of the Erymanthus and, in the heat of the day, it would anchor by some

shady spot, where Lady Hester would preside over a gay alfresco
meal where the two rival cooks, her own Persian and Lord
Sligo's Turk, would outvie one another in the preparation of
Oriental delicacies.

At Corinth Hester received for the first time the visit of a
Turkish Bey, who paid her the singular honour of allowing his
harem to visit her. This visit was the cause of an incident at
which in later years she would have been profoundly shocked,
an incident arising from her misguided wish to indulge the
high spirits of her young companions. She allowed them to
remain in an adjoining room while she received the Corinthian
beauties who, imagining themselves to be in the safe privacy
of a lady's chamber, unveiled their faces and exposed their
bosoms to the delighted eyes of Lord Sligo, Bruce and Meryon,
who were peeping through the wainscoting. Soon their suspicions were aroused by sounds of smothered laughter, and
Lady Hester had the greatest difficulty in appeasing their fears.
Luckily they had the sense not to arouse oriental jealousy by
relating the story to their master, the Bey. It was an act of
deliberate irresponsibility on the part of Lady Hester, the
irresponsibility of one who, no longer young herself, is bent on
emphasizing the careless attitude of youth. She was surrounded
by men, the oldest of whom was not yet twenty-five, and she
set herself out to dazzle her tiny court by employing the same
methods she had used for over fifteen years. As soon as she
landed at Patras she began to enjoy herself. The British transport sailed back to Zante, and her cloak of decorous spinster-
hood was thrown to the Ionian winds. Long before they reached
Corinth Michael Bruce realized that the prelude of their
love affair was rising to a climax, and Peter Sligo, the tempting
bait of hundreds of match-making mothers in London and
Dublin, adapted himself to the somewhat incongruous rôle
of confidant. He displayed a very charming trait in his nature
by making friends with the doctor whom he invited to accompany him whenever he went on shore, so as to give the lovers a
little privacy.

In an age of consummate hypocrisy, when duchesses slipped their bastards quietly and unobtrusively into gilded cradles and heirs-apparent committed secret bigamy, no woman had her honour more besmirched, her chastity more questioned than Hester Stanhope. She had been judged and condemned merely on account of her disregard for public opinion, and every town gossip would have laughed incredulously had they been told that at the age of thirty-four she was still a virgin. It was characteristic of her that when finally she became the mistress of Michael Bruce, she proclaimed it to the whole world, for she would have regarded a clandestine liaison as shoddy and second-rate. It was not an easy step for her to take, for though in Pitt's house she had been allowed so much latitude and freedom, she had always adhered to his strict moral principles, and there was a strong religious side to her nature that believed in the rigid doctrines of the Old Testament, which as a child she had been taught by her Scottish grandmother. The hard, definite religion that was preached to the children of the eighteenth century was the tree on which in later years she grafted the exotic flowers of a hundred Eastern sects.

Lady Hester and her fantastic retinue rode across the sun-baked isthmus of Corinth, and the ragged population of the fishing villages turned out in the broiling midday heat to stare at the white-faced woman in her high plumed hat, riding between two beautiful young milords. At the end of the long multi-coloured procession of couriers, servants, interpreters and guides, came Anne Fry, her Ladyship's only female servant, for Elizabeth Williams had remained behind at Malta. Mrs. Fry, a well-trained English lady's maid, was now expected to grapple with Turkish servants, heathen rites and vermin-ridden houses, not to mention the vile tempers of two German valets, who at Patras had provided the inhabitants with a novel spectacle by indulging in a duel with sabres. Bravely she bumped along on her mule, too meek to question the strange destiny which had sent her among murderous-looking Albanians with shining *yataghans*, and slit-eyed Tartars beating their beasts of burden.

That night the party slept on board the two-masted vessel which was to take them to Athens the following morning, and Dr. Meryon received the somewhat disarming information that Mr. Bruce and Lady Hester were going to lodge in one house, while he would be a guest of Lord Sligo in the quarters which his Lordship had occupied during his previous visit. In his published works Dr. Meryon was careful to omit the fact that Lady Hester and Michael Bruce lived under the same roof in Athens, and it is not the only time that the reader pays the penalty for his discretion. How much more he might have told us of his heroine had he not been awed by the presence of her august family.

The boat cast anchor in the early morning, and with the help of a fair wind the Piræus was reached by midday. In those days what is now a great port, with teeming docks and dense forests of masts and funnels, was but a small, narrow harbour, with a bedraggled customs-house, from where a long, white track led through fields of corn and olives to the sacred hill of the Acropolis.

As the ship passed the mole head, Lady Hester caught sight of a naked figure about to dive into the sea. There was a loud splash, and from the waters emerged the curly, chestnut head and freckled face of a beautiful youth. Sligo called out, "That's Byron," and Hester gazed with her cool, critical eyes at the young poet who was soon to become the idol of the gay, superficial society which had proved so fickle to her. Like her, he would feel secure on his pinnacle of fame; and his fall would be more sudden and more dangerous than hers.

Byron gave her one laughing look and remembered John Hobhouse's unflattering description. Sligo and Bruce were old Cambridge acquaintances and he was sorry to see Michael in the thrall of such an overwhelming female. Then Sligo shouted to him to go and dress and meet them at the customs-house. This was the beginning of an intimacy which

93

could only flower on foreign soil, where people of the same nationality and class cling together even when there is no sympathetic link between them. Byron was a constant guest at Lady Hester's house, but he came not so much for her sake as for that of her companions, and soon there was a slight coldness in the air when her Ladyship discovered that the few English travellers who visited her every evening regarded Lord Byron as the centre of attraction. He was still at the age when he wanted to impress and startle his audience, and she was bent on putting him in his place. She contradicted and argued with him, and soon the poet had enough of the woman whom Bruce described as "the most superior creature in all the world." Lady Hester told her doctor that she saw "nothing in him but a well-bred man like many others, for as for poetry—it was easy enough to write verses, and as for thoughts, who knows where he got them? Perhaps he had picked up some old book that nobody knew anything about and stole his ideas out of it." She did not even praise his beauty, for she insisted that there was a good deal of vice in his looks with the eyes set so close together, and the contracted brow; the only point of his appearance which she admired was the fine modelling of his cheeks and neck and the curl on his forehead. The severity of her judgment was probably due to some underlying jealousy, for both Bruce and Sligo made much of his talents and treated him as a prodigy of genius.

Byron's tongue was as sharp as hers and his eyes were as critical, and there was nothing he considered so tiresome as a clever woman, so after a few days of arduous sight-seeing and evening *conversazione* at her Ladyship's house, the poet suddenly pleaded urgent business at Patras. Athens was not large enough to hold two such decided and egotistical personalities as were Lord Byron and Lady Hester Stanhope.

From Patras his Lordship wrote a long and candid letter to his friend Hobhouse. "I saw the Lady Hester Stanhope at Athens and do not admire that dangerous thing—a female wit! She told me (take her own words) that she had given you a good set-down at Malta in some disputation about the navy; from this, of course, I readily inferred the contrary, or, in the words of an acquaintance of ours, that you had the best of it! She evinced a similar disposition to arguefy with me, which I avoided either by laughing or yielding. I despise the sex too much to squabble with them, and I rather wonder you should allow a woman to draw you into a contest in which, however, I am sure you had the advantage, she abused you so bitterly. I have seen too little of the lady to form any decisive opinion, but I have discovered nothing different to other she-things, except a great disregard of received notion in her conversation as well as conduct. I don't know if this will recommend her to our sex, but I am sure it won't to her own. She is going to Constantinople."

CHAPTER ELEVEN

"MAKE way for His Majesty the Sultan, the Commander of the Faithful," cried the *bostangis*, cracking their knotted whips, while on the right and left of the street tall janissaries raised a wall of spears to keep back the congested crowds. It was Friday, the Mahomedan Sabbath, and the narrow streets wore a festive air, while the bazaars were crowded with holiday-makers waiting to see the Sultan Mahmoud pass on his way to prayer. First in the procession came the water-carriers, sprinkling the dusty ground. Then followed four gigantic, bearded figures, mounted on magnificent horses, surrounded by a glittering retinue; His Majesty's coffee, stool, sword and pipe-bearers outvieing one another in the gorgeousness of their apparel.

An awed silence fell on the crowd as the great ministers of the Sublime Porte passed by, the Captain Pasha, the Reis Effendi, and the Grand Vizier. Muffled in pelisses covered in fur, bending under the weight of their jewelled turbans, mounted on horses whose bridles were studded with emeralds and diamonds, they paraded the wealth they had extracted from the public coffers, but all the time they were in constant fear of their lives, terrified of the very janissaries who guarded the streets. Now the Commander of the Faithful was at hand, and every pious Moslem folded his hands on his breast and bent his head in prayer for Allah and Mahomet to protect the royal race of Othman. Like a jewelled idol he was carried through the streets on the back of a milk-white stallion, and the high tossing plumes of his negro slaves screened him from the vulgar gaze. Behind him fell the crooked shadow of the hideous blackamoor who ministered to his imperial pleasures, the Kislar Aga, guardian of the Harem and master of the hundred black and white eunuchs who followed in his train.

Amongst the crowd of his cringing subjects, one figure sat proud and erect on horseback, watching his august Majesty with a calm, steady look. A white woman dared to ride at midday through the streets of Stamboul and to show herself unveiled in the presence of the Grand Signior. Not even Lady Mary Wortley Montagu who, a century earlier, had captured the imagination of the Turks, had dared to expose herself to such a risk, yet there was something so proud and yet so respectful in her demeanour, something so unfeminine about that firm, white face and those serious blue eyes, that there were many in the crowd who swore that she was not a woman. Pride is the quality most appreciated by an oriental, and it was Hester Stanhope's queenly dignity which compelled the admiration of the fastidious Osmanlees. This was her first public appearance in the capital of the Empire where she was going to make her home; and this was the only glimpse she ever had of the Sultan whose power she defended to the last days of her life. The man who disobeyed the tenets of his religion by indulging in drunken orgies, who gave way to fits of ferocious sadism and perverse debaucheries, was hardly worthy to be upheld by such an honourable and upright woman. The daughter of 'Citizen' Stanhope was a rigid upholder of the divine right of kings, and in the furthest corners of the Turkish Empire, on the banks of the Orontes and in the hills of Judea, she preached loyalty to Arab chieftains.

Lady Hester arrived at Pera in the late autumn of 1810, and she took an instant dislike to the restricted quarters of the European city; it required a good deal of courage to flaunt a liaison under the disapproving eyes of Stratford Canning, England's twenty-four-year-old Minister Plenipotentiary to the Sublime Porte, a well-meaning, zealous young man with a tremendous sense of his own importance and none of his cousin's Irish humour. The name of Hester Stanhope, however, still conjured memories of the glories of Downing Street, and the Minister (no Ambassador having been appointed for the moment) was only too ready to offer her the hospitality of the British Embassy and to swallow his private scruples. She herself admitted that he treated her with the utmost civility, and yet she was always quizzing his pomposity and 'primosity.'

Lady Hester was on the defensive, for her emotional affairs had reached a crisis. Though one cannot help thinking that she made a good deal of unnecessary fuss about a perfectly normal happening, one respects the feelings which prompted her to write a full confession both to her brother and to General Oakes, who proved such a loyal friend to her and Bruce. There must have been moments when she realized the absurdity of having fallen in love with a boy, who neither in rank nor in talents could compare with the men she had known in her youth. It is a curious thing that the two lovers never seem to have had the least desire to be left on their own, for Lord Sligo was always of their party, and failing his Lordship, Dr. Meryon, whose jealousy of Bruce smouldered beneath a submissive exterior. Bruce did not have pleasant manners towards his inferiors. He was hard and conceited, and his selfishness was apparent to everyone except Hester. This selfishness was his only defence against a stormy and tyrannical passion. In her state of erotic hysteria Lady Hester found social life at Pera quite unbearable, and, though winter was advancing rapidly, she decided to hire a villa at Therapia on the banks of the Bosphorus.

The house which took her fancy was a delightful summer villa, with high vaulted rooms, stone floors, and fountains playing in marble basins. Built by some Turkish pasha to keep out the heat of July, it was hardly the ideal December residence. Luckily for them, both Lord Sligo and Michael Bruce were impervious to discomfort, but the icy winds sweeping down the Bosphorus soon attacked Lady Hester's lungs, and it is typical of Bruce that she was hardly convalescent before he suggested accompanying his friend to Smyrna. Perhaps bitter experience had taught Hester not to bind her lover with too firm a chain, perhaps she needed to be alone to readjust her mental balance, to reflect over the strange sensations and emotions of the last few months. Whatever may have been her motive, she let him go at a time when many women would have tried to keep him at their side, and, during some happy weeks, Dr. Meryon was allowed to revel in the exquisite pleasure of *tête-à-tête* talks and noonday rides.

It was not only selfishness which prompted Bruce to go to Smyrna, for he was fascinated and enthralled, as well as genuinely in love with Hester. He left her in order to deliberate over the future and to plan his course of action, for in his youthful idealism he contemplated marriage, and Sligo was romantic enough to encourage him in this mad idea. From Smyrna he wrote to his father declaring his intentions, but old Mr. Bruce, regardless of Lady Hester's rank and position, was furious to hear that his handsome, petted son should have entangled himself with an elderly spinster, when even the great Lord Wellesley, India's proudest Viceroy, had hinted that his charming daughter would not be averse to marrying the heir to an income of twenty thousand a year. Michael Bruce was not the kind of man to fall in love with a pretty debutante. His success with Hester had been a triumph for his *amour propre*. Whenever he dined out at Pera he was openly congratulated on a difficult conquest and he did not realize that the very men who complimented him on his success added under their breath, "I had rather it should be you than me."

He regarded his mistress as the most beautiful and most brilliant member of her sex, and, considering his exalted opinion of her talents, it says a good deal for his courage that he never allowed her to ride rough-shod over him in the manner which was so characteristic of her. On certain occasions he even dared to put her in her place. One day he and Sligo had been forced to listen to her holding forth on her favourite subject, a panegyric on her famous grandfather. Finally they succeeded in changing the subject and began to discuss the translations of Theocritus. Lady Hester resented any conversation of which she was not the centre. "Who on earth is Theocritus?" she asked, and her tone implied that she could not understand anyone bothering to discuss such a dull, obscure person. "Madam," replied Michael Bruce, "I may say of you what was once said of the great Lord Chatham, as you call him, and whom you have been talking about these last two hours. I hardly know which most to be astonished at, your extraordinary genius or your extraordinary ignorance." It was a brave thing for a boy of twenty-two to say to a woman who had never been told the truth in her life, and it was his courage and cool self-assurance which changed the relationship from Queen and Prince Consort to that of man and woman.

Lady Hester had many anxious hours during her winter at Therapia. The Stanhope pride was a family failing and she dreaded what James would have to say to her becoming the mistress of the young man he had casually introduced to her at Gibraltar. Communication between Constantinople and Cadiz was difficult in war time, and the plane trees on the shores of the Bosphorus were in full spring dress long before she received her brother's answer.

Meanwhile, she slowly and diffidently tried to make friends with the proudest and most exclusive people in the world. There was no intercourse between the European society of Pera and the great Turkish families. Even the Ministers had no direct dealings with the Seraglio, for all diplomatic transactions were handled by the Embassy. Lady Hester enlisted the help of Mr. Pisani, the interpreter to the British Embassy, who introduced her to a few minor officials, but Dr. Meryon's well stocked medicine-chest was her chief letter of introduction to the powerful pashas, and the doctor's services were soon in great demand in the latticed harems of Stamboul. Gilded barges bore him down the Bosphorus to the mouth of the Golden Horn, where the great Captain Pasha himself waited to consult him at the Arsenal, and there were closely guarded visits to the gardens of Eyoub and Buyukdereh, where armed eunuchs conducted him through marble courts to overheated harems in which frail beauties, stricken with consumption, lay gasping for breath.

While Lady Hester waited for her lover, Dr. Meryon made the most of his professional capacity in familiarizing himself with the soft, rounded forms of the attendants of the harem.

Lord Sligo and Michael Bruce made a triumphal return to Constantinople at the head of a cavalcade of fourteen horses. They were accompanied by an old Cambridge friend of theirs called Henry Pearce, who, tired of peregrinating alone in the Levant, had been only too willing to join their party. Sligo had been called back to Malta and he only stayed a few days at Therapia in order to witness a successful finish to the first act of Michael's love drama. It was somewhat of a shock to male susceptibility when the quixotic proposal of marriage was kindly but firmly refused. Lady Hester never went back on her steps. She had made a brave gesture and now she refused to take the safety exit; besides, she was shrewd enough to guess that Bruce's father would not approve of his son marrying a woman fourteen years his senior, and what a slur on her pride it would be to feel that a rich commoner disapproved of a Stanhope. She knew that Bruce would not be faithful to her for ever, so she just snatched at a temporary happiness, justifying herself in her own eyes by the fact that she was harming no one but herself.

There are times when lovers, as well as losing their sense of humour, lose all sense of proportion. Normally Hester would never have dreamed of confiding all her troubles to any one as young and as irresponsible as Lord Sligo. But he had been so sympathetic and understanding about the whole affair that she empowered him to tell General Oakes everything that had passed between her and Bruce. She herself wrote to the General, "He will answer you every question you may ask about me, even should they be very curious ones. He has my leave for so doing." Sligo was only too anxious to prove worthy of her implicit trust and confidence, and in a somewhat exaggerated burst of kindness he offered to sail from Malta to Cadiz in order to interview James Stanhope, whose eagerly awaited answer had arrived at Therapia a few days before his Lordship's departure.

There is very little excuse for Major Stanhope's hard and cruel condemnation of his sister's conduct. In his defence one can plead that he took the typical attitude of most young men of his class, but surely he, of all people, might have made allowances for the violence of her emotions. He had witnessed so many of her hysterical enthusiasms, her hero-worship for Sir John Moore; her suicidal despair when she was jilted by Granville Leveson-Gower. Surely he might have adopted a more temperate point of view towards the sister who had mothered him and looked after him ever since his earliest childhood. His rage, however, blunted all his tenderer feelings, and in his bitter, disapproving letter he hit hard at the one quality they had in common—their pride. Hester, who had been living in a state of tension all during the winter, now collapsed completely, and Sligo, who could not bear to see anyone unhappy, set himself the ungrateful task of interfering in other people's affairs. He had enough worries of his own, for rumour had reached him that the high naval authorities were taking a black view of his case.

Bruce could ill-afford losing his friend; he was ambitious, and hoped with his wealth and talents to play a prominent part in politics, while if it became known in England that he was trailing round the East as Lady Hester's *cher ami* it would seriously endanger his future career. He had been the first to flaunt their liaison when he had thought that it would culminate in marriage, but he had not yet acclimatized himself to his new *rôle*. The puritanism of the middle classes lurked beneath the veneer of the gay young man of the world. When one respected a woman as he respected Hester, one married her and begot a family by her. There was already that latent domesticity in his nature which in later years inspired him to marry an elderly widow with several children.

Lord Sligo sailed away to Malta, leaving a couple of his most obstreperous Albanians in Lady Hester's charge, and, though the wise and kindly Governor was delighted by his charm, he was sincerely distressed to hear that the people whose flirtation he had so innocently encouraged should have now taken such an irrevocable step. When one reads the correspondence which passed between Lady Hester and General Oakes one realizes what a serious offence she had committed in the eyes of the world. Even the most tolerant and broad-minded of men could not hide his disapproval. "It was, as you may easily imagine, a very great surprise to me, and the circumstance is what I cannot do otherwise than greatly deplore, for, viewing it in every way and well aware of the prejudices of the world, I fear it must hereafter cause both you and Bruce much trouble and distress. I can, however, assure you I make every allowance. I shall be very glad to be of service to you in any way you can point out and I shall, believe me, have a satisfaction if I am at all the instrument in promoting your comfort and happiness. At this distance, and without knowing a great deal more than I do at present, it is quite impossible for me to give any advice or opinion that ought in the smallest degree to have weight; yet, from all that Lord Sligo has told me, I will so far venture my sentiments as to say that I am rather inclined to take Bruce's side of the question for ameliorating the evils and difficulties, which must I fear, from the general usage and customs of the world, and of our country in particular, be naturally produced by such an event as has occurred."

When Sligo announced his intention of going to Cadiz in order to mollify James Stanhope's outraged pride, the general deplored the fact that he was not a little older 'with a greater knowledge of mankind and of the world.' Lord Sligo had a warm heart and the best intentions, but patience and discretion were not his strong points.

General Oakes was one of the many people who believed that Bruce had a great career ahead of him, and he knew that there was nothing more unsettling for a young man of his age than to adopt Lady Hester's restless mode of life; a life of constant excitement and fantastic grandeur, a glamorous, preposterous existence, suitable to Chatham's granddaughter, but most demoralizing for a prospective Tory M.P. No one was more anxious than Hester that he should have a brilliant future. She even went so far as to write to his father assuring him that she lay no claims on his son and that she would never try to keep him by her when the time came for him to return to England. She firmly believed that she was an uplifting influence for any man, and when in later years Bruce failed to realize her hopes, she never thought of reproaching herself for having encouraged him in his absurd dandyism and reckless extravagance. She meant to be so noble and honourable about the whole affair, even General Oakes should not be allowed to endanger his public position through his private sympathies, and she wrote to him, "I have no sort of defence to make for that conduct which surprised you; all I can say is, had I acted differently I should have had to reproach myself and altogether give up a person whose attachment appears to me as extraordinary as I have since found it uniform and sincere. I fairly tell you I had not courage to do so. I know how to make the best of my situation and have sense and feeling enough never to force myself forward so as to make it at all awkward for him; all the society I want is that which if I had been nobody I could equally have enjoyed—a few of his men friends, and those of my own, who this nor any other imprudence would not have deprived me of; yet I never wish them to commit themselves, particularly those in a public situation, which was one of my reasons for having candidly mentioned this business to you."

Now that Lord Sligo had departed, Dr. Meryon again found himself in the unenviable position of being the unwanted third, for Henry Pearce preferred the delights of Pera to the somewhat strained atmosphere of the villa at Therapia. Towards the end of May Lady Hester decided to try the sulphur baths of Brusa for the sake of her health, and the jealous, touchy doctor was again offended when he was sent in advance to make all the necessary arrangements for Milady and her young lover.

CHAPTER TWELVE

THE minarets of Brusa rose amidst the purple haze of Judas trees, and rivers of white irises fell down the slopes of Mount Olympus, rivalling the snows of its lofty summits. Every coffee-house was wreathed in garlands of wistaria, and by every wayside khan the chestnuts flared their tasselled candles. Nowhere does spring show herself in a more exquisite and more fragile garb than in the valleys of Asia Minor, in those meadows starred with flowers which inspired the carpet weavers of Ushak and Konia. There was no sound except the tinkle of the muleteers' bells, re-echoing in the mulberry groves, and the soft splash of water in the streams of melted snow which meandered through orchards of apricot and cherryblossom.

The peasants working in the cornfields and vineyards were quiet, conscientious people, and they took little interest in the Europeans who had hired a group of cottages on the slopes of Mount Olympus. They knew they must be great people in their own country, for they were honoured with the Sultan's *firmans*, and all the exiled pashas who congregated in Brusa at a safe distance from the suspicions and intrigues of Stamboul, offered hospitality to the large, blue-eyed Englishwoman who rode about the countryside dressed in a costume which resembled that of a seraglio page. The first time Hester Stanhope entered the ladies' baths, women fled in dismay, covering their faces, marvelling at the audacious young Bey who dared to disturb their privacy, but soon they discovered their mistake, and the Turkish ladies, with their fluttering hands and bird-like voices, made timid overtures of friendship to the English princess, who, usually so critical of her own sex, now went into raptures over the beauty of Asiatic women. It amused her to go to the hammam and to watch them bathing with all their trinkets on, squatting cross-legged in the drying-rooms, binding their hair with flowers, while attendants served them refreshing sorbets cooled by the snows of Olympus. She liked their shy, diffident questions and the shallow, tinkling laughter which greeted every one of her answers, and soon she was a constant visitor in the great harems of the neighbourhood.

In one of her gay, quizzing letters to Stratford Canning she writes, "You ought to see this beautiful place, but when no longer a great man you might fall in love with some of these very beautiful Turkish women, and that would be a great sin." "When you are no longer a great man," referred to the fact that Mr. Liston, the new Minister, was due to arrive in a few months. Canning was delighted to relinquish his tiresome and difficult post, and Lady Hester trusted that on the day of his departure his serious face would for once be softened by a smile. She appreciated his good qualities, but she could not resist giving little digs at his impeccable virtue and restrained Foreign Office manner, and though he was notoriously impatient he took her teasing in good part. Couriers were constantly bearing messages between Pera and Brusa, where the latest news from Spain and old copies of the *London Gazette* were eagerly awaited.

Hester had left Constantinople in a nervous, unbalanced condition. Her brother's disapproval of her conduct had been sufficient to break the taut threads of her self-control, and Michael Bruce had been dismayed at the Greek Tragedy airs which she had assumed over an inevitable occurrence. For the second time in her life she had hinted at suicide, but this time one suspects that it was but an idle threat uttered to the winds in order to gratify her sense of melodrama. Whether melodrama or hysteria, it was sufficient to alarm her lover, and he had taken her across to Asia in the hopes that a change of scenery might calm her nerves, while the sulphur baths proved beneficial to her health. But he had never expected such a mercurial rise in her spirits as he witnessed during the first week.

She was enchanted with Brusa. Under the soft, green shade of hundred-year-old plane trees, which cast fan-like shadows over the marble walls of silent mosques, she found a peace she

had never known before. The feverish energy of the Stanhopes
and the ambition of the Pitts died in the sunlight of an Asiatic
spring. Hester was born again; she was young, alluring,
mischievous as the child who had climbed the trees at Chevening, as gay and irresponsible as the girl who had paraded a
masculine costume at London masquerades. Everything that
was a novelty held charm for her. To live in a wooden cottage
belonging to an old Greek priest; to eat pilaffs and meat-balls
wrapped in vine leaves; to tame young Arab foals brought to her
by handsome Anatolian peasants, and to pay long, ceremonious
visits to grave and formal Beys, were new experiences which
satisfied her craving for romance.

The strangest and most enthralling sensation of all was to
lead this simple and pastoral existence with a boy of twenty-
two, a spoilt little London dandy, whom she had taught to
forget the delights of civilization. Michael Bruce must have
been a very charming companion to have made himself so
indispensable to her, but there was a side to his nature in which
she played no part at all. While Lady Hester paid her visits to
Turkish harems and Dr. Meryon treated phlegmatic pashas for
boils and eye trouble, Bruce spent hours dreaming on the terrace
of the Green Mosque, where even the heat of the midday sun
could not penetrate the dense, rustling shade of plane trees
nor kill the soft reflections of turquoise and emerald tiles. The
Green Mosque, the Holy of Holies, with its dome floating in the
thin, clear air like a balloon of shining snake-skin, with its
carved doorway dripping cool, white stalactites of stone, and
poppies blowing their frail red petals on its crumbling marble
steps, was a perfect place to escape from a passion which threatened
to annihilate him in its ardour and intensity, to escape from a
woman whom he adored, yet at moments found impossible to
live with.

One's heart goes out to Michael Bruce when one pictures
him trying to satisfy the whims of a highly-strung, temperamental creature, who insisted on her doctor being present at
every meal and every excursion. No wonder he was irritated by

Meryon's jealous and watchful eye, and how bored he must have been by his lengthy platitudes! Hester had no intention of offending the doctor, who prided himself on introducing her to all the important Turks of the neighbourhood, including the Governor; and though Bruce was annoyed that Meryon should come in for so much attention, he was glad enough to accept the pashas' invitations. Nowhere does friendship and esteem take such a material form as in the Ottoman Empire, and the presents which the rich Osmanlees bestowed on their European visitors were outvied by Michael's generosity.

Occasionally an adventurous English traveller would cross the Sea of Marmora, land at Mudania, and ride through miles of flowering orchards to Lady Hester's cottage. Mr. North (the future Lord Guildford) and his nephew, Mr. Douglas, came mainly to recount their exploits in Syria and Arabia, but they had to confess to one great disappointment—they had never reached Palmyra. For once the piastres of the English milords had been of no avail. The fanatic Wahabees of the desert were at war with the Anazé Arabs, and not even the boldest Bedouins dared to promise them a safe convoy. This was the first time that Lady Hester heard of Zenobia's capital, and it was Frederick North's failure which now tempted her to contemplate a journey which so many Europeans considered to be impossible.

These English visitors were few and far between, and when towards the end of June the doctor was despatched to Constantinople to find his patient a summer residence on the Bosphorus, Hester and Michael Bruce indulged in a blissful though belated honeymoon. Both their natures were too restless and too complicated to allow this simple idyll to last more than a few short weeks. In the middle of July they moved to Bebek, a village only ten miles from Constantinople, within easy reach of any English tourist who chose to present his respects to his notorious countrywoman. Stratford Canning, whose departure had been postponed till the winter, paid punctilious calls, and Hester was forcibly reminded of her family by the inopportune appearance of her 'disagreeable' cousin, Henry William Wynn, whose long, full chin betrayed his Grenville blood. She had only seen him once in her life, and all that she remembered was that he was ugly, but she made up her mind to dislike him, and when he arrived at Bebek she greeted him with a long diatribe against his relations. Grenvilles, Chathams and Carringtons were abused in the most outrageous manner. The only one for whom she had a good word to say was Lord Ebrington, who had been fortunate enough to please her during her stay at Malta.

She realized the unfavourable light in which her affair with Bruce would be regarded by her family, and she made haste to criticize before they had a chance of condemning her behaviour. There was always something unbalanced in her attitude towards her relations. Her sudden enthusiasms and unfair antipathies were apt to be bewildering; one day she would write friendly letters to Lord Buckingham and General Grenville, signing herself 'your affectionate cousin,' and the next day no words were too bitter with which to denounce that proud, cold-blooded race. Henry Wynn did not appreciate her malicious remarks at the expense of his mother's family, but he was sensible enough to laugh at her jokes, and, to her surprise, they became excellent friends. He wrote to his mother: "She even does me the honour to say that my foreign education has a little counteracted the Grenville blood. I must, however, say that at the time when she is abusing everything which is most dear to me, she does it in a manner that it is impossible to be angry with her, and I believe that it proceeds more from a love of ridiculing than from the heart."

Michael Bruce must have found life at Bebek rather tame after the exalted passion of the last few weeks. Hester had given him many proofs of her love, but though there were moments when she physically prostrated herself before him, parading her infatuation openly in front of strangers, yet at the same time she was capable of forgetting him and becoming wildly excited just because some dull sea captain who happened to have been a friend of Lord Camelford came to visit her at Bebek. Nothing was good enough for Captain Barrie, and for a few days her unfortunate cousin's mad exploits were the sole topics of conversation. Bruce, who resented the ghost of the bony giant being present at every meal, took a short trip to Adrianople.

Lady Hester was very content in her Turkish villa, with its handsome marble hammam attached to the harem and its shady gardens sloping down to the Bosphorus. She declared to General Oakes that, in spite of all the misery and suffering caused by her brother's conduct, she was "now happy and comfortable and quite another creature to what she had been at Malta." The chief attraction of Bebek was that there were no Europeans living in the village, for her genuine predilection for the Turks had now developed into a form of snobism. The very fact that they did not want to have anything to do with infidels and foreigners, especially women, made her determined to over-rule their prejudices. In the days when she travelled in Germany and Italy she had never taken the slightest trouble to get to know any of the inhabitants, but now even Michael was ignored when the Captain Pasha's brother announced his intention of honouring her by dining at her house. The former mistress of Downing Street was as thrilled as a child when four Ottoman Effendis sat at her table and ate English dishes with knives and forks, even going so far as to break the laws of their religion by tasting the delicious foreign wines she had prepared for their benefit. Proudly she asked Stratford Canning if he had ever heard of another case when four Turks, and one the brother of a Captain Pasha, visited and dined with a Christian woman. She told him, "I bore my sword with such an air that it made a conquest of them all, and they begin to find their own women rather stupid (at least they say so, but men fib sadly)." And when the Minister failed to appreciate her success she accused him of being jealous. Relations were becoming somewhat strained between them, for though Canning was willing to make allowances for her eccentricities, he was profoundly shocked when he heard that her Ladyship had visited the Turkish fleet dressed in men's overalls, a military greatcoat and a cocked hat. The Captain Pasha had given her permission to view the boats, provided she was not dressed in women's clothes, and she delighted in making herself the cynosure of hundreds of eyes by inspecting Turkish sailors in the uniform of an English officer. For days the drawing-rooms of Pera resounded with exaggerated tales of the Englishwoman's daring.

It is difficult to explain Lady Hester's success with the Turks. Her fabled riches helped her considerably, for what had been a mediocre fortune in London was unbounded wealth in the Levant, where a summer palace on the Bosphorus could be hired for twenty pounds a month. But it was not her fantastic generosity which paved her way to favour and won the affection and confidence of a taciturn and reserved race. It was her strange impersonal charm; her masculine attitude to life, guided by a feminine instinct, which appealed to the ambidextrous sexuality so prevalent in the Turkish male. Soon, through unforeseen circumstances, she was to pander still more to their perverse tastes by adopting masculine attire, and in the last years of her life she told Prince Pückler-Muskau "that the Arabs and the Turks had never looked upon her in the light either of a man or woman, but as an *être à part*."

In the eyes of Stratford Canning she was merely a tiresome, overbearing female, but no real trouble came between them till the late summer, when she suddenly decided that the one place really beneficial for her health would be the South of France. The very fact that France and Italy were forbidden territory made her long to go there, though it is hard to believe that the niece of Pitt, who during the anxious year of 1803 had helped her uncle in recruiting volunteers for the coastal defence, should really have asserted "that she was dying to see Bonaparte with her own eyes." Already, in Malta, she had informed the doctor that she intended to get a passport for France, where she could study Napoleon's character with a view to returning to England and plotting against him. The whole idea was so preposterous as to be hardly credible. But she had nursed it during many months and now she intended to put it into action.

Unknown to the Minister, she opened negotiations with Monsieur Latour Maubourg, the French *Chargé d' Affaires*. Diplomatic etiquette forbade any kind of intercourse between French and British subjects, so Lady Hester had to be very careful in arranging her secret assignations. The Frenchman was charming and courteous, and promised to do all in his power to procure her the necessary passports, for not only was she a very delightful and fascinating woman, but it was also a marvellous opportunity of annoying that priggish and conceited Mr. Canning. Hester revelled in those clandestine meetings on the Asiatic shores of the Bosphorus, where their two caiques lay safely hidden in the shadow of overhanging willows. One day she noticed that she was being spied upon and the next morning she received a very unpleasant visit from His Excellency the British Minister, demanding an explanation of her conduct. His high-handed tone had no effect on her and she refused to promise that she would give up seeing Monsieur Maubourg, adding that if he had been older and more experienced she would have told him of her intentions, only she did not want to give trouble to one so young. At the same time she congratulated him on the efficiency of his spies.

Mr. Canning left in a fury, and when Michael Bruce returned from Adrianople he was informed that the doors of the British Embassy were shut against her Ladyship and her suite. Bruce was highly amused by the whole affair, but Hester was not one to submit silently to open affront, especially as she suspected that Canning would send in a complaint to his Government. She sat down and wrote a letter to the Foreign Secretary, Lord Wellesley, which to this day remains a masterpiece of kindly malice. After recounting the whole story, she writes, "Although it is evident that Mr. Canning has not been educated in your

Lordship's school of gallantry, yet I give him full credit for acting from the most upright and conscientious principles, and if his zeal has carried him a little too far, there is no one so willing to forgive it as I am, or so little inclined to attempt to turn him from what he considers to be the execution of his duty. Affectation nor fear has in no degree influenced my line of conduct towards him; and if I have acted with more moderation than is usual to me, it proceeds from what may (though true) sound like conceit to confess—the persuasion that Mr. Canning and I do not stand upon equal grounds and that he is by no means a match for me, were I determined to revenge what to others carries the appearance of insult. But as he is both a religious and political methodist, after having appeared to doubt my love for my country, he will next presume to teach me my duty to my God! Before I conclude, I must request your Lordship not to receive Mr. Canning with dry brows or wry faces, or to allow the fine ladies to toss him a blanket. The best reward for his services would be to appoint him Commander-in-Chief at home and Ambassador-Extraordinary abroad to the various societies for the suppression of vice and cultivation of patriotism. The latter consists in putting one's self in greater convulsions than the dervishes at the mention of Bonaparte's name."

Lady Hester despatched one copy of this letter to General Oakes, asking him to forward it to London, and another copy was sent to the British Embassy at Pera; for she did not believe in saying behind a man's back what she did not dare to say to his face. No one enjoys being made a fool of, especially in official circles, and Canning blushed with shame as he pictured the mirth which this letter was bound to arouse in the Cabinet. Napoleon's imperial government did not bother to answer Monsieur Maubourg's application for his English *protégée*, and Hester had to remake her plans for the winter.

Her inability to obtain a passport for France was the turning-point in her life. Had she gone there it is almost certain that in the end she would have returned to England, but the far-reaching tentacles of the Ottoman Empire, which stretched from Athens to Baghdad, from Jerusalem to Bessarabia, tempted her to seek paths of travel which later she had neither the inclination nor the power to retrace. Bruce suggested wintering in Egypt, and his suggestion was warmly seconded by Henry Pearce, who was now tired of doing the social round of Pera; and towards the end of October Lady Hester and her suite set sail for Alexandria. It speaks for Stratford Canning's magnanimity that he and Lady Hester patched up their quarrel before her departure.

CHAPTER THIRTEEN

NEVER in the greatest flights of her imagination had Hester Stanhope pictured that she could be a wet, shivering castaway huddled in the cave of a barren rock, surrounded by an angry sea, with her only chance of safety depending on a set of rascally Greek sailors.

Accompanied by her suite of debonair young men, she had sailed so blithely out of the Golden Horn, through the Dardanelles, into the Aegean. But the sea which had waged inveterate warfare against Ulysses now stormed and raged against her intrepid Ladyship. Contrary winds delayed the party at Chios, and when they had already passed Rhodes and were making good headway for Alexandria, a violent tempest burst. The wind changed and the ship was beaten back on its course. For two days it rolled and pitched in a howling gale, then it sprang a leak, and in despair the pilot headed it towards Rhodes. But not all the united efforts of the crew and of the passengers could save them from shipwreck. It was useless for the captain to cry "All hands to the pump," for, as is the case with most Levantine ships, the pump had been so little used as to be quite unserviceable. The sailors lost their nerve, and fell on their knees praying to the Virgin, while Bruce, Pearce and the doctor did their best to stem the stream of water which came rushing into the hold. There was no longer any hope and the long-boat was lowered into a threatening sea. Clothes and medicine-chests, jewels and valuable pelisses, rare Oriental conserves brought as presents—nothing could be saved, not even her Ladyship's pet dog, who was too sick and frightened to jump into the boat. Only the doctor had the presence of mind to provide himself with a bag of dollars and a brace of pistols. Hester seemed calm and unruffled, issuing directions as clearly and as firmly as if she had been ordering boatmen on the terrace of Walmer Castle; but even her courage must have failed her for a moment when she was carried down into the lifeboat which tossed and rolled amidst high, black waves.

Night comes suddenly in the Levant, and though only about five o'clock it was already pitch dark. The wind lashed the heavy clouds of rain and beat the waves into white showers of spray, which at every instant threatened to swamp the frail and overweighted craft.

Poor Mrs. Fry—was this the last journey on which she was to follow her eccentric mistress? Even her Ladyship's words of comfort could not reconcile her to her fate, though she was determined not to give way to tears in front of those despicable Greeks. Dashing, handsome Michael Bruce, was this the miserable end to all his love of adventure and sensational excitement? And conciliatory little Dr. Meryon—did he not now regret that he had not stayed in his city lodging-house instead of trapesing after a spoilt and wilful valetudinarian? Hester was the only one who refused to believe that God, that egotistical God who gave especial privileges to those in whose veins ran the blood of Pitt and Stanhope, would allow her to die an obscure and untimely death in an Aegean storm.

Years ago it had been foretold that she was to be crowned in Jerusalem as Queen of the Jews. Brothers, the mad fortune-teller, whose uncomfortable prophecies against the House of Brunswick finally led him into Bedlam, once begged to be allowed to see the niece of Pitt. Lady Hester condescended, partly out of mere curiosity and partly out of genuine belief in his supernatural powers, and it was in a padded cell that she first heard that she was to be crowned as Queen in the East. All during these years she had remembered the words of a raving lunatic; it was the key to her frustrated ambitions and to her dreams of future grandeur—and she was the only person in the precarious little boat who was convinced that they would be saved.

Lunging, plunging through the blue-black waves, driven by a screaming gale, the boat finally struck against a rock. Soaked to the skin and battered with fatigue the party scrambled ashore. But what they had hoped might be a promontory of Rhodes was only a bare, stony crag surrounded by water on every side. Lady Hester and her maid were transported to the shelter of a cave which opened out of the cleft in the rock, where they had managed to moor the boat, while the men remained exposed to the mercy of the storm, and waited for daylight to come. Unless they were able to reach the island they were faced by the prospect of a slow death by starvation. For there was no fresh water on the rock, nor were there wild birds or living things of any kind.

Shortly after midnight the wind abated a little and the captain suggested making an attempt to reach the island. Even the cowardly Greeks preferred to run the risk of perishing at once than that of dying from sheer hunger. He added that, if the whole party insisted on coming, they were bound to sink at once; whereas, if he went alone with the crew, they might be able to return within the space of a few hours, bringing both provisions and boats for their deliverance. Lady Hester had no choice but to let them go, and the small group of Europeans, surrounded by their motley troupe of Asiatic servants, strained their eyes till they finally saw the beacon of fire with which the sailors signalled their safe arrival.

Daylight came, and the storm renewed its violence. After a short period of fitful and uneasy sleep the travellers woke, cold and shivering and ravenously hungry. There was not a sign of a sail on that grey and angry sea, and the coast of Rhodes lay shrouded in a mist of rain.

No one talked much, though Bruce and Pearce made a few pathetic attempts to show that they were not frightened of dying, and Hester chose an unfortunate moment to tell them how her uncle used to dislike the rich dishes served up at grand banquets, and how happy he was to eat hunks of bread and cheese in a clean Kentish farmhouse. Then even her conversational powers failed through exhaustion and want of food, and, wrapped in a pelisse, she fell asleep on the wet stones.

Towards evening the doctor saw a black spot on the sea—

117

it was the boat coming to their rescue. The Captain had remained behind, for he was not such a fool as to risk his life a second time, and the sailors had profited by their few hours on land by bracing up their spirits with several pints of arrack. By now, they were willing to brave the perils of any storm, and they had no sooner landed on the rock, before the travellers discovered that they had to deal with a drunken and unruly crew. But they had remembered the provisions, and for the moment nothing mattered, provided there was enough bread and cheese, arrack and water to satisfy appetites which had starved for thirty hours.

As soon as the meal was finished Lady Hester calmly prepared herself for another night of wind and rain, while Bruce and the doctor began to be uneasy.

The entire crew was riotous and insolent, but the only alternative was to stay behind and perish on a barren crag, and even drowning was preferable to starvation; then there was the fear that at any moment the wind might turn and they would run the danger of being swept off the rock. Once more they were hoisted into the rotten, creaking boat, muttering nervous prayers. The lantern swayed in the high wind, the candle blew out, leaving them in utter blackness, trusting to the sense of direction of a drunken pilot. The sailors had to pull hard in the very teeth of the gale, and the rain lashed against their faces. But at the very moment when a giant wave covered the boat from stem to stern, they touched land, and found themselves in a deserted swamp at the southernmost point of the island.

In spite of the terrible ordeals of the last two days, Bruce and Pearce still had enough energy to carry Lady Hester (who was no mean weight) across the marshes, till they finally reached a small windmill, where they decided to spend the rest of the night. The miller was woken up and despatched to the nearest village to procure some kind of conveyance, and while the women retired to rest in the granary the men gathered round an open fire. They were soon joined by Mrs. Fry, whose overwrought nerves could not stand the scratching of the rats, and Michael Bruce elected to watch over the bedside, where Chatham's granddaughter lay fast asleep on a pile of dirty straw, blissfully unconscious of the hordes of scuttling vermin.

Morning came. It was one of those luminous, shining days born from the fury of a storm, when all the world looks cleanly washed and new. The travellers woke with sore, aching limbs, and covered themselves with their rain-bespattered pelisses while their linen dried in the sun. It was characteristic of Hester that, instead of bewailing the loss of her clothes and jewels, she only regretted the poor little dog who had been too frightened to jump into the boat. All that she had saved from the wreck was a miniature of General Moore, the blood-stained glove he had worn at Corunna, forty golden guineas, and a valuable snuff-box which Lord Sligo had given her on his departure; but, in spite of the tremendous losses she had suffered and her physical exhaustion, she set herself out to comfort the rest of the party, promising her servants that as soon as they reached the town of Rhodes she would compensate them by dressing them in new clothes. The miller returned from the village, followed by numerous peasants leading mules and asses. They had already been told of the doctor's bag of dollars, and each in turn offered her Ladyship the hospitality of his cottage, but the village was so dirty and neglected and the habitations were so wretched and bug-ridden, that she decided to spend the following night in a stable. Under the circumstances even a bed of straw and a dinner of unleavened bread and goats' cheese were welcome.

Charles Meryon, who seems to have combined the functions of doctor and courier, was despatched in all haste to the town of Rhodes to procure money and a few necessities of life from the British agent, for the bag of dollars could not keep eleven people alive for very long. The rest of the party were to follow him by more leisurely stages, but Lady Hester had barely done eight hours of the journey before her strength gave out and she fell ill at Lindo.

The Doric town of Lindo, once a centre of the oldest Grecian civilization, lies on the Eastern side of the island. It is built on a promontory of rock shadowed by a ruined acropolis, and the arms of the knights of Rhodes are still carved over the doorways of the Turkish houses. The road over which the travellers passed was a stony mountain track leading through forests of pine carpeted with salvia and wild thyme, rising to giddy heights above the blue Aegean, circling by rocky crags crowned with the ruins of Crusader castles, where tufts of yellow liquorice grew among the stones. After being shaken for eight hours on a badly saddled mule, Hester arrived shivering with high fever. By this time the news of the shipwreck had spread all over the island, and an exiled Greek named Philipaki offered her hospitality at his house which lay among the orange groves of Malona.

'Philip Parker,' as Mrs. Fry insisted on calling the archon, did everything in his power to make her Ladyship comfortable, and after a few days' rest she was well enough to pursue her journey. It was a strange, motley-looking crowd which rode through the gates of Rhodes; the servants were half naked and the masters were attired partly in the stained European clothes they had worn before the shipwreck, partly in old shawls and native silk shirts lent them by their Greek host. Yet they refused to be downcast, and at Archangelo, the little Greek village which lies between Rhodes and Lindo, the peasants witnessed the fantastic spectacle of a tall, large Englishwoman in tattered, trailing garments, and two blonde, pale-faced young men joining in the Pyrrhic dance.

The British agent was only too willing to help Lady Hester in every way, but Hassan Bey, the Turkish Governor, did not share the courtesy of most of his countrymen. He was a rude, uneducated man, with a prejudice against Europeans, and he refused to advance her more than thirty pounds. A courier was immediately despatched to Constantinople, soliciting the help of Stratford Canning, and the doctor was despatched to Smyrna to procure medicinal supplies and household stores.

Meanwhile, a kindly Turk offered Lady Hester the use of a summer villa situated among the gardens of Trianda, only three miles distant from the town, and as "the Frankish houses of Rhodes were only fit for poultry," she was delighted to accept his hospitality. The island certainly deserved its title of 'the rose of Helios,' for even in January the climate was delightful, and the travellers were all quite contented in their temporary home, in spite of the numerous difficulties of procuring new equipment and the unpleasantness of the Captain of the ship who, after leaving them to their fate, now claimed enormous compensation, refusing to be satisfied with the generous rewards which had been distributed among the crew. Lady Hester's cheerful mood was chiefly due to the fact that, while they had been detained at Chios, a ship from Malta had put into harbour bringing her a forgiving and conciliatory letter from her brother. Fortunately James had realized the foolishness of his conduct without the help of Lord Sligo's mediation.

The most urgent problem to solve was that of clothes. It was impossible to procure European garments of any kind, and Hester was faced by the alternative, either of dressing as a Turkish woman, which would mean giving up her entire freedom, otherwise she would lay herself open to criticism and abuse; or of adopting the attire of an Asiatic Turk. Dire necessity forced her to assume one of those fanciful masculine costumes which she had taken so much pleasure in parading at London masquerades. Even now she liked making herself conspicuous and she took as much pleasure as a child in choosing her variegated leather cartridge-belt, her chased sword and yellow *babooshes*, vowing that "no costume had ever been so becoming to her." And when by chance her cousin Wynne appeared at Rhodes, he found her in one of her gayest and most fascinating moods, looking very charming in her wide trousers, short embroidered jacket and shaped waistcoat, surmounted by a multi-coloured turban, decorated with a bunch of flowers. Even plump, bustling Mrs. Fry was made to wear Turkish robes, though she never attempted to assume as dashing a costume as her mistress.

Dr. Gell, the famous archæologist, landed on the island, accompanied by a bevy of fine young gentlemen bent on treasure-hunting among the Mycenæan ruins. Bruce was delighted to see his former master and some of his old college friends, but Hester sneered at "the wise faces they would probably make over every crooked stick and worn out stone which might meet their eye." And they in their turn had little sympathy for their compatriot who strutted about in men's clothes and curried favour with the Turks.

Then Dr. Meryon returned from Smyrna, bringing her equipment, and the servants rioted because it had been impossible to procure enough cloth in the town to provide them with new clothes, so, with the exception of a young Greek called Georgiaki Dallegio, they were all dismissed. When Captain Hope, hearing of Lady Hester's sad plight, arrived at Rhodes on the frigate *Salsette* and offered her a passage to Alexandria, he found a very diminished household at Trianda. Her Ladyship christened him 'Chivalry' Hope, for none of the old Knights of Rhodes, whose mediæval palaces lowered among the flowering trees of Turkish gardens, could have been more chivalrous to a lady in distress. Hester was not one of those helpless feminine creatures at the mercy of a retinue of servants. She personally supervised the packing as well as sealing herself all the new stores which had arrived from Smyrna, and she told the doctor that "if she had a duke as a son she would teach him to saddle his horse himself." She revelled in her new masculine impersonation, but her young lover, though he laughed at her bizarre appearance and congratulated her on the enchanting effect of her turban, must have wondered nervously whether, at the same time as thrusting a *yataghan* and pistol through her silken sash, she would adopt a new attitude to life and take her pleasures in her own way and at her own time.

CHAPTER FOURTEEN

IN the harem gardens of the Usbekieh Palace, on a gold embroidered divan of scarlet velvet, Mehemet Ali entertained Hester Stanhope with sorbets and coffee. It was the first time that the Albanian adventurer, whose strategic brilliance and subtle cunning had raised him to the pashalik of Cairo, had received the visit of an English lady. The rocks on the citadel hill were still stained with the blood of the murdered mamelukes, but the consular agents of France and England, instead of remonstrating in horror at the ghastly massacre, had outvied one another in congratulating the unscrupulous instigator; and Lady Hester could be duly honoured when Mehemet Ali condescended to receive her at his palace, for never since the days of the Pharaohs had any ruler sat more securely on the Egyptian throne than this sturdy little man of humble origin, born on the sea front of Kavala, schooled in the discipline and hardship of the Turkish army.

He must have smiled his mocking, foxy smile in the shadow of his silken beard as he watched his guests coming down the garden path, for, unversed in the etiquette of Turkish apparel, where every class and calling has its own particular costume, Lady Hester and Michael Bruce had only thought of choosing the most gorgeous and spectacular garments. The court dress of a Tunisian Bey had taken her Ladyship's fancy and she never looked more magnificent than in her pantaloons of purple and gold, her turban and girdle made out of the finest cashmere shawls. To the eyes of an oriental there must have been something slightly ridiculous about the blue-eyed Englishwoman parading herself in a costume of the Barbary States.

The Pasha had sent his own horses to conduct her to the palace, with a retinue of honour, bearing silver sticks. The number of the sticks testified to her Ladyship's high rank, as also the fact that he rose from his divan to greet her on her arrival. Sorbets were served in finely cut crystal glasses, and coffee in delicate china cups studded with jewels, while the *narghileh* was presented but declined, for Hester had not yet learned to smoke. Through his small ferret eyes, Mehemet Ali surveyed this strange creature of indeterminate sex, whom the women of his harem had mistaken for his young son, Tussun Pasha. She spoke French, and Boghoz Bey, the Pasha's confidential secretary, acted as interpreter. In her drawling, musical voice she asked straightforward, intelligent questions about the State monopolies of grain and cotton and the new fortifications of Alexandria, and soon the Pasha realized that this woman, with her feminine intuition and her masculine breadth of vision, might be very useful in helping him to cement his friendship with the English. He promised that he would do for her what he had never done for any woman before—he would review his troops in her honour. He little knew that, in spite of all his flattery and courtship, she was to prove his most inveterate enemy during his Syrian campaign.

In May of 1812, as they sat in the gilded and painted kiosque, with the fountains leaping over arbours of jasmine and roses, Mehemet Ali and Hester Stanhope were enchanted with one another's company. He never once betrayed his humble origin by a single uncouth word or gesture and she never allowed her Western prejudices to influence her in her appraisal of an Eastern tyrant. Many a delicately nurtured woman would have shrunk from contact with one who in cold blood had butchered his former masters. But Hester Stanhope admired the power and strength of the man who had set himself out to re-organize a country which for hundreds of years had been ruined and ravaged by licentious and extravagant rulers. Her friendship with him did not prevent her from visiting the widows of the murdered Beys, and in a letter to Stratford Canning she writes, "Mehemet Ali was civiler to me than he ever was to anybody in his life, he always received me *standing*. I rode with him, paid him visits when I chose, where I chose, and at my own time; I talked to him for hours together, and everything I asked was done. But did this make me mean? No!

I visited the widow of Mourad Bey; I was on terms of great intimacy with all the wives and widows of the mamelukes, who were murdered or who fled, and I gave him myself an account of my visits. Mourad Bey's widow is the most charming woman (though not young) I ever knew, the picture of a captive queen with extraordinary talents, the tenderest heart, and the most affectionate manner."

Mehemet Ali overwhelmed her with honours and at the military review she showed off her intrepid horsemanship before the appraising eyes of Bedouin and Arab tribesmen, while Colonel Seve, a deserter from Napoleon's army, who, as commander of the French mamelukes, had adopted the Mussulman religion and the title of 'Sulaiman Pasha,' congratulated her on her equestrian powers. After the review, both Mehemet Ali and his favourite courtier, Abdul Bey, presented her with two fine Arab chargers, while Bruce received a magnificent sabre and a Kashmir shawl.

In spite of her personal successes Hester was disappointed with Egypt. As soon as she landed at Alexandria she took a dislike to the country, which she considered 'quite hideous,' and neither the gardens of Rosetta nor the mosques of Cairo could wholly obliterate that first impression. At the end of her stay she admitted that she liked Egypt, notwithstanding 'the narrow streets, the stinks and bad eyes,' and the doctor, who was usually a faithful echo of her opinions, wrote that "Alexandria was more dusty than Blackfriars Bridge on a windy day, and more crowded with blind than a hospital for the ophthalmania; Rosetta was more full of fleas than a beggar's tent, and Cairo more stinking than a butcher's slaughter house."

Now that she had adopted oriental attire, Lady Hester cast away the last remnants of convention. When her cousin Wynn appeared at Cairo after having crossed the desert from Gaza, he found her living alone with Michael Bruce, while Pearce and the doctor were billeted in the house of a rich Italian merchant. The despised Grenville relation, who on first acquaintance had been summarily dismissed as 'my disagreeable cousin Wynn,' was now given a warm welcome, and when Lady Hester chose to make herself charming, no one could withstand her for very long. Henry Wynn wrote to his mother from Cairo, "I had constant society in my cousin's house, and to me she made herself very agreeable. She has many faults, but I believe an excellent heart. . . . We went, a very large party, to the Pyramids. . . . Lady Hester attempted to go in but the undertaking was too great even for her, who is superior in exertion to any woman I ever saw."

This party to the Pyramids very nearly ended in disaster, for as they were being ferried across the Nile, a leak sprang in the bottom of the boat, and they would have all been drowned, but for the forethought of Henry Wynn's servant, who plugged the leak with his turban and shouted to the boatman, who had dropped his oars in consternation, that he would kill him if he did not row them across as fast as he could. In those days an expedition to the Pyramids was a hazardous undertaking. There were always marauding Bedouins on the edge of the desert waiting to attack some unsuspecting traveller and, before setting out, Lady Hester hired a guard of French mamelukes. These troops were composed of men who had twice been renegades, first to their Emperor and religion, and secondly to the mameluke Beys whom they had deserted at the time of their downfall. They were a corps of quarrelsome desperadoes, who, while adopting polygamy and the Koran, still played at billiards, and drank and gambled in the European quarters of Cairo. Mehemet Ali found plenty of employment for soldiers who had been disciplined in the *grande armée*, and when Lady Hester left Egypt, as an especial mark of favour, he allowed two of these Frenchmen to accompany her as a mounted guard. It was no idle boast when her Ladyship declared "that she had made her own way with the Turks."

After a month spent at Cairo Lady Hester and her suite departed for Damietta, where they hired a boat to take them across to Jaffa. Henry Pearce, who by now had got tired of sharing lodgings with Meryon, while Bruce and Lady Hester led their idyllic love life in a house of their own, decided to leave the party at Jaffa. Once more Bruce found himself faced by the prospect of an ill-assorted triangle with the doctor. At first there had been a chance of Sligo rejoining them in the summer. But poor Lord Sligo, in spite of the protection of General Oakes, who at Lady Hester's instigation had done everything in his power to help him, was on his way home to England, where a trial at the Old Bailey awaited him.

Bruce was beginning to feel the first twinges of home-sickness. The ardent young lover wilted under the strain of pandering to Lady Hester's megalomania. He was harsh and irritable with his servants, who were constantly being dismissed for no fault of their own, and his frayed temper vented itself on Meryon, whose slow, pedantic manner must have been infuriating to anyone who was nervous and highly-strung. Hester still loved Michael with all the intensity of her passion-ate, possessive nature, but though she allowed him to play the *rôle* of master in her house, he was never permitted to interfere or to compete in her relations with the pashas. The generous gifts, which he very often paid for, were given in her name, and it was she who carried the *firman* which made consuls, agents and governors prostrate themselves in her honour. All this could not have been very gratifying for someone as vain and as quick-tempered as Michael Bruce. It could hardly have been inspiring to make love to a woman who rode about all day in a mameluke travelling dress and seriously contemplated shaving off her curls in order to wear the turban with a better effect, and any sane and normal person must have felt slightly em-barrassed when Hester began to discuss, half seriously, half laughingly, the possibility of her being crowned in Jerusalem as Queen of the Jews.

The travellers landed at Jaffa on the 15th May, when the terraced, white-walled town was still crowded with Easter pilgrims, bartering the cheap goods of European Turkey against

Eastern perfumes and Damascus silks. The hundred tongues of the Levant were to be heard in the stony, narrow streets, where Nestorian and Chaldean Christians rubbed shoulders with Catholic priests and Greek patriarchs, and the whole of the Levant was incarnate in the person of Signor Damiani, the British agent, who had come down to the harbour to meet her Ladyship. He was of Italian extraction, born in Syria, and his father had already served under the English flag. He presented a somewhat ludicrous figure in his greasy Turkish robes, with his matted grey hair tied in a fat pigtail surmounted by an old-fashioned cocked hat which dated back to the days before the French revolution. It must have been a preposterous but rather charming scene to have witnessed this bent old man of sixty offering, in his broken English, British protection to the niece of Pitt, who towered over him in her scarlet trousers and flowing *burnous*.

While Lady Hester moved to the Consul's house, Bruce and the doctor were once more thrown together and forced to lodge in the Franciscan monastery; but as soon as the necessary preparations were made, they left for Jerusalem. It was an imposing cavalcade which set out on the road to Ramlah. Hester Stanhope, attended by a groom on either side, rode at the head of a procession of eleven laden camels, seven servants, two mamelukes, and a bodyguard of janissaries which had been provided by the Governor of Jaffa. Through undulating fields of barley and irrigated meadows planted with water-melons, the travellers proceeded to Ramlah, where the peasants were suffering from a plague of locusts. The governor of the town begged her Ladyship to tell him of some method of ridding his fields of the pest, and Lady Hester, who could never resist giving advice, told him of the ways in which English farmers exterminated cockroaches.

Between Ramlah and Jerusalem they had to pass through the territory of Abu Ghosh, the Arab sheik who levied taxes on every traveller bound for the sacred city, but when he saw the magnificent retinue descending the stony mountain path which led to the village, he realized that here were no poor, timid pilgrims, but rich grandees, with whom courtesy would be more profitable than strength. It was not often that beautiful Englishwomen came riding over the hills of Judea, and for the first time Lady Hester partook of true Arab hospitality. A sheep was killed in her honour, her animals were supplied with corn, and her dinner was prepared by the sheik's four wives. The gaily flowered marquees that had been procured in Egypt were pitched in a grove of olive trees, and as she tasted the minced meat rolled in vine leaves, the vegetable marrow stuffed with rice, the pilaffs of lamb and boiled chicken, she entranced her host with the charm of her conversation and the dignity of her manner. His delight was unbounded when he found that she was a friend and distant cousin of Sir Sidney Smith, who had captured the Arab imagination by his handsome appearance and brave demeanour during the siege of Acre.

In a wild mountain valley in the heart of the Holy Land, warming her hands over the fire which had been lighted to frighten away the jackals and hyenas, Lady Hester listened to the Arab chieftain extolling the admiral on whose arm she used to make such effective entrances into crowded London drawing-rooms. As a mark of honour to the cousin of Sir Sidney Smith, Abu Ghosh himself mounted guard at night over the encampment.

In Jerusalem Lady Hester was lodged in a house adjoining the Franciscan convent where again Bruce and the doctor had to share lodgings. Michael was beginning to realize that it was not easy to keep up an ardent liaison while travelling through the Holy Land, where the male members of the party were invariably expected to lodge in a monastery while the women were sequestered in adjoining houses. Relations were becoming somewhat strained between him and the doctor, and the discomforts and difficulties of the journey did not help to improve his temper. It was at Jerusalem that they met Ismael Bey, that legendary being whose existence has so often been discredited. The only survivor of the mameluke Beys,

he had escaped destruction at the hands of the Albanian troops
by leaping on horseback over the walls of the Cairo citadel.
After living for months as a fugitive in the desert, at the mercy
of every Bedouin robber, he had managed to reach Jerusalem.
Even now there was a price on his head and he was only secure
as long as the Pasha of Acre remained an enemy of Mehemet
Ali. This pasha was the just and benevolent Soliman, who had
succeeded the terrible El Djezzar, who even in the East had
earned the title of 'Butcher.'

Lady Hester, who could never refuse anyone in distress, gave
the unfortunate mameluke all the help in her power, at the
same time writing to Stratford Canning to solicit his protection. The few European travellers in Jerusalem were shocked
and disgusted to see an Englishwoman, accompanied by her
lover, visiting the grave of Our Lord attired in what to their
eyes looked like a fancy dress in the worst of taste, but after two
years spent in countries where Christians and Europeans were
openly despised, Lady Hester did not bother about the opinion
of her compatriots and co-religionists. The Governor of Jerusalem received her with pomp, and when she returned to Jaffa,
Mahomed Aga redoubled his attentions, having heard of the
honour paid her by Mehemet Ali. Legends of her generosity
and courage, and poetical descriptions of her beauty spread
through the whole of Syria and Palestine, and though she
condescended to be the guest of the European agents, it was
to the native chiefs that she showed the 'ineffable smiles of
her countenance.'

From Jaffa the party proceeded to Acre, across sandy tracks
and forests of Aleppo pine, past little white-walled towns
stretching out to sea, shadowed by the ruins of Crusader
castles, till they came to the rocky bay where the English
fleet had broken the power of Bonaparte. Djezzar Pasha, Acre's
sadistic ruler, had left his imprint on the inhabitants of the
town, and mutilated men and women stood at every street
corner. To deprive a man of eyes, ears or sexual organs was a
favourite form of oriental vengeance, and no one in the

entourage of the suspicious pasha had escaped his blood lust. The despot who through jealousy had tied every lady of his harem into a sack and dropped them into the sea, was hardly likely to be merciful to his servants. When Lady Hester visited Malem Haym, the Jewish banker, who fulfilled the post of private secretary and minister to the reigning pasha, she was horrified to find he had been deprived, not only of his nose, but of his right ear and eye. The Haym brothers had a unique position in Syria where Jews were usually hated and despised, for they controlled the affairs of both the pashas of Acre and Damascus, and Hester Stanhope had many occasions on which to be grateful for their friendship.

At Acre the travellers lived in the house of Mr. Cattafago, the Austrian Consul, one of the few Levantines who enjoyed the confidence of both Europeans and Arabs. Lady Hester, who in later life waged such inveterate warfare against all consuls and agents, always made exceptions in favour of him, Mr. Barker and the Chevalier Guy, the French Consul at Beyrout, who protected her during the last lonely years.

Acre was not a happy summer resort and soon the party, accompanied by Mr. Cattafago, left for Nazareth. At Nazareth, Bruce and Meryon had their first open quarrel. It was hard for the doctor to remember his dependent position when he was faced by the intolerable arrogance of a young man two years his junior. He regarded his patient as a wonderful and mysterious heroine and he hated to see her stepping off her pedestal by pandering to the whims of Michael Bruce. In Michael's opinion the doctor was the unwanted third, and he was always trying to persuade Hester not to include him in their expeditions. One day Meryon dared to contradict him, and he left in a rage for Tiberias. Hester realized that soon it would be impossible for her to keep both her lover and her doctor, and she knew that at her time of life the latter would be more easily replaced. After a few days Bruce returned in high spirits, accompanied by a great, burly man dressed in peasant robes. He introduced him to Lady Hester as Sheik Ibrahim, but when she saw a pair of blue eyes looking out of a heavy German face, and when she heard herself addressed in perfect English, with only the slightest trace of a foreign accent, she realized that this humble stranger, for whom Bruce showed so much enthusiasm, was none other than the celebrated Burckhardt.

The explorer adopted an unfortunate tone towards Lady Hester. He treated her as the rich eccentric amateur, who had no real knowledge or understanding of the country, and he believed that, in common with most of her compatriots, she had merely come to the East to treasure-hunt among the ruins of ancient civilizations. Hester was the last woman in the world to brook his air of kindly condescension, and she resented him for having made his own way with the Arabs, without expending large sums of money and without putting himself under the protection of any local pasha. He had been accepted as one of themselves by the people whom she had set herself out to startle and astonish. Her path was the more spectacular but the more expensive. Gorgeous gifts for the nobles and bags of piastres for their dependents were no small item in her travelling budget, and a considerable portion of the pension paid by Parliament contributed towards the costly pleasure of being crowned as 'Queen of Palmyra.' Bruce's enthusiasm was another and more personal reason of her dislike of Burckhardt. While the explorer remained at Nazareth she did not play the leading rôle; even the doctor trailed after him, asking him pedantic questions about the fetid carbonate of lime found in the Dead Sea, and she was the only one of the party who did not regret Burckhardt's departure for Egypt.

Lady Hester's stay at Nazareth was protracted owing to an accident she had on the day of her departure. Her horse slipped on a stone and fell, and she was thrown to the ground and severely bruised, but after a week she was well enough to proceed, and the travellers set out for Acre en route for Tyre and Sidon. At Tyre, Michael Bruce was the only member of the party who bothered to look at the ruins of the Phœnician capital, for his mistress had no interest for what she termed 'a heap of old stones.' From Acre up to Sidon the coast is bounded by the high crests of Lebanon, and as soon as her Ladyship arrived at Sidon she was greeted by a message from Emir Bechir, the Prince of the Mountain.

The Lebanon, with its limestone crags, its snowy peaks and fertile valleys, where flourished Asia's most mysterious sect, took an instant hold on Hester's imagination. Sidon, which, according to the doctor, was a dull town, having nothing to boast of but its gardens which were fruitful, and its water which was excellent, was rendered interesting through the fact that it was on the very borders of the Druse country. Magnificent mountaineers, with light eyes and curling beards, accompanied by veiled women with silver head-dresses shaped like horns, came down from their villages to sell their cattle in the market place. Monsieur Taitbout, who entertained the travellers in the French khan, had many tales to recount of the sect which admitted no proselytes, which believed in the transmigration of souls and allowed incestuous relationships. But the strangest tales were those recounted of the Emir, who had recently become a convert to Christianity. By some he was deemed to be a hypocrite and tyrant, by others a saint and just ruler of his people; and Lady Hester was dying of curiosity to see this redoubtable prince. Even the excitement of re-meeting 'Chivalry' Hope, whose ship was anchored in the harbour, faded before the prospect of visiting the Emir Bechir in his palace of Ibtedin, and on the 29th July, a cavalcade of twenty-two camels, twenty-five mules and eight horses left Sidon for the Druse capital of Deir El Kammar.

CHAPTER FIFTEEN

WATERFALLS dashing over the rocks of the Lebanon formed clouds of spray round the palace of Ibtedin, where sculptured colonnades supported galleries of fretted marble, and the fountains in the courtyards re-echoed the music of a hundred streams. The crenellated towers of the Emir's residence rose above the rock-bound terrace, shadowed by high mountain peaks, overlooking the fertile valley.

After a day of parching heat among the glare of chalk and limestone, it was with relief and joy that Lady Hester reached the green shade of the mulberry trees in the valley of Deir El Kammar. All the inhabitants of the tiny town came out to stare at the painted Englishwoman, for the Druses declared that no skin could be as white as hers without artificial aids. The Emir's minister accompanied her to a palace, once the chief residence of the Shaab family, now but a rest-house for the accommodation of the Prince's guests. It was only the next day that she was admitted to the great courtyard of Ibtedin, with the painted ceiling executed by an artist whose hands had been cut off, so that he could never reproduce his work of art, and the marble grille which guarded a watchful tiger, a fitting pet for the wily and cunning ruler.

The Emir Bechir rose to meet his guest. He was a tall, handsome man of fifty, with a flowing beard and great pale eyes, which stared out of a dark, sombre face. Every traveller who visited the Lebanon during his long reign fell under the magnetism of those strange, light eyes. Even Hester, who flattered herself to be a judge of character, succumbed to his suave charm. It was so easy to be charming to European travellers, who never stayed long enough to interfere in local politics or to make unpleasant inquiries into the administration of the country, but Bechir did not reckon with the mad caprices of an Englishwoman; those dreams of extravagant eccentricity in which the British aristocracy allow themselves to indulge.

134

How could he guess that the whim of a moment would inspire Lady Hester Stanhope to rent a ruined castle on one of the most inaccessible rocks of his territory, and how could she guess, when she passed the little village of Djoun which lay between Sidon and Deir El Kammar, that the peasants at the doors of the white-washed cottages would one day acknowledge her as 'the Lady of the Manor'?

The Prince, whom Lady Hester described as a 'mild, amiable man,' was a crafty and consummate hypocrite. Past-master in the art of conspiracy and intrigue, he had outwitted the jealous suspicions of Djezzar Pasha and had secured his throne during one of the most stormy periods of Syrian history. Born of Mussulman parents, converted to Christianity, he practised religious toleration in the widest sense of the word, and he participated in the sacred ceremonies of Christian, Mussulman and Druse. The hospitality which he accorded to Lady Hester and her suite was princely and magnificent. During her month's stay at Deir El Kammar every one of her meals was prepared by the Emir's head cook, while his secretary saw that her smallest need was gratified. After her first visit to Ibtedin, an Arab charger, splendidly saddled, was brought to the door of her house as a gift from Bechir.

Syrian hospitality was by no means gratuitous. The Prince's secretary was not above mentioning the sum which her Lady-ship would be pleased to present as a gift and which would help to defray the heavy expenses which his Highness had incurred on her behalf. Lady Hester was a poorer woman when she left Deir El Kammar, for not only had she presented Bechir with a sum of a thousand piastres, equal to fifty pounds, but she had distributed presents and *vails* (tips) among his enormous retinue of dragomans, secretaries and servants. Even the Arab stallion did not compensate for her losses, for he proved to be so vicious that she had to present him to one of her followers.

But when she returned to Europe (for she still had full intentions of ultimately going back) what a sensation she would cause by saying that she had lived for a month among the

Druses. She had visited their *aakels*, and in her correspondence she was fond of hinting that she had been initiated into some of their deeper mysteries; whereas, in reality, she was the last kind of woman to pry into the secrets of a strict religious sect. She was satisfied with far more simple pleasures, such as testing the truth of the legend that the Druses ate raw meat. One day she gave a strange feast. A sheep was killed, blown, skinned and cut up, and, while still reeking, was placed on large dishes made of matting and served to a crowd of peasants. The whole animal, as well as the tail, which was a mass of fat, was swallowed in the space of half an hour.

For a whole month the Emir managed to live up to his character as a kind, gentle Prince, while he led Lady Hester to believe that it was his chief minister, the sheik Bechir, who held the power of life and death in his hands, and who was very often responsible for the cruelties committed in his name. The Sheik was the head of the house of Djunblatt. With him there were no conflicting strains of religion and race, for he represented the proudest of all the Druse families; and his palace at Moukhtara had none of the overpowering ostentation of Ibtedin.

Lady Hester spent two days at Moukhtara and revelled in the fact that she was the first traveller whom the sheik had allowed to walk over his palace; she was even naïve enough to enjoy the thought that the hall where she dined so peacefully had been the scene of several massacres. Though the dinners were amicable and friendly, there was always an officer at her elbow, to drink from her cup and taste of her food before it was handed to her. The sheik lived in constant dread of being poisoned, for poison was a favourite weapon of the Emir Bechir when he became jealous of a too powerful minister.

Michael Bruce was the first member of the party who got bored with life at Deir El Kammar, and he proposed travelling north to Aleppo, but Hester, who was not a little proud of her transparent complexion, refused to go there on account of the Aleppo tetter, an eruption on the skin which affected nearly every traveller who visited the town. Two brothers of French origin, named Bertrand, who combined the careers of doctor and dragoman, had been engaged at Sidon, and one of them now accompanied Bruce to Aleppo, while the other one was to escort her Ladyship across the mountains to Damascus. For the first time, Hester saw her lover go without the slightest misgivings or regret. She was so intoxicated by her success with the Arabs that she had little time to spare for sentimental dalliance. Lately Bruce had been difficult. He had not only quarrelled with the doctor to such an extent that she had seriously contemplated dismissing the faithful Meryon, but he had started to interfere in her plans, and she knew that if he remained at her side he would never allow her to stage a sensational entry into Damascus.

From Deir El Kammar she wrote flattering letters to the newly nominated pasha at Damascus, who sent back a messenger bearing a courteous invitation to his city. The first thing this messenger did was to warn her Ladyship that it was impossible for her to appear unveiled in the fanatical city; her dragoman re-echoed these warnings, but Hester refused to pay any attention, and on the 31st August, in the stillness of a summer afternoon, she rode with an uncovered face through the gates of Damascus. The doctor, who had been sent ahead to prepare her a house in the Christian quarter, was full of nervous trepidation. Monsieur Bertrand feared for the safety of her life, for if a single man in the crowd grumbled at the effrontery of a woman daring to show herself unveiled under the shadow of the Mosque which sheltered the Prophet's sacred flag, not even the Sultan's *firmans* would protect her from the anger of the people. But the calm, dignified bearing which had shielded her from insult in the streets of Stamboul now stood her in good stead. All eyes were turned towards her. "Her feminine looks passed, with many, without doubt, for those of a beardless youth. More saw at once that it must be a woman; but before they could recover from their astonishment she had passed on." She was neither man nor woman, but a being apart.

The Christian quarter of Damascus was far removed from the tiled mosques and flowering gardens on the banks of the Barada, and Dr. Meryon was not given time to recover from his nervous ordeal before Lady Hester declared that she refused to take up her abode among the despised Greeks and Armenians. Instead of being thankful that she had been allowed to pass in safety through the streets, she now sent a polite but imperious note to the pasha, demanding a lodging in the Turkish quarter. At first her request was refused, but she was obdurate, and before forty-eight hours had passed she had obtained a splendid palace in the vicinity of the bazaars, within a stone's throw of the pasha's seraglio. Purse-strings were opened, and timely gifts in the right places helped to secure many of the honours, which Lady Hester regarded as the result of her personal success.

Even the *baksheesh* could not account for the tales which were circulating round the bazaar—tales of the English Queen with a face as pale as the moon, who rode like an Arab and whose eyes were as sharp as a Bedouin's, for Lady Hester's remarkable eyesight was regarded by the Syrians as one of the greatest gifts of God. Every day crowds congregated round her house to watch her mount her horse, and many an Arab boy would look appraisingly at the narrow foot with the high instep, the proud, arched instep which the Swiss governesses in the Chevening nurseries had tried in vain to crush. There was so much space between the heels and the toes that, when she placed her foot on the ground, water could flow through without wetting her. "It was an Arabian foot, the foot of the East," and people began to murmur that, though the *Melika* was so white, she was of Mussulman descent. When she rode through the streets unaccompanied save for her small Greek interpreter, the women came out of their houses to strew coffee in her path; when she entered the bazaar everyone arose from their seats as if she had been a pasha or a *mufti*, and Sayd Solomon paid her the honour of receiving her during the feast of *Ramadan*. But she was tired of receptions in marble courtyards with sorbets and coffee served by cringing slaves; she was tired of fountains echoing the slow cadenced rhythm of the harems. The black tents of the Bedouins attracted her and the tawny deserts which stretched beyond the apricot orchards of Damascus. She was more ready to admire the rugged chief of the mercenary troops than the haughty pasha, who received her on a velvet divan and whose pride of rank would not allow him to stand before a woman. When her janissary commented on the splendour of her reception, she replied, "Yes, but this is all vanity," and he remarked, "Oh, my Lady, you carry the splendour of royalty on your forehead, with the humility of a dervish at your heart."

The Superiors of the Franciscan and Capucine monasteries came to offer their services to her Ladyship, who begged them not to repeat their visits, as the presence of monks would be unwelcome in the Turkish quarter; but she accepted the gift of a fine *abah* from the wife of the English Consul at Baghdad, and cultivated the friendship of Dr. Chaboceau, the French doctor, who was a privileged guest in the most exclusive harems. Chaboceau had known the famous Volney, and assured Lady Hester that the explorer had never reached Palmyra. Already at Brusa she had been fired with a desire to visit the ruined city in the desert. The very danger of the expedition appealed to her. Even an experienced traveller like North had been forced to turn back, and Burkhardt had reached the town in triumph only to make an ignominious return to Hamah, after having been stripped to the skin by a party of Bedouin robbers. Now it came to light that the great Volney himself had never set foot in Zenobia's capital but had merely pirated the descriptions in his book from the account given by Wood and Dawkins.

The Pasha of Damascus, a lethargic, elegant Turkish gentleman, raised his eyebrows in surprise when Lady Hester asked him for an escort for Palmyra. His Jewish bankers, the brothers of Malem Haym, strongly dissuaded her from such a hazardous undertaking. At that time the Syrian desert was in a state of turmoil, for the constant guerilla warfare between rival

Bedouin tribes was aggravated by ominous rumours that 50,000 Wahabees were within four days' journey of Damascus. Added to this, the pasha had quarrelled with the Captain of the hired mercenary troops, which protected the feeble representatives of the Sublime Porte. The Captain Hamed Bey was the son of a deposed pasha, and refused to obey anyone except Moulai Ismael, the great military chief, who lived at Hamah on the borders of the desert. Lady Hester had met Hamed Bey at Cairo, where he had been helping to discipline Mehemet Ali's Coptic troops, and now was the occasion to cement their friendship. The qualities which had endeared her to the English cavalry, from the Duke of York to the youngest subaltern, insured her popularity amongst the troops which were held in dread by the civilian population of Damascus. Moulai Ismael arrived from Hamah, and many a Turk quaked in his bed, while the pasha made a show of civility which he was far from feeling. Hester dubbed him the 'Sir David Dundas of Syria,' and described him as a 'sensible, popular and active old fellow,' though her courage faltered for a moment when he summoned her for an interview.

It must have been an ordeal even for the most brazen of women to dismount in the terraced courtyards, crowded with horses, to walk past a thousand soldiers and to present herself to fifty officers, who paid tribute to her arms and masculine demeanour by treating her as an equal. The old chief was delighted with her; he offered her an escort of a hundred men to conduct her all over Syria, and put one of his confidential officers at her disposal. For the first time since Pitt's death, Hester recaptured the glory of the old days at Shorncliffe. Even drilling Kentish recruits and criticizing the uniforms of the Berkshire militia was dull in comparison with watching a fantasia performed by the most daring horsemen of the Turkish Empire. Every one of these visits to the great chiefs and pashas meant the giving and receiving of splendid presents, and Lady Hester's stable was now well-equipped with Arab horses from the finest Syrian studs.

Even Moulai Ismael could not guarantee a safe convoy to Palmyra, and he advised Lady Hester to secure the protection of Mahanna El Fadel, the chief of the Anazé Arabs, a tribe outside the jurisdiction of the Sublime Porte. Meanwhile, news of her Ladyship's doings reached Bruce at Aleppo. It was obvious that in the excitement of meeting military chiefs and Bedouin sheiks she had not found the time to miss him, and if her sense of fairness had allowed her, she would have been quite capable of starting off on her expedition without waiting for his return. Michael Bruce had every right to feel injured. The trip to Aleppo had been a failure in spite of the warm friendship he had founded with the Consul, Mr. Barker, the only British agent in the Levant who helped to further his country's interests. The glamour of the Orient was beginning to fade and Michael was tired of uncomfortable khans and incompetent servants. The inhabitants of Aleppo managed to combine the most unpleasant characteristics of East and West, and the autumn rains transformed the famous gardens into fields of churned mud.

Mr. Barker was amazed to hear of Lady Hester's project. He said that it was madness for any woman to attempt riding across twenty leagues of desert and suggested the *tacterwan* as the only possible means of transport. The *tacterwan* was a kind of sedan-chair drawn by mules, and Michael, realizing that he would have some difficulty in persuading her Ladyship to relinquish the saddle, resorted to his old plan of securing a male support, and invited Barker to accompany him to Damascus. Their departure was unavoidably postponed; plans had to be changed and express couriers bearing pages of good advice were despatched to Lady Hester, who complained in a letter to General Oakes: "It seems very cross to be angry at people being anxious about you; but had Bruce and Mr. Barker made less fuss about my safety, and let me have had perfectly my own way, I should have been returned by this time from Palmyra." Inadvertently Bruce caused a further delay by falling ill on the journey, so that he was laid up at

Hamah. There is no evidence that Lady Hester was worried over her lover's illness, for she made no attempt to accompany the doctor whom she sent to look after him.

She was far too busy with her own plans and she remained at Damascus to receive the visit of Emir Naser, the twenty-five-year-old son of Mahanna El Fadel. This Arab chieftain, dressed in a dirty sheepskin and ragged satin robe, pillaged from some travelling merchant, dined with Lady Hester, and a banquet was served consisting of Arab, French and English specialities, including a plum-pudding which caused a great deal of mirth. Naser came as an emissary from his father, saying that he had heard of Lady Hester's intention of going to Palmyra under the protection of the mercenary troops, and that it would be fatal for her to try to force her way through the desert. If she did, Mahanna would consider himself at liberty to treat her and her escorts as he did all those who presumed to cross the desert without his permission—namely, as enemies. But if she put herself under the protection of the Bedouins and relied on their honour, they would pledge themselves to conduct her there and back in safety. What he did not mention was the fee he would request for this safe conduct. His manner was eloquent and convincing; his flattery subtle and inspired. No woman, least of all Lady Hester, is averse to being called 'Star of the Morning' and 'Daughter of the Sultan.' Laden with gifts, Naser and his followers returned to the black tents with the message that in a few weeks' time the *Melika* would pay a visit to Mahanna El Fadel.

The doctor found Bruce and Barker at Hamah, and for once the arrogant invalid must have been grateful that his hasty tongue had not induced Lady Hester to dismiss her physician, while Meryon found it advantageous to forget his past grievances. At one time his departure for England had seemed perilously near, so near that he had to envisage the dreary prospect of a country practice as an alternative to toadying to some gouty nobleman. Here at least the natives treated him as a young milord, even if Bruce never allowed him to forget that he was a social inferior. After a few days the patient recovered, and he and Barker set out for Damascus *via* Baalbek, while Meryon pursued a mysterious errand on behalf of her Ladyship.

On the edge of the desert, in the little village of Nebk, lived a strange individual called Lascaris. Born of a good Maltese family of Piedmontese origin, he had hitched his wagon to a somewhat perilous star by following Bonaparte to Egypt after the capitulation of the island. There he ruined his career by marrying, in a romantic mood, a Georgian slave, whom he tried unsuccessfully to launch in Parisian Society. In France the Emperor found no suitable post for his talents, and he returned East and became involved in unsuccessful trading in the Crimea and Armenia, till finally he drifted to Aleppo, where he ran a line of cheap barter with the Bedouin villages on the borders of the desert. His outward appearance was poverty-stricken and pathetic; he entertained every passing traveller with the tales of his woes, begging them to help him to secure a pension from Malta, and to everyone he was careful to add that he had quarrelled irretrievably with the Emperor Napoleon.

Neither Lady Hester nor the doctor realized that Lascaris was one of the astutest of French agents, quietly planning the overland route which the genius of Napoleon had drawn from the banks of the Nile to the Hindu Kush.

When Hester first heard of his existence, she immediately thought of him as a useful chattel, a liaison officer between her and the Bedouins, and she was delighted with the doctor's accounts of his simple Arab life.

Bruce took an instant dislike to Damascus. He and Barker were lodged in the Christian quarter, in the house which had been despised by Lady Hester, and, with the exception of doctors, no man, under pain of death, was allowed to wander through the streets two hours after sunset. These two cir-cumstances managed to give the death-blow to an incongruous and unsatisfactory liaison. Lady Hester's masculinity was not a matter of superficial pose. Her outlook, moral code and bodily needs were those of a normal, temperate Englishman.

Her ardent nature was not absorbed with sex, which occupied but a subsidiary position in her life. The physical strain of her tiring journeys, the mental excitement of a constant change of environment, left her little inclination for love-making. The adulation of the Damascene crowds had awakened that formidable ego which for a short while had been forgotten in her love for Michael Bruce. Once again it strutted and spread itself, swollen with self-importance, trampling on the naïve, delicate emotions aroused by the tender affection of a sensitive lover.

It was now Barker's turn to fall ill, and Hester unreasonably accused him of being a troublesome patient "with a fever that did not seem inclined to leave him, or rather that he had fixed a certain term for its duration." She was bored with Damascus; it never struck her for one moment that she might stay and keep Bruce company while he nursed his friend, and she had no compunction about announcing her intention of leaving for Hamah, where Michael could join her as soon as Barker was fit to travel. No one was taken into her confidence, for the love of mystery had always been one of her strongest characteristics, and though officially she went to Hamah, in reality her first destination was Nebk, where she visited Lascaris whom she engaged as her interpreter before setting out for the camp of Mahanna El Fadel.

The adventuresome instincts of the child on the beach at Hastings, who had planned to row alone across to France, now impelled Hester Stanhope to throw herself, unarmed and unprotected, at the mercy of an Arab chief. She cast aside the gold embroidered vestments of a Turkish Bey and appeared before Mahanna in the sheepskin pelisse and white *abah* of a Bedouin sheik. Her simplicity and courage won his admiration. She told him quite openly, "I know you are a robber and that I am now in your power, but I fear you not, and I have left all those behind who were offered to me as a safeguard, and all my countrymen who could be considered as my protectors, to show you that it is you and your people whom I have chosen as such."

Then she partook of a Bedouin banquet and allowed the Emir to present her with the most succulent morsels of roasted sheep, impervious to the fact that he tore them off with his hands, which were covered with the grime of weeks. How unreal were those memories of London nights and those crowded routs, when the pompous Lord Buckingham ran to fetch her an ice; when she followed George Brummel's lead and refused to dine with some rich city peer unless he provided certain fantastic dishes and sauces of which the unfortunate host had never heard. Now she followed the example of her companions and dipped her long, aristocratic fingers with the delicate, tapering nails, into the mould of rice reeking with melted fat, while, hiding her distaste, she managed to swallow the gritty coffee made with brackish water. Later in the day she accompanied Naser to see the horses and mules being fed with camel's milk; the women, with their dyed blue lips and red-stained nails, came out of their tents to stare at her in amazement, and that night, squatting round the camp fire, she listened to poets from the banks of the Euphrates reciting the old tales of the Arabian Nights.

Aglow and triumphant she returned to Hamah, where she was joined by a very disgruntled Bruce, and as it was impossible to attempt the expedition to Palmyra until the early spring, they settled into Moulai Ismael's house where, according to Michael Bruce "they spent the most disagreeable winter, the coldest that had been known in Syria for thirty years."

CHAPTER SIXTEEN

HAMAH, 'a very quizzical town upon the banks of the Orontes,' was not an ideal winter resort, and Lady Hester's retinue of Egyptian grooms, Syrian cooks and Greek interpreters suffered from the cold to such an extent that many of them fell seriously ill. The first to succumb was poor Mrs. Fry, who was shaken with a violent attack of pleurisy at the very moment when her Ladyship chose to send her doctor into the desert in order to attend the Emir Mahanna. Consideration for others had never been Lady Hester's strong point, and she thought nothing of making Meryon trek off into the wilds at a time when the Syrian desert was white with snow and swept by icy gales. She told him that it was a unique opportunity for a young man of his age to study Bedouin life, and incidentally she suggested that he might make an excursion into Palmyra and come back and tell her if the road was practicable.

When one reads the doctor's painstaking and unimaginative diary, one feels that there were occasions when he was very near to being an involuntary hero.

He had one consolation, for however cold and primitive it might be in the Bedouin tents, it was no better at Hamah, where six inches of snow lay on the ground and not a single habitation was rain-proof. Lady Hester was settled in Moulai Ismael's house; and even though she had to walk on stilts through the muddy streets; even though Bruce grumbled from morning to night, and his friend, Mr. Barker, left for Aleppo after having supplied them with the necessary funds for their journey; even though the four wives and fifty concubines of Moulai Ismael got on her nerves, she was determined to stay there until the weather permitted her to go to Palmyra. Then her only maid fell ill, and she had to allow herself to be dressed by negro slaves, and the doctor was lost in the desert, so that she had to hire a Bedouin guide and send Georgiaki in search of him. And to complete a series of misfortunes, on the very day that he returned to Hamah, Monsieur Beaudin had a bad fall from his horse. Beaudin was a capable young Levantine from Aleppo and had taken the place of the two Bertrand brothers, who had been dismissed and sent back to Sidon, and he had already made himself so invaluable that when he took to his bed, the household became a pandemonium; that strange, motley household to which recruits were added at every halting-place. The latest addition had been made at Deir El Kammar, where Meryon found himself a new valet in the shape of a shabby, cringing Syrian who addressed him in a French that had obviously been learned in the streets of Marseilles. This man declared that his name was Pierre, that he was of Latin origin and that he had served as interpreter in Napoleon's armies. He even went so far as to add that as a child he had been taken to Versailles, where he had attracted the notice of Louis the Sixteenth. Arab and Provençal imagination flowered expansively in his conversation, and his garlic seasoned cooking and stock of stories entitled him to a prominent place in Lady Hester's travelling staff.

During the whole of the winter only one European traveller passed through Hamah, and Lady Hester's social life consisted of the occasional visits of Bedouin chiefs and the dreary company of the one or two deposed governors who had retired to the obscurity of this desert town. Still she kept up her spirits and teased both Bruce and the doctor, who, on his return from Palmyra, affected many of the strange customs of the country. In a letter to Mrs. Fernandez she wrote, "Oh, I forgot to tell you that the gentlemen have all long beards, and the doctor is such a quiz you can have no idea of, his head shaved and a pigtail coming out of the crown a yard long, a copper-coloured sheepskin and a pipe, six feet long, never out of his mouth. He never stands two minutes and squats about all over the house, sometimes upon the roof, sometimes upon the stairs, the court and all the house; when in the air, pulls a mat after him to sit down upon, washes his hands every five minutes and always eats with his fingers."

Lascaris, who had been living part of the winter at her Ladyship's expense, was now given enough money to carry out a cherished plan of settling at Palmyra. In her kindness of heart Hester even went so far as to ask General Oakes to procure him a small pension, and it is to her credit that she was one of the few English people travelling in the East who realized the importance of Napoleon's secret service. She was right in saying that Lascaris would be a useful British agent to send out into the desert, but in later years it must have been humiliating for her to learn that he had been in Napoleon's pay at the very time she asserted that "his sentiments were quite English and that it would be worth while to keep him so." Her intimacy with Lascaris was of very short duration, for he was tiresome and cantankerous and the last kind of man to submit to her imperious whims.

The snows melted and the Orontes overflowed. It was impossible to move from one quarter of the town to another, and water poured through every house. Lady Hester's health was far from good, but the doctor did not dare to dissuade her from attempting a journey she had set her heart on. There was good news from the desert, for Mecca had been recaptured from the fanatical Wahabees, who had been forced to retreat to their own capital of Dariya; but the good news from the interior was counteracted by bad tidings from the coast, where the plague had broken out at Sidon.

At last spring came, and the almond trees burst into blossom on the banks of the Orontes. Young kids and lambs frolicked round the Bedouin tents, and even the stony desert was carpeted with flowers of a hundred hues.

The time had come for Lady Hester's journey. Forty camels and seventy Arabs waited for her orders. Supported by Moulai Ismael, she bargained with Mahanna for the price of her safe convoy; and she agreed to pay 3,000 piastres (£150), one-third only to be deposited in advance, the rest on her safe return. Legends of her fantastic wealth had spread all over the country. She was said "to ride a horse worth forty purses, with housings and stirrups of fine gold, to receive every morning one thousand sequins from the English Sultan's treasurer; to carry a book indicating where hidden treasure was to be found (this book was Woods and Dawkin's plates of Palmyra); and to possess a herb that transmuted stones into gold."

Though neither Michael Bruce nor Hester knew the meaning of fear, several members of their entourage trembled for their safety. Even the inhabitants of Hamah, who lined the streets on the day of their departure, were full of gloomy prognostications.

On the 20th March, 1813, Chatham's granddaughter set out on her journey to Zenobia's capital. She rode at the head of the caravan, surrounded by a guard of Bedouin chieftains mounted on lean mares, flaunting long lances tipped with ostrich feathers. Her apparel was the same as theirs, a striped *abah* and a gaily-coloured *keffiyah* bound to her head by a rope of camel's hair. Bruce no longer had the place of honour at her side. Her sense of the dramatic would not allow any other European in her immediate vicinity, and he and the doctor were left to cover the rear of the procession. It is small wonder that one finds a somewhat ironical note creeping into one of Bruce's letters to General Oakes. He writes, "If Lady Hester succeeds in this undertaking she will at least have the merit of being the first European female who has ever visited this once celebrated city. Who knows but she may prove another Zenobia and be destined to restore it to its ancient splendour? Perhaps she may form a matrimonial alliance with Ibn Saud, the great Chief of the Wahabees. He is not represented as a very lovable object; but, making love subservient to ambition, they may unite their arms together, bring about a great revolution both in religion and politics, and shake the throne of the Sultan to its very centre. I wish you would come and assist them with your military counsel." The humour is tinged with bitterness, for Bruce realized that what he had imagined to be a deep and genuine affection had been little more than a physical infatuation. A pride which amounted to megalomania now rendered Hester Stanhope utterly self-sufficient.

Added to this, Bruce had made himself very unpopular with the Arabs by treating them as inferiors. The Emir Mahanna, in the midst of a friendly conversation, had told Hester quite plainly that if the young lord ventured out into the desert unaccompanied by her, no one would answer for his safety, while Naser's reply to Michael's arrogance was to ignore his existence and to take his orders only from the *Melika*.

At first Hester was enchanted with Naser; she declared "that he had manners that Lord Petersham would die of envy before, as he was as *éveillé* as a Frenchman, and presented himself with the air of Lord Rivers or the Duke of Grafton." The London dandies would have been pleased if they could have heard themselves being compared to a tough, sinewy Bedouin in a ragged satin robe and dirty sheepskin. Naser's compliments beguiled Lady Hester's ears, but terror fell on her servants whenever he came into their vicinity; nothing was safe from his thieving hands—clothes, pistols, provisions, everything was seized, and in less than an hour thrown carelessly to one of his followers. This was in the best Bedouin tradition, and only the menacing battle-axe of her Ladyship's negro slave, who kept watch over her tent at night, kept her possessions inviolate.

After two days' travelling they reached Mahanna's tents, where a great feast awaited them of roasted camel's flesh and bowls of leban (a kind of sour milk) and cakes of unleavened bread served with dibs, a treacle extracted from the juice of grapes. The old Emir was anxious to hear the latest news of Napoleon, whom the Arabs regarded in the light of a Saviour who might protect them from Russia, the one country the Turks had taught them to fear; and when Lady Hester had exchanged the necessary civilities with her host, they set out again at dusk.

There was no monotony in the journey across the Syrian desert. Sometimes they passed through miles of stony desolation,

Chevening Manor, Hester's childhood home.
Private Collection/Bridgeman Art Library

Hester's father: the republican Earl, Charles
Stanhope. His support of the French Revolution
led to him being lampooned and caricatured.
Getty Images

William Pitt, the Younger, was Prime
Minister and Hester's uncle.
Time Life Pictures/Getty Images

Walmer Castle, where Hester lived for a while with her uncle, William Pitt. She was responsible for landscaping the gardens.

Lord Granville Leveson-Gower, afterwards First Earl Granville, was a notorious flirt. Hester's infatuation with him was the scandal of London and she was bitterly hurt when he refused to marry her.
© *Yale Center for British Art, Paul Mellon Collection, USA/Bridgeman Art Library*

Lieutenant General Sir John Moore KB was Hester's first real love but was tragically killed in battle in 1809. His last words were, 'Stanhope, remember me to your sister.'
Courtesy of the Director, National Army Museum, London/Bridgeman Art Library

Mehemet Ali, the Albanian adventurer who became the pashalik (ruler) of Cairo. He entertained Lady Hester upon her arrival in Egypt but they later became implacable enemies.
Getty Images

After being shipwrecked in the Aegean Sea Lady Hester, having lost her possessions, adopted a version of the Turkish male dress which she was to wear for the rest of her life.
Getty Images

Dr Charles Meryon in Eastern dress. Dr Meryon was Hester's private physician for many years and one of her most loyal friends.

Lady Hester's Lebanon home, Dár Djoun.
Mary Evans Picture Library

Sidon looking towards Lebanon by David Roberts, 1843. Hester could see the shores of Sidon
from Djoun.
Stapleton Collection, UK/Bridgeman Art Library

George Gordon, Lord Byron by Thomas Phillips, 1815. Byron visited Hester in Athens several times but they did not like one another. Hester sneered at his poetry while Byron wrote of her '[I] do not admire that dangerous thing – a female wit!'.
Time Life Pictures/Getty Images

Tertrachm (obverse) of Zenobia, Queen of Palmyra, *c.*274. Hester enjoyed being compared to this legendary queen.
Private Collection/Bridgeman Art Library

The remains of Zenobia's Palace, Palmyra, 1859 by Carl Haag. Hester was the first European woman to set foot in Palmyra. The inhabitants welcomed her with a fantastic reception and hailed her as 'Queen of the Arabs'.
Private Collection/Bridgeman Art Library

The remains of
Dâr Djoun.
Photo Børre

by ruined castles and forests of turpentine trees; sometimes they climbed perilous mountain paths and descended into a flower-scented oasis alive with the sound of droning bees. Then the road would lead back to dreary, tawny wastes strewn with boulders of orange limestone.

Their Bedouin escort had a varied programme of entertainments to offer them on the way. Throwing off their *keffiyahs*, with their long hair flying in the wind, they would break out into some elaborate *fantasia*, riding at one another furiously, pointing their lances, while their strange war-cries re-echoed in the silence of the desert; or as an alternative one of them would recite some long, heroic poem, which none of the travellers understood, for Lady Hester's knowledge of Arabic was still very limited, and though her gestures were eloquent, she always had to rely on the tempered translations of the dragoman.

All went well till the fifth day, when they pitched their tents in the lovely vale of Mangoura at the foot of the Belaz mountains. Every evening it was customary for Naser to visit Lady Hester's tent and to ask for her orders, but now he refused to appear, saying that even if the Lady was the daughter of a *vizier*, he was the son of a prince, and it was for her to wait on him. Surrounded by seventy tribesmen, at the mercy of the guides who knew the secret wells and by-ways of the desert, it was useless for Hester to lose her temper or for Michael to resent this lack of courtesy to a woman. Utter indifference was the only line to adopt, and Naser, who hoped to intimidate her Ladyship so as to extort a larger sum of payment, found that not the slightest notice was taken of his behaviour. The tribesmen whispered to the frightened servants that their chief was in a black mood and liable at any moment to order them back. Even the capable Beaudin lost his head while the imaginative Pierre regaled the company with highly-coloured tales of Arab vengeance. Lady Hester made her own arrangements without consulting Naser, and the doctor, together with a guide, was sent ahead to Palmyra to prepare her lodging.

The following night there was panic in the camp, when rumours spread that a party of Faydan Arabs, sworn enemies of the Anazés, were hiding near the encampment. Some mares had broken loose and there was not the slightest doubt that they had been stolen. Without giving any warning, Naser and his followers rode off into the night and left Bruce and Lady Hester and a group of cowardly servants alone in the middle of the desert. Hester remained calm and unmoved. She ordered everyone to take up their pistols and stationed them at various points of the encampment. She consoled tearful Mrs. Fry, and, faced by actual danger, she and Bruce were once more drawn together, for their undaunted courage was the strongest link between them. In less than twenty minutes Naser returned, with an unconvincing tale of having surprised the enemy, who had fled at his approach. It was fairly obvious that it had only been another ruse on his part to test Lady Hester's morale. Bravery is a quality greatly appreciated by the Arabs, and from now on Naser was Miladi's submissive and admiring slave.

It was a hot, sunny day when the caravan crossed the mountain pass that formed the gates of Palmyra. Under the imposing mass of the ruined Turkish castle, past the grey fortified towers that guarded the pass, they came to the valley of the tombs—great piles of masonry, rocks of an older world in a green, shadowed hollow where the sun had no place. Behind lay the desert and in front was a stony ridge. Suddenly the silence of the valley of the dead was broken by the sound of galloping horses and the beat of kettle-drums. The Palmyrenes, naked to the waist, wearing petticoats of tanned skins and cartridge belts of cowrie shells, had come out to welcome their English visitor. In her honour they performed a mock attack and defence of a caravan, and the clear desert air was heavy with the smell of gunpowder.

Now Lady Hester stood on what seemed to be the ridge of the world, and below lay Palmyra, the ancient Tadmor—a forest of mutilated columns carelessly scattered on the tawny plain, fragments of white and orange limestone crushing the frail desert grasses. Only the proud sweep of the colonnade, which terminated in Zenobia's triumphal arch, still stood erect, catching the reflections of the sun, and only a thin green fringe of palm trees still stood in memory of Zenobia's gardens. Against the ruins of Apollo's temple huddled the mud huts of the modern Palmyrenes, and in the sunlight the yellow clay and orange limestone merged into gold. The whole town was of gold, unreal and fantastic, sinking back in a drift of sand, with its treasures destroyed by the vandalism of marauding Bedouins. Hester Stanhope rode under the great colonnade, the first European woman who had ever set foot in this crumbling capital. The inhabitants had prepared her a reception in the tradition of those which they had once awarded to their empress. On the columns with their projecting consoles, where the mark of cramp irons testified to the former existence of marble statuary, stood the most beautiful girls of the place, with their pointed breasts and slim thighs but faintly concealed by transparent robes and their heads swathed in long white veils. Some carried garlands, while those on the side of the triumphal arch and under the gateway bore palms in their hands. As the caravan advanced, they remained inanimate as if carved in bronze; then, when Lady Hester had passed, they leapt to the ground and joined in a wild dance at her side. Under the triumphal arch, built by Zenobia to celebrate her Egyptian conquests, the procession came to a halt, and the loveliest of all the living statues bent down from her pedestal to place a wreath on Lady Hester's head, while bearded elders recited odes in her honour and young boys followed in her train playing on Arabian instruments. Fifteen hundred people, the total population of Palmyra, acclaimed her as their *Melika*.

The words of the Bedlam prophet, "You shall be crowned as Queen in the East," had been fulfilled; but her empire was but the sands of the desert instead of the teeming streets of the sacred town. That day the blood of Diamond Pitt 'which came all aflame from the East' burned in Hester's veins. It was the crowning point in her aimless, restless life. As the Queen of Tadmor, built by Solomon thousands of years before the clanking feet of the Roman legions re-echoed in the Syrian desert, she was to appeal to generations of romantics. For twenty-five years her name would serve as a pass-word to every adventuresome traveller who crossed from Syria to Persia. It was she who gave the orders to the sheik that no European should be allowed to visit the ruins without the payment of a thousand piastres. This exorbitant tax was deliberately fixed by her, so that only a few of her compatriots could share in her glory. Even in the wilds of the desert, Hester Stanhope worshipped before the altar of her colossal egotism. She saw herself reflected in Zenobia's fame; she had her beauty and personal charm, her masculine bravery and undaunted courage. But where were the legions for her to command? Where were Longinus and the laden elephants bearing her the spoils of Egypt and Palestine? She had nothing on which to expend her restless, feverish energy. That everlasting search for health, a health at the mercy of her tormented nerves, was the only real motive for her constant wanderings. There was very little of the explorer or the archæologist in her make-up. All she searched for was power, and the unquestioning admiration of a tribe of ignorant Arabs was more gratifying to her than the friendship of her equals.

The sense of the dramatic which is inherent in every Bedouin had inspired the Palmyrenes to stage a charming pageant. But Hester Stanhope took it in deadly earnest. From now on she styled herself 'Queen of the Arabs,' and as she paid handsomely for that privilege, no one bothered to contradict her.

CHAPTER SEVENTEEN

THE plague was raging all along the coast from Acre to Tripoli, and Latakia at the edge of the Ansary mountains was the only port still free from infection. After their triumphal journey through the desert it was somewhat of an anti-climax for Michael Bruce and Hester Stanhope to have to shut themselves up in a sleepy little Syrian port and wait for the brave captain who would dare to sail his ship down that plague-infested coast. Their plans were vague, for they were suffering from an inevitable reaction after the excitement of the past few months. One day Hester would talk of returning to England, the next day she would propose undertaking a journey to Mecca; at one moment she amused herself by planning an expedition overland via Basra to India, at another moment she toyed with the idea of doing some unofficial spying in Russia, for she believed that country to be the great menace in the continental balance of power.

After the crippling expenses of the last year she did not have the necessary means with which to carry out any of these fantastic plans. If Hester Stanhope had been a rich woman, there is no doubt that she would have played an important part in the politics of the Near East. She had inherited her grandfather's breadth of vision and amazing flair for foreseeing the possibilities of colonial expansion. But her pension of twelve hundred a year, which was rarely paid up to date, owing to the difficulty of procuring her life certificate, which had to be signed by an English Consul, coupled with the interest of the ten thousand pounds left her by Charles, and her comparatively small reversion on the Burton Pynsent estate, constituted practically the whole of her income. The shipwreck had entailed stupendous expenses, and instead of living a quiet life until she had saved enough money to recuperate from her losses, she set herself out to outvie the orientals in the magnificence of her retinue and the generosity of her gifts. When Mr. Coutts, who was not only her banker but one of her grandfather's oldest friends, remonstrated with her on her extravagance, she excused herself by saying that she did not want to remain quietly in one place on account of Bruce, who had to make the most of his few years of travel. She sorely taxed the conscience of a banker by relying on the liberality of a friend, who found it hard to refuse anyone who had Pitt blood in her veins. Money fell through her hands like water. Her journey to Palmyra had been heavily paid for, not only in cash but in every kind of present, from gold-chased pistols and English watches to Damascus silks and Aleppo stuffs. But her vanity had been satisfied, for her name was known from Stamboul to Baghdad. She had succeeded in spite of the warnings of Frederick North, who had written to her from Sidon just before she set out for Hamah, saying, "Pray, dear Empress, do not travel with too few attendants in the desert. Your predecessor, Zenobia, would have avoided captivity had her suite been more numerous, and as you are allied both with the pashas and the Anazé Arabs, why should not you be escorted with the troops of both?"

She dreaded the thought of returning to England and having to pick up the threads of her old life. She would amuse her friends for a few weeks with the stories of her journey and then she would be ignored as a fading old spinster with a tarnished reputation. Here she was famous. The Anazé Arabs had enrolled her as one of their family, Mahanna El Fadel had granted her the freedom of the desert, she had met the fanatical Wahabees and had ridden their fleet-footed dromedaries and listened to their tales of the great Ibn Saud, with his eight hundred wives and his spacious palaces in the palm-fringed oasis of Dariyah. Who knows that she might not venture there one day and add yet another name to the list of the Eastern despots who had fallen to her charms? How could she go back to England, to a country ruled by a set of despicable toadies and place-seekers, headed by Lord Liverpool, that prince of opportunists? How could she, who had lived in the deserts and

156

who had seen herds of over a thousand camels descend the Belaz mountains to the enchanting vale of Mangoura, be content with the 'grandeur and dullness of Stowe and the confined, missified beauties of Dropmore?'

During that summer at Latakia, Hester realized that the time was approaching for Bruce to return home. She still believed in his future, though not with the same ardent conviction as when she had written to a friend from Therapia, "The country is going, though a few men like my dear companion might save it; he, if not put forward too soon, will make a real *statesman*, he has all the capabilities, only wants a little more knowledge and experience of the world."

She knew it was no good for a young man to idle away his time in bathing and shooting quails with Mr. Barker, who had taken a cottage in the neighbouring hills, and when a letter arrived from England saying that old Mr. Bruce was seriously ill, she enforced the necessity of his immediate return. She now kept the promise she had made years ago at Therapia; she was sending Bruce back to England for the good of his career, and she tried to make herself believe that he would achieve fame and glory. She had to believe it, for to her it was the breaking of the last human ties, it was the end of her life as a normal healthy young woman, and she needed some kind of justification for the tremendous sacrifice she was making. He was the only man who had ever satisfied her as a woman. Except for one short episode, a brief infatuation over which the doctor preferred to draw a veil, there is no evidence that she ever had another lover.

Bruce had spent over four of the most impressionable years of his life in her company. The rottenness and corruption of the Levant, the constant lying and thieving of the inhabitants, the avid money greed of the proudest sheik, combined with Hester's bitter cynicism, had destroyed his youthful enthusiasms. He was now older and more experienced. His health, which had always been delicate, was much improved through enforced abstinence from wines and condiments. In a letter from the doctor to Lord Sligo, one reads that at one time "Mr. Bruce brought up every meal he ate," which is not a very attractive sidelight on a smart young man of fashion. But there can be no doubt that the last four years had been disastrous for the formation of his character. He assessed his talents at a high value, but so far he had achieved nothing. The grand tour had been fatally dragged out. At a time when his contemporaries were already in working harness, he was still playing the *rôle* of an Eastern dandy. He was demoralized and unsettled, too proud to compete with men whose abilities he considered inferior to his own. He was no longer in love with Hester Stanhope, for all emotion had died during those sleepless nights in uncomfortable beds in the monasteries of the Holy Land; during those dreary evenings in the Christian quarter of Damascus when he had to spend his time playing cards with Mr. Barker. Her lack of consideration and consummate selfishness would have managed to exhaust the patience of the mildest and most sweet-tempered of men, and Michael Bruce's temper had never been one of his assets. No woman of her age could have taken less pains to hold a young man's love, but though she was already thirty-seven there was still something extraordinarily magnetic and fascinating about her. Her charming smile, her lovely hands and soft, white skin would have been sufficient for many to call her beautiful, even if she had not possessed that overflowing vitality which dominated her surroundings. And though there must have been moments when Michael longed to find a tactful and easy exit from a tiresome and difficult liaison, he still depended on her and admired her.

Life at Latakia was dull and uneventful, for the plague had frightened away every English tourist, and Bruce was tired of those white-roofed towns baking in the glaring Syrian sun, tired of those endless orchards of sycamores and figs and those miles of neatly planted vineyards. Even the blue Mediterranean became monotonous, when day after day he looked in vain for the sight of an English frigate.

158

Letters arrived after many months of delay in the lazaretto of Constantinople, where the plague was raging at its fiercest; letters from his friends and contemporaries in London, telling him of the gaieties of Brighton and the balls at Carlton House; letters from Peter Sligo, who, after serving a short time of imprisonment at Newgate, was once more pleasure cruising in the Mediterranean; long, affectionate letters from his father reminding him of the brilliant career which awaited him at home. Old Crawford Bruce had never become reconciled to his son gallivanting in the East with a woman, tales of whose eccentricities were already beginning to circulate round London. The news of Hester Stanhope having adopted masculine attire had dumbfounded her relations; Grenvilles, Haddingtons and Harringtons deplored and lamented the indecency and depravity of her behaviour, but not one of them thought of sending her out a new wardrobe of European clothes.

Only her brother James, whose own income was hardly sufficient to meet his requirements as a major in the Guards, set himself the task of saving five hundred pounds in order to procure his sister a new trousseau. Hester was touched by his devotion, but she refused to pander to his conventional outlook, and James's careful savings were spent in purchasing elaborate presents for subservient pashas. She was completely unscrupulous in money matters, and in 1813 Bruce advanced her a considerable sum out of his own private funds in order to prevent her from overtaxing her banker's generosity. According to the doctor, "Bruce had greatly profited by her Ladyship's experience and knowledge of the world," but his education had been an expensive one. Hester had inherited her uncle's habit of borrowing vast sums of money from her friends without making the slightest attempt to cut down her personal expenses. She was robbed and swindled at every turn. The merchants who allowed her credit worked at a hundred per cent profit, and though in those days Syria was considered to be one of the cheapest places in the Levant, she complained that it was too expensive to live there on account of the exorbitant demands which were made on her purse.

She and Bruce had left Hamah in the spring and had travelled by slow stages up the lovely Orontes valley. As soon as they arrived at Latakia they hired the largest house in the town, while the doctor, who never liked reminding his patient when his salary was overdue, installed himself in a small cottage, where he collected a large practice among the local European and chief Moslem families. All during the summer Bruce had vague plans of going back to England, and though Hester had allowed him to believe that they were returning together, she was clear-sighted enough to see that he was no longer in love with her. She knew that as long as he remained in her vicinity he would never have the strength to break with her, but she had no intention of going back to England, and in a letter to Mr. Coutts she writes, "If I deceived him, it was only to render parting less painful and to do the thing by degrees, for, after he had opportunities of forming other intimacies upon the Continent or elsewhere, what he would have considered at one moment with agony of mind, at another he might have considered as a release I know the human heart too well not to know also how to foresee and tolerate all its changes."

She needed all her courage during those last weeks, for the fact that she was about to lose him rekindled the love which had been swamped in the self-deification she had indulged in during the past year. Unconsciously she set herself out to charm and fascinate him, to strengthen the physical bond, which she had allowed to slacken through her own carelessness. Though she used all her powers of argument and persuasion to induce him to return to England, she allowed him to see her own misery and unhappiness, for she could hardly bear to face the loneliness of a life without him. Meryon, whom she considered to be one of the stupidest men in the world, would now be her only companion, and even he dreaded the thought of being left alone with her and longed for the convivial Oxford taverns and the homely comforts of family life. Gone were the days when he was proud and happy merely if her Ladyship condescended to take a walk with him. She had sadly changed. The self-absorption which in early middle-age had come over Lord Stanhope had been inherited by his daughter. She was not only self-absorbed; she was self-obsessed and she drained the vitality of everyone with whom she came into contact.

Yet she abided by the promise she had once made to Bruce's father, offering to give up his son when the time came for him to take up his career, and it was she who formed all the plans for Michael's journey, which, owing to the plague, had to be made overland via Aleppo, Constantinople and Vienna. All differences and quarrels were forgotten during the last weeks. They were both so nervous and highly strung that they worked themselves up to a state of exalted passion. Even Meryon, who had suffered so much from Bruce's arrogance, was sad on the day when he said good-bye to him on the high road to Aleppo.

For the first time in her life Hester was frightened; the plague was encroaching on every side, yet she lacked the strength and vitality to tear herself away from the country where she had already taken root, and one day she informed the astonished doctor that she intended to settle down at Sidon, where she had hired a Greek convent in the foothills of the Lebanon. This convent was one of the residences of the Patriarch of the Greek Catholics, and it had taken her fancy on one of her mountain rides during her stay at Deir El Kammar. She remembered it as a quiet, peaceful spot on a lonely mountain side, commanding a wide view of the sea; a fitting home for a hermit who was tired of the vanities of social life.

Before she could move into her new home, the plague came to Latakia and panic was in every heart. People shut themselves up in their houses and corpses lay unburied in the streets. Amongst the grief-stricken parents who clamoured at Dr. Meryon's doors were Mr. and Mrs. Barker, whose two small children were stricken with the disease. All his medical training could not help the doctor to contend against the terrible malady of the East. The children died and he himself was so harassed and worn out that he fell seriously ill. As he lay weak and exhausted with high fever, Anne Fry brought him the news that her Ladyship was the latest victim to the plague.

CHAPTER EIGHTEEN

THE plague attacked Hester Stanhope with a violent inflammation of the brain. In the same way as the poison of the gout had affected her grandfather's mental equilibrium, so now the delicate tissues of her mind gave way under the ravages of disease. She was doomed to suffer from mental aberrations and strange obsessions and the first dark shadow of insanity fell across her path. The poison went straight to the two most delicate parts of her constitution—her brain and lungs. When she rose from her sick bed, Dr. Meryon heard for the first time that gasping, tearing cough which was to haunt him during all the years of his life. How much misery and unnecessary humiliation might have been spared her if her illness had proved fatal. But then the world would never have known that glamorous, legendary figure—the white-robed Sibyl of the Lebanon. Her normal life was finished; her natural emotions had run dry. From now on her existence was one of fantastic delusions and imaginary triumphs. When men deserted her she resorted to God; not the solid, rational God whom she had worshipped in her childhood, but a glorified Messiah, bearing the prophet's sword and endowed with all the fearsome splendours of the Apocalypse.

She kept to her bed during the rainy months of November and December. The roof of her house leaked and there were pools of water in her room; her maid fell ill, and she was left to the care of native women; there was a scarcity of provisions, and she lived on a diet of asses' milk, while all the servants, including the doctor, had to be satisfied with the humble fare of goats' flesh. Poor Doctor Meryon—there was no longer any question of his going back to England, for how could he desert her Ladyship in her present condition? He himself was in a sad state of health, for he had got up in the middle of a fever to nurse his patient, and since then disaster had followed upon disaster. Dragomans and maids had fallen ill one after the other, and no physician in a crowded London hospital could have been more overworked than he. Finally, in the middle of January, 1814, Lady Hester summoned up enough strength to move to her new house.

The convent of Mars Elias cannot have been a very attractive spot, for when Meryon viewed it for the first time his thoughts turned involuntarily towards England. A dilapidated convent on the slope of a limestone mountain, with no garden except a small cloister, must have been very far removed from his loving memories of comfortable Georgian country houses with neat stucco doorways and green paddocks. There was one particularly unprepossessing feature about the interior of Mars Elias—the most venerated of all the local patriarchs had been embalmed within its walls, sitting upright in an armchair. The embalmer cannot have been very proficient in his profession, for an ominous stain and strange odour clung to the hallowed spot; but this was one of the paltry details which had no effect on Hester Stanhope.

She remained at Sidon while the necessary repairs were being made to what she only intended to be a temporary home. It was about this time that she wrote to Mr. Coutts, "I must remain here till the spring. How to get away? Neither my strength nor my purse will allow me to go a thousand miles on horseback to Constantinople in the rainy season; there are no vessels but bad Greek traders, mostly infected by the plague. However, I hope to get to Smyrna or the islands in the spring."

The spring came and found her settled in her new home. She lived in the most rigid seclusion, for the plague had now spread to the neighbouring village of Abra and corpses were piled high in the mountain caves. She was nervous and querulous and obsessed by the fear that she might once more fall a victim to the disease. Even the doctor was banished from her presence when he became contaminated through nursing the unfortunate peasants.

Never had the Turkish Empire been so decimated by the plague as during the year of 1814. While European potentates, ambassadors and ministers galloped post-haste to Vienna to reclaim the spoils of their fallen enemy, the Turks fought against a foe more deadly than all the armies of Napoleon. While Castlereagh revived Pitt's glorious memory at the conference table of Schönbrunn, Pitt's niece lamented the humiliation of Bonaparte and inveighed against the "England who put weeping humanity in irons, who had employed the valour of her troops destined for the defence of her national honour, as the instrument to enslave a free-born people." Across the centuries came the faint echo of Chatham's voice, the words of the Great Commoner challenging Britain's right to tax her colonies.

The only Englishman whom Lady Hester condescended to receive was Captain Forster, of His Majesty's sloop *Kite*, who brought her messages from Robert Liston, the new Ambassador to the Porte. The purport of these messages were kept strictly secret from the doctor, who little knew that her Ladyship had asked the Ambassador for the loan of a warship, in order to carry out one of her fantastic daydreams which assumed such extravagant proportions in her brain. While she had been living at Latakia she had discovered an old manuscript belonging to some Italian monks. This manuscript described the exact site of a store of secret treasures hidden among the ruins of Ascalon. Many have accused Lady Hester of being mad in believing such an Arabian Night fairy tale, but in the East, where property was insecure and where a rapacious pasha was capable of seizing the worldly goods of some poor wretch who had only been guilty of a slight offence, it was not unusual for prudent men to lay by a secret hoard of wealth. But there was an element of madness in the proposition that she should hand over the whole of the treasure to the Sultan, while the search was to be entirely financed by the British Embassy at Constantinople. All she asked for herself was the glory of conducting the expedition; all she asked for her country was the added prestige it would gain in the eyes of the Turks through this unselfish and generous attitude.

When she asked Robert Liston to send a ship to survey

the coast, with a view to the practicability of landing at Ascalon, she never told him that she expected the bills to be sent in to his Government. She regarded herself as Ambassadress in Syria, and she asked no one's advice. Sir Arthur Paget had charged Pitt for his servants' new liveries during his mission to Vienna, so why shouldn't she expect Lord Liverpool to pay for an expedition which would cement the friendship between Great Britain and the Sublime Porte?

Captain Forster informed her Ladyship that it was impossible to land at Ascalon; and after he had sailed away from Sidon the matter was temporarily dropped. Lady Hester now set herself out to court and flatter her two neighbours—Soliman Pasha of Acre and Bechir, Prince of the Druses. Soliman, seconded by his secretary, Malem Haym, remained a loyal friend up to the day of his death in 1818, but the wily, cunning Emir was beginning to be suspicious of the Englishwoman who had chosen to settle on the very borders of his territory. The peasants treated her as a queen and her *firmans* entitled her to give protection to any of his rebellious subjects. He had enough difficulties to contend with in ruling over people of different races and religions, without having a meddlesome stranger interfering in his affairs; yet as long as Soliman Pasha chose to honour her with his friendship he could do little else but follow his example. He invited her on his hunting expeditions and presented her with some of the finest horses from his famous stables. A slight coolness came between them when, in the summer of 1814, she applied to him for the use of a cottage situated at Meshmushy, on the higher slopes of the Lebanon. The Emir's consent was somewhat half-hearted, for he did not relish the idea of a turbulent Englishwoman spending several months in one of his Druse villages. His reluctance was so obvious that it roused Lady Hester's indignation, and she wrote to him saying that, even if she did not have the loan of a cottage, she would pitch her tents on the mountain top. He had no alternative but to give way.

Before Hester left for Meshmushy she received the sad tidings of Lady Lucy Taylor's death, and though she had cut herself off from her family and was on bad terms with most of her relations, the sudden death of her younger sister made a profound impression on her. She was in a nervous, unbalanced condition, when any excitement or emotion was sufficient to unhinge her mental equilibrium. The first sign of her abnormality manifested itself by the sudden dislike she took to her devoted maid. Nothing Anne Fry could do was right. Her Ladyship's bath had to be prepared half a dozen times in one morning, because one minute she insisted it was too hot and the next minute she insisted it was too cold. She screamed and shouted at her, and when the poor woman attempted a mild remonstration, she declared that she had been insulted, and told the doctor "that he had no more spirit than a louse, else he would have knocked that damned woman flat a thousand times rather than stand by while she was being insulted." Finally she refused to allow Anne Fry to accompany her to Meshmushy, and the whole burden of the domestic arrangements fell on the doctor's shoulders, for Beaudin, the French dragoman, found it impossible to argue with her Ladyship when she was in a rage.

The journey was made by slow stages, so as not to exhaust her, and every evening as soon as the tents were pitched she worked herself up into a tantrum over some trifling detail. There were moments when even Meryon's patience became exhausted and when he could have wept from the humiliation of seeing the woman whom he had admired and venerated making an exhibition of herself in front of the neighbouring villagers. He had always regarded her as his ideal of a great lady, and now he saw her helpless with fury, screaming out that she wanted to bastinado Pierre; giving way to uncontrolled sobbing just because Beaudin had made some slight mistake in the managing of the caravan. It was useless for Meryon to try to pacify her, for it only made her fly out at him, calling him 'a brute' and 'bear' for trying to provoke her. And in the end he decided to return to Abra and to remain there until she settled down into a more reasonable state of mind. The bracing mountain air and peaceful life soon calmed Lady Hester's nerves, and the long-suffering doctor returned to his post and ministered to her with selfless devotion.

He wrote in his diary that "during her fits of temporary madness, all that bore the name of England or was English increased her rage. The bare remembrance of what she had been and how she was now left seemed to light a fire in her brain." Hester had deliberately destroyed every link with her old home. Letters from faithful friends remained unanswered, and her lawyer, Mr. Murray, received nothing but the bitterest vituperation as thanks for his painstaking efforts in dealing with her debts. Even generous Mr. Coutts was at one moment forced to refuse her credit, thereby provoking her to unjust and cruel words. The doctor stated in his memoirs that her first debts were incurred in 1815, but already in the previous year she had borrowed fifteen hundred pounds from Michael Bruce and two thousand pounds from Lord Lonsdale, the son of the wealthy peer who had secured Pitt his first parliamentary seat. For a few months she practised rigid economy, declaring everywhere that if she had to depend on her friends in England they would be content to let her starve, while she was obsessed by the idea that she was neglected and unfairly treated by her family.

The wound inflicted by Bruce's involuntary desertion had not yet healed, and it was hard for a woman of her temperament to settle down to a single life. There can be no doubt that this unnatural physical privation was largely responsible for the strange fantasies which developed in her brain. The chief trouble was that she refused to consider herself as an ordinary woman with the normal cravings and desires. Even to herself she had to keep up an elaborate pretence, posing as the detached philosopher, who had renounced the world. But occasionally this artificial attitude broke down, and she would give herself away pathetically to one of her old friends.

She had every right to complain. Old Crawford Bruce, who

had recovered from his illness, had not appreciated her honourable behaviour. She had confessed her relationship with Michael in order to appease "the feelings of an old man wrapt up in his son," and she had expected him to have, not only more confidence in her, but more consideration. There is something very sad about the letter to General Oakes, in which she writes, "Now it is all over it is not worth talking about, and those who know me well know that I am better able to make great sacrifices than little ones." During the summer she received a message from Michael Bruce suggesting a meeting on the Continent, and for a few days she contemplated a happy reunion; but there was not very much warmth or genuine affection in his words, and she ended by refusing an offer made more out of honour and loyalty than out of love.

By the autumn she had recovered her health and spirits, and her old restlessness returned. One morning she informed her dragoman that he was to make the necessary arrangements for an expedition to Baalbek, and though in Syria everyone of consequence travelled on horseback, she insisted on undertaking the whole journey by mule. Mars Elias was well stocked with thoroughbreds, but she wanted to proclaim her poverty throughout the length and breadth of the country so that the English agents and Consuls would marvel at the way in which the wealthiest members of the British aristocracy allowed their cousin to live. This cult of poverty was mere ostentation on her part. The mules had to be hired, while her own horses remained idle, and provisions had to be supplied for the ten men and five female servants, without whom her Ladyship refused to stir. She herself supervised every detail of the expedition. She was present when every trunk was corded, when every mule was laden. Like her father, she had a passion for exercising her talents in every field, and though she had never been allowed to step inside the kitchen at Chevening, she knew enough about cooking to instruct her French and Arab cooks in the mixing of English puddings and pastries. She had inherited her father's flair for designing clothes and cutting out paper patterns, and she had already given proof of this talent in the old days at Walmer, when she had provided the Berkshire militia with a new and dashing uniform. She had an elementary knowledge of medicine and a good deal of practical information on the subject of crops and farming. If she had been born in a humbler station of life she would have been an admirable wife for a colonist, but her pride of rank prevented her finding satisfaction and happiness in useful occupations. A retinue of inefficient servants trembled at her slightest nod, and there were days when she was so fastidious that no one except her drago-man or doctor was permitted to prepare her lemonade; days when she recoiled from the clumsy touch of inexperienced negro slaves, and cried because Anne Fry failed to adjust her turban to her liking.

Magnificently proud and pathetically lonely she set out on her expedition to Baalbek. The road descended through narrow mountain gulleys and ravines to the great russet coloured plain of Bkaa. The first snows had already fallen on the giant crests of Mount Hermon and Sannin and cold winds swept across the valley. Even the grandeur of Baalbek, with its proud Corin-thian columns rising out of the green oasis which stretched up the slopes of the Anti-Lebanon, could not compensate Hester for the cold and discomfort of living in tents. She was not yet the fatalist which she became in later years, and in order to avoid contagion from the plague none of her servants were allowed to enter any native house or to touch any other food except their poor, scanty provisions which had been brought from Meshmushy. The doctor had a characteristic tale to recount of her Ladyship's tiresome exactions when she forced all her servants to swallow some particularly dry and un-appetising meat dumplings which had been cooked at her express order.

It was not a satisfactory journey, and Meryon was glad when they re-crossed the mountains and saw the famous cedars of Solomon disappear behind the horizon. Almost with regret he thought back upon the times when the cool, arrogant young voice and boyish laugh of Michael Bruce enlivened the caravan. Hester was too immersed in her daydreams to pay much attention to his conversation. She had a dark, clouded look in her blue eyes and the little doctor felt slightly uncomfortable, slightly uneasy, for there was something strained and queer about that look. Hester's thoughts were among the stones of Ascalon; already the golden bullion lay before her waiting to be shipped to Constantinople—an Englishwoman's gift to the Grand Signior. The country which neglected her, the ministers who ignored her, how they would all humble themselves when she alone held the power of obtaining concessions from the Sublime Porte! Riding along the road to Tripoli she allowed the wings of her imagination to take flight, till she was brought back to reality by her dragoman asking her whether she would spend the night at the guest house of Mars Antonious.

This convent belonged to a strict Maronite order and no living creature of the female species was allowed to cross its holy threshold. Even the hens were kept cooped up and not allowed to stray among the cocks in the yard. But the monks still upheld the laws of hospitality, and a house had been specially built where female guests could be accommodated. For over three years the Sultan's *firmans* had enabled Hester Stanhope to sleep in any house which took her fancy, while governors and sheiks had been forced to supply her with horses and guides and to comply with her exacting and imperious demands. The spoilt, capricious woman of fashion still lurked beneath an authoritative and masculine exterior, and Hester had the bad taste to insist on the Father Superior receiving her in the monastery. Instead of helping to support the Christian dogmas and superstitions she deliberately flouted the Catholic religion by relying on the Sultan's *firmans* to force her way into the sacred precincts. The monks had no alternative but to receive her with as good a grace as possible and she had the vulgarity to ride into their courtyard on a she-ass, to examine every one of their private cells and to preside at a banquet in the refectory

to which she had invited two of the local sheiks. Dumbfounded and terror-stricken, the monks waited for her to be
stricken by the vengeance of their Saint, but she remained
smiling and impervious and the fame of her exploits spread
across the mountains till it reached the ears of the Emir
Bechir, who frowned at the Englishwoman's insufferable
impertinence.

CHAPTER NINETEEN

THERE were ominous whispers in the bazaars and coffee-houses of Beyrout. A *Capidgi Bachi* (or *Zaym*) had landed from Stamboul, and everyone knew that the arrival of a confidential officer of the Sublime Porte boded no good, for an important mission from the Grand Signior usually entailed either the confiscation of property, an execution or an arrest. Monsieur Beaudin on his way back from Tripoli to Sidon, where he had been ordered to make the arrangements for Lady Hester's homecoming, heard the news at the French *khan*, and a little later in the evening he was joined by Giovanni, the doctor's servant, who was almost in tears because his mule had been pressed into the service of the *Capidgi Bachi's* Tartar. These Tartars had the power to commandeer, in the name of the Sultan, any mule, horse or camel they found on the road. Giovanni had still more unpleasant information to impart, for the *Zaym* was bound for Sidon and his business concerned Lady Hester Stanhope. It would be a bad day for the country if he had come to arrest the *Sytt*, for from Tripoli to Acre the people fattened on her *baksheesh*, and it was only foul-mouthed gossip which accused her of being a spy in her country's interests.

Instead of pursuing his journey, Beaudin galloped back to the mountain village where her Ladyship had stopped to pay a visit to a learned Druse Princess. Covered in perspiration and trembling with fear, he broke her the dreadful news, but she told him calmly that she was expecting the *Capidgi Bachi's* visit, and she had barely returned to Mars Elias before a messenger came from Sidon requesting her presence at the governor's palace. Great men like the *Capidgi Bachi* did not demean themselves by entering the domain of a Christian woman, but Lady Hester refused to submit to Moslem prejudice. As self-appointed Ambassadress in Syria, she had every right to expect even the Reis Effendi or the Grand Vizier to wait upon her at her own house, so she answered the governor's message with a polite invitation to the *Zaym*, begging him to honour her by being her guest at Mars Elias.

A little before midnight there was a great trampling and noise in the courtyard and a hammering at the gates, requesting admittance in the Sultan's name, while the lonely mountain-side re-echoed with the shouting of grooms and servants.

Neither Beaudin nor the doctor were reassured by Lady Hester's imperturbable manner, and they both slipped pistols into their girdles, so as to defend her with their lives in the case of her being taken prisoner. The money-greedy Syrian Christian, who over a year ago had put a manuscript into Lady Hester's hands in order to earn a handsome tip, had little guessed the consequence of his action. During long, delirious nights, when she lay raving with high fever, during peaceful summer days at Meshmushy, and autumn evenings at Baalbek and Tripoli, she had dreamt of the store of treasures hidden beneath the stones of Ascalon. It was now several months since she had written to Constantinople petitioning for the Sultan's authority to dig among the ruins, exciting Mahmoud's cupidity by the prospect of three million dollars to swell his private coffers. Robert Liston, a suave, amicable diplomat, was the intermediary between her and the Grand Signior. Ever since his appointment as Ambassador to the Porte he had treated her with great indulgence, chiefly on account of her having been recommended to him by his old friend, Mr. Coutts. If she chose to waste her patrimony on carrying out these fantastic operations it was not incumbent upon him to interfere, and never for one moment did it strike him that she could expect his Government to pay for her expenses.

His Majesty the Sultan, who had everything to gain and nothing to lose by pandering to her schemes and who on many occasions had employed agents of his own to rifle secret treasure hoards, made haste to despatch one of the most trusted officers of his household to make inquiries on the Syrian coast and to invest Lady Hester Stanhope with *firmans* granting her power over the pashas of Acre and Damascus and all the governors of Syria. These *firmans* entitled her to royal honours, giving her the right to enforce unpaid labour and to live at the expense of the pashalik of Acre. At the same time the *Capidgi Bachi* was warned that he was to keep a close watch on her Ladyship's movements, so as to prevent her from appropriating half the treasures for herself—for no oriental could believe in motives which were entirely disinterested.

With subtle flattery and soft spoken words the *Zaym* tried to discover what was her Ladyship's true reason for offering to the Porte treasures which others would have kept for themselves.

This was the period when many English travellers came to the East for the sole purpose of collecting precious relics from the ruins of the ancient world. If the *Sytt* had not come to look for treasures, why was she here? She was not banished from her country, she had no mercantile affairs, and if it was really true that she lived here for the sake of her health, surely there were more attractive spots in the Turkish Empire than the barren slopes of Lebanon. Soon the *Zaym* found that he had to deal with a high-minded fanatic, who for some mysterious reason of her own had sworn implicit allegiance to the Sultan. When he had made all the necessary inquiries he proposed setting out for Acre, but Hester had just returned from a long and fatiguing journey and she refused to leave before she had replenished her wardrobe and equipped herself with every household necessity. The unfortunate doctor was only allowed to spend one night at Abra, before he was despatched to Damascus with a long list of commissions, and his departure was followed by that of the *Capidgi Bachi*, who left Mars Elias on the 1st February, 1815, in order to make all the necessary arrangements for her Ladyship's reception at Acre. As soon as the doctor returned Hester gave orders for the caravan to start. She was extraordinarily sanguine about the success of the expedition, and not even Meryon dared to damp her high spirits. No wonder she was joyous and elated with pride when

Soliman Pasha greeted her with the Royal honours which she had sought after all her life.

Her spectacular figure had already taken hold of the Syrian imagination; already the smallest children rolling in the mud knew the name of the English princess, but now that she was conducted by a *Capidgi Bachi* with governors following in her train, fear, which to a Syrian means far more than love or respect, filled every heart. The Pasha of Acre, whose ill-health prevented him from accompanying her on the expedition, provided her with a regal retinue. There were twenty tents in addition to the six with which she had departed from Sidon, and among them was the famous green silk gold-starred marquee, which in the following year sheltered the injudicious *amours* of the unfortunate Princess Caroline and her Italian courier during their tour of the Holy Land. When the peculiar shape of this tent aroused discussion in the House of Lords, and Granville, Grey and Castlereagh criticized Bouverie's defence of his princess, they little knew that this same marquee had once harboured Hester Stanhope, the most dazzling and most brilliant of their youthful companions.

It must have gratified Lady Hester's vanity that a tent which had been built especially for her should be offered second-hand to a royal princess.

Water-carriers, tent-pitchers and torch-bearers followed in the procession, which was escorted by a troop of Hawary cavalry and heralded by fleet-footed couriers. A resplendent *tacterwan* with a palanquin of scarlet cloth decorated with gilded balls was provided for her Ladyship, but she showed her old aversion to what she considered to be an undignified mode of transport and she insisted on travelling either on mule or horseback. Mr. Cattafago was invited to accompany her, for she needed someone to protect her interests, in case the *Zaym* should accuse her of keeping part of the treasures for herself. It is very hard to fathom why Lady Hester should have taken all this trouble to put money into the hands of the Sultan, whose misdeeds were already common gossip in the bazaars of his most distant pashaliks. Was it in order to consolidate her position in Syria, where, by strengthening her ties with the central government, she could command greater respect from the local governors? Or had she deeper and more far-reaching schemes of Arab domination? Did she see herself as a Queen, an ally of the Sublime Porte, or was she merely out to gratify her cravings for adventure and romance?

Difficulties beset the expedition from the very beginning. To start out on a treasure hunt during the rainy season was not a happy idea and, from Acre down to Haifa, black storms swept the Mediterranean. Meryon, who had been detained at Acre owing to the illness of the Pasha of Tripoli (one often wonders how he still had the nerve and stamina to doctor all the poor unfortunates who sought his aid), rejoined her Ladyship at Haifa, and found her huddled beneath the *débris* of her starred marquee, which had been blown down by the gale. It was an evening of momentous happenings, for, at the very moment when the storm was at its height, the doctor stumbled into the dinner tent where he was greeted by a strange, ragged individual with grizzly, uncombed hair and wild, burning eyes. This uncomfortable apparition saluted him in French and proceeded to declaim fearsome prophecies on the fate of Bonaparte. Then he vanished, and the flabbergasted doctor returned to Lady Hester, who was now safely installed in a smaller and securer tent. When he questioned her about the curious madman who was wandering round the encampment, she answered that he was a wonderful old man, named Loustenau, who, during the last two years, had been living on charity in a cowshed near Haifa, that once he had been a general, commanding the Mahrattan armies, but that now he had turned to religious contemplation, drawing direct inspiration from the Bible. And she added in all seriousness that, when she saw him for the first time, he greeted her, saying, "Madam, at this very moment in which I speak to you, Napoleon has escaped from Elba." The doctor laughed a somewhat uneasy laugh, for he could not help wondering who was the more mad, her

Ladyship or the prophet. But many weeks later, when the news of Napoleon's flight from Elba reached the Syrian coast, he realized that the general's prophecies had tallied with the exact date of the Emperor's escape.

There was no chance of any rest or respite during that stormy night. Both the *Zaym* and Mr. Cattafago had been sensible enough to procure quarters in the town, and Meryon envied them bitterly as, buffeted by the wind, he fought his way from tent to tent. A little before midnight another fantastic stranger appeared in the encampment, a swash-buckling, mustachioed Dalmatian, swaggering about in the uniform of an English naval officer. This man introduced himself as Tomaso Coschich, one time dragoman to the Princess of Wales, during her journey of 1813, now in the service of Admiral Sir Sidney Smith, who had appointed him the bearer of especial messages to his cousin, Lady Hester Stanhope. The wretched doctor had to rouse the cooks and provide him with supper, which was no easy matter in a howling gale; and while Coschich satisfied his hunger, he informed his host that he had come to conduct Lady Hester in safety back to England, and in order not to be delayed at Acre owing to the closing of the gates at sundown, he had exaggerated the importance of his mission and had told the Pasha's secretary that he bore despatches proclaiming the declaration of war between Turkey and Russia. This ruse had been highly successful and had enabled him to secure the escort of a treasury messenger all the way to Haifa.

Meryon was disgusted at such a vulgarian daring to suggest that he was a fit escort for her Ladyship. He was not only disgusted at his vulgarity, but he was shocked at the indelicacy of Sir Sidney Smith for sending such a low type of foreigner on a confidential mission, and he lost no time in presenting Lady Hester with her cousin's letters, advising her to dismiss the troublesome messenger as soon as possible. Hester, who was unable to sleep owing to the fury of the storm, was delighted to have some occupation for her restless mind, but

she was justly irritated when she found that the Admiral
expected her to be the intermediary in soliciting money from
his Syrian friends.

Sir Sidney Smith was one of the many heroes who refused
to settle down to a quiet old age. All his life he had been a
reckless spender, and his principal object in attending the
Congress of Vienna had been to escape from his creditors.
He was inordinately vain, and as a retired Admiral he found
that he did not play a very important part in that brilliant
galaxy of European celebrities. It was vanity which first
prompted him to play the compassionate humanitarian in
planning a crusade against the Algerian Corsairs, who held
the monopoly of the slave trade and ruined the commerce of
the Southern Mediterranean. In the corridors and alcoves
of Schönbrunn, Sir Sidney could be seen buttonholing Metter-
nich or Talleyrand, soliciting audiences from crowned heads,
who signed their names to his petitions but dismissed him
with a smile when he asked them for financial aid. Perforce he
had to turn to his Syrian friends, to the Emir Bechir, whom
he had once sheltered on his ship, and who in an unguarded
moment had promised to furnish him with fifteen hundred
men at the first call to arms.

Sir Sidney made a sad mistake in seeking his cousin's intervention and in asking her to distribute the presents which he
intended as bribes. In the old days he had been famous for the
liberality of his *baksheesh*, but now he displayed crass stupidity,
as well as meanness in the choice of his gifts. Abu Ghosh, the
Chieftain of Judea, was sent a pair of Persian pistols, when the
one thing an Arab really prized was English firearms. The Emir
Bechir was presented with a satin cloak, and for a Syrian to
wear a satin cloak was the same as if an Englishman were to
appear in chintz breeches. And the most incongruous of all the
gifts was a Bible destined for the public library of Jerusalem,
when no such institution existed.

Lady Hester had always had a flair for discovering people's real
motives. She took little notice of her cousin's tender inquiries

179

about her health, for it had taken him a year to answer the letter which she had written from Latakia, asking him to send a ship to take her away from Syria. Now that she had no immediate intention of leaving the country, he wrote grandiloquently, saying that his nephew, Thurloe Smith, was only waiting for a suitable opportunity to come and fetch her in his frigate. In order to gratify his ridiculous vanity, Sir Sidney had no scruples about embroiling her in difficulties with the Porte and in endangering the life of the Emir Bechir, whose head would not be safe on his shoulders if he was known to lend out troops without direct permission from the Sultan. The very idea of transporting a regiment of Syrian mountaineers to the coast of Barbary was absurd, "for those hardy peasants only knew how to fight on their own dunghill." Hester's sense of humour, which had been strangely absent of late years, returned in full force when she unpacked the cheap cotton flags which were to serve as standards for Sir Sidney's Syrian regiment, and she immediately dubbed him 'the king of pocket-handkerchiefs.'

The next morning her Ladyship commanded a halt of three days at Haifa, so as to give her time to compose her answer to her cousin's dispatches. The *Zaym*, who had already been informed by his spies that a mysterious stranger had appeared at midnight, immediately suspected an intrigue, and, to avoid complications, Hester ended by showing him the Admiral's letters. This was one of the many occasions on which she identified herself with the Turks at the expense of her countrymen. Sir Sidney was not only her cousin, but an English Admiral, and it is hard to forgive the indiscretion which she showed over his private affairs.

Altogether she took a very high-handed attitude. The Emir Bechir not only never received his letters, but Mr. Barker was asked to hold up every letter coming from Sir Sidney Smith. She herself wrote to the Emir, saying that she wanted to see him on some private matter as soon as she returned from Ascalon. On this occasion Bechir had every reason to be grateful for her interference, for woe betide if the Porte ever suspected him of making a secret alliance with a European power. In the tactful and diplomatic letter which Lady Hester wrote to her cousin, she advised him to make a direct application to the Sultan and not to endanger his subjects by asking them to act contrary to his orders. She added: "Not to admire your intentions in the cause of humanity, and the feelings which dictate your conduct, would be impossible, but I could wish you to reflect a little, and if the thing is to be undertaken to do it in the most open, fair, honourable way possible. I am much too proud to care for popularity, you much too vain not to like it."

Careful copies, both of her letters and those of Sir Sidney Smith, were sent to the British Ambassador, and as soon as she had sealed her dispatches, Mr. Coschich was graciously requested to take the next boat for Cyprus. The Admiral's presents for the Syrian potentates were packed away in her trunks, for there was time enough to send them to their destinations when she returned to Mars Elias. Then Sir Sidney's affairs were forgotten and she proceeded on her journey.

After a week's stay in Jaffa, Ascalon was reached on the 1st April, and the doctor could not help thinking it was a suitable date on which to embark on a fantastic treasure hunt.

The deserted ruins of Herod's birthplace, where snakes and lizards crawled among the stones, now assumed the appearance of a fashionable race-course. Gaily coloured tents and marquees sprang up in the shadow of the crumbling walls, on the site of Astarte's Temple, while the dirty little village on the outskirts of the ruins was able to boast of two clean cottages, which had been swept and garnished for the reception of the *Sytt*. Lady Hester, who only a few months previously had been indecorous enough to violate the sacred precincts of a Maronite monastery, now adhered to the strictest tenets of the Moslem faith. No wine was served at her table while she was travelling with Turks, and Mrs. Fry was forbidden to appear out of doors without a veil. It would have offended the susceptibilities both of the *Capidgi Bachi* and of Mahomed Aga, the Governor of Jaffa, who had been commanded to superintend the excavations, if she had planted her tent in their midst, and on this occasion she had the tact not to assert herself. Every day a hundred and fifty peasants were pressed into service to gratify a Sultan's greed and an Englishwoman's whims. And as they toiled in the broiling sun, digging for the fabled gold, either the doctor or one of the Consuls acted as overseer.

From the very first Meryon doubted the success of the enter-prize. There were traces of recent excavations, which looked as if the Governor had already been conducting a private search and Djezzar Pasha had ransacked every ruin from Ascalon to Sidon, to find the columns of porphyry and granite with which to rebuild the famous Mosque of Acre. The *Zaym* was too phlegmatic to care whether the expedition ended in success or failure; he was chiefly interested in his meals, and the cooks had a hard task to satisfy his fastidious palate. Three meals a day were served in the open dinner tent, and these meals were considered ample reward for the unpaid workmen. Every afternoon, at two o'clock, Lady Hester mounted on her ass and made a tour of the ruins. Her presence helped to reanimate the peasants, who already regarded her as a semi-deity, and sometimes she ordered music to raise their spirits.

On the fourth day of the operations there was great excite-ment throughout the encampment. The treasure had been located, but the disappointment was intense when it was found to be nothing more than a superb statue of the late Roman period, representing an armed warrior. Mahomed Aga, whom Lady Hester had offended during her previous visit to Jaffa, lost no time in saying that her Ladyship, like all her country-men, had merely brought them here in order to search for antiquities. Charles Meryon was the only one who rejoiced at the discovery of this master-work, and with his timid, conciliatory air, he informed his patient that "her labours, if productive of no golden treasures, had brought to light one more valuable in the eyes of the lovers of the fine arts, and that future travellers would come to visit the ruins of Ascalon, rendered memorable by the enterprise of a woman who, though digging for gold, yet rescued the remains of antiquity from oblivion."

Poor Meryon never had any success in his attempts to pour balm on troubled waters, and when after fourteen days of fruitless digging Lady Hester decided to stop the excavations, she insisted on having the statue destroyed and thrown into the sea, in order to prove to the Porte that she was entirely disinterested. She was miserably disappointed, and though probably she committed the vandalism in a fit of childish rage, there is also the supposition that she may have imagined the gold to be concealed in the torso. Even now she believed in the existence of the treasure, and was only bitter that Djezzar Pasha should have preceded her in his search. It only remained for her to pack up her trunks and to dismiss the troop of astrologers and magicians, with their magic stones and crystals, who had gathered together from the farthest corners of Syria to augur her success. It only remained for her to scatter *baksheesh* among the workmen, to appease the *Capidgi Bachi* with the gift of a handsome negress, and to distribute lavish presents among her suite of governors and Consuls. It had been an expensive holiday and she still fondly imagined that the British Government was going to foot the bill.

Many years later, when a young French traveller named Poujoulat visited the ruins of Ascalon, where the sands encroached on the crumbling ramparts, the Arab guide showed him the traces of the English lady's excavations. And the *débris* of the statue, which Hester Stanhope had ordered to be thrown into the sea, still littered the pavement of Astarte's Temple.

CHAPTER TWENTY

HESTER STANHOPE returned to Abra a discouraged and frustrated woman and for a few weeks she seriously contemplated leaving Mars Elias and settling down in Crete or another of the Greek islands. But when she received Robert Liston's letter from Constantinople, which gave her to understand that the British Government had no intention of defraying the expenses she had incurred at Ascalon, she found that not only was it impossible for her to indulge in any new journeys, but that she would even be forced to take a loan from Mr. Barker.

It was useless for her to try to economize. In her largehearted generosity she made her house into a refuge for the friendless and the homeless. General Loustenau, whom she had taken under her protection at Haifa, was now a permanent inmate of Mars Elias, for his sad story appealed to her incorrigible romanticism. A Béarnais adventurer, he had left his home as a young man to seek adventure in the East, and he had found himself in Poonah at the time of the Mahrattan wars, when any European soldier of fortune could gain honour and riches as a general in Scindiah's armies. Loustenau's strategic talents were speedily recognized by the French agents, who, in the interests of their country, persuaded the Rajah to give him the command of a regiment. His victories over the English were so spectacular that in a few years the Béarnais peasant had become one of the wealthiest and most venerated men in the country. A hand which he lost in the wars was replaced by a silver stump. Pigeon-blood rubies and enormous diamonds were showered on him by a grateful Rajah, while he earned the titles of 'Lion of the State' and 'Tiger of War.' But in spite of all his glory he was homesick, and in spite of being offered the pick of the Rajah's concubines, he married a French girl, who bore him several children, and as soon as they were old enough to travel he returned to France, after an absence of eighteen years. In his native land his luck deserted him, the revolution swallowed his store of gold, he launched out in unfortunate speculations and, after a few disastrous years, he decided to leave his family and to sail back to India. He had only got as far as Acre, when he fell seriously ill; the disease affected his brain, and from now onwards he became a religious mystic, a raving prophet with mad eyes, foretelling the doom of Europe. He gave away what little money he had left and lived on charity and he had been wandering about Syria for two years when Hester Stanhope found him among the orchards of Haifa.

She was fascinated by the mad soothsayer who evoked the awful visions of the Apocalypse, who told her of the Messiah destined to ride into Jerusalem on a horse which was born saddled, and who prognosticated the downfall of the monarchies of Europe, when men would turn once more to the civilizations of the East. The doctrines of the Old Testament, so simply expounded by old Lady Stanhope, now received a new and strange significance, and the prophet had certain moments of lucidity when his cunning peasant mind prompted him to make vague references to a white woman who would reign as the Messiah's bride and ride at his side into the new Jerusalem. These prophecies never failed to be rewarded by handsome presents.

Loustenau was not the only friendless exile who found refuge at Mars Elias. Two Abyssinians who had been shipwrecked off the coast were discovered by the doctor in a Maronite monastery, and when Lady Hester heard of their misfortunes she immediately offered them a home till they could find the means of returning to their native country. Her compassion for these wretched castaways involved her in a long correspondence with Lord Valentia, the eccentric Irish peer, who had made a life study of Abyssinia, which was at that time an almost unknown country.

In spite of these passing interests the days seemed very long and blank to a woman who had always been used to adventure and excitement. She was too ill to rouse herself from her physical lassitude, and she was unable to walk up the stairs

without the help of two men, while she never went out riding
without a groom walking at her side in order to support her
back. She was lonely and homesick during the spring of 1815,
and she was too proud to remonstrate with the doctor, when he
tentatively suggested his returning to England. Why should
she remonstrate? Meryon's desertion meant nothing to her,
for in spite of all their years of intimacy she had never considered him as a friend.

Georgiaki Dallegio was dispatched to London with boxes
full of presents and a long list of commissions, of which the
most important was to bring back a new doctor. The young
Greek interpreter was armed with introductions to the greatest
families of England, and in order to ensure him a kind reception, Lady Hester equipped him with Druse, Bedouin and
Turkish male and female costumes, which were bound to
arouse curiosity among her fashionable friends. She relied
on Georgiaki to recount them picturesque tales of her mode of
life and to contradict the strange stories circulated by English
travellers. In 1815 a paragraph, copied out of a French journal,
appeared in an English newspaper, describing her as leading a
retired life in the Lebanon hills, surrounded by a swarm of
adopted children. And immediately there were a hundred
voices ready to vouch for the existence of her Ladyship's
illegitimate offspring. Though Hester held her head high and
professed to be impervious to criticism and slander, she was
far too nervous and sensitive not to resent the foul gossip which
circulated round her name.

Georgiaki was to remain several months in London, so as
to acquaint himself with the customs of the country, and
Doctor Meryon was expected to wait patiently for his return.
In order to distract his thoughts from England, Hester sent him
off on a short trip to Alexandria, where he had been summoned
to attend on the Consul-General, Colonel Misset, and she
invited an Italian doctor from Tripoli to come and stay with
her during his absence.

Summer dragged slowly on. Living on the solitary heights

of Meshmushy, Hester had very little to do except to cultivate the somewhat dour friendship of the Sheik Bechir and to resume amicable relations with the Emir. Her health improved, and once more the Syrian peasants became familiar with the tall equestrian figure in a mameluke costume, who accompanied the Emir on his hunting expeditions and galloped across the rocks with the boldness of an Arab. But as her body regained strength her mind became restless. She was now absorbed in a wild chimerical scheme of forming an association of literary men and artists, whom she proposed inviting from Europe for the purpose of making discoveries in every branch of knowledge and of journeying over different parts of the Ottoman Empire. Perhaps she dreamt of emulating Zenobia, who had surrounded herself with the greatest scholars of the ancient world, only she forgot that, instead of the resources of an Empire, she had but a small and inadequate pension. It is strange that she should have had this sudden yearning for culture, for even now she was no great reader, declaring that "books filed away the mind." It was from vanity that Sir Sidney Smith took up arms against the Algerian Corsairs, and it was from vanity that Hester Stanhope proposed to found an Eastern academy, an academy greater than Napoleon's Egyptian institute. In her megalomania she was convinced that she was destined to play a leading part, when Loustenau's prophecies were fulfilled and men forsook the rotting civilizations of the West and migrated again to the East; yet there were always those sordid financial worries to hamper her grandiose plans.

At the end of the summer she paid Bruce back the fifteen hundred pounds he had lent her, but she was in such difficulties that she was forced to accept his generous offer of an additional income to be paid her at regular intervals. How galling it must have been for her pride to take money from her ex-lover, and she had no sooner accepted his offer than she regretted her lack of independence. Owing to some unavoidable delay the drafts were not immediately forthcoming and she wrote bitterly to Mr. Coutts, "It is the first time in my life that I ever allowed persuasion or entreaty to hamper my independence, but the fear of what might be said by the world at seeing me left in a strange and distant country ill-provided for and under ten thousand unpleasant circumstances without the possibility of my extricating myself, the unwillingness I felt to hurt those whose feelings I foolishly compared to what my own would have been at leaving anyone so unprotected, induced me to reluctantly agree to proposals which have not been abided by. This is the truth, the plain truth which I could prove to you any day I pleased from documents in my hands. I am speaking to you now as an old friend, not as a banker, as I am not going to ask you anything, but to keep this business to yourself. I mention this to you to account for my own conduct and not to lower another's, whose terrible, flighty, capricious disposition has occasioned me many an uneasy hour, but yet whose reputation is dear to me."

A few months later she was all tenderness and compassion for her darling Michael, who had got himself involved in a very serious scrape in Paris. Together with Captain Hutchinson and Sir Robert Wilson, he connived the escape of Count Lavalette, who at the restoration of the Bourbons had been condemned to death for high treason. It was an act of knight-errantry, worthy of Lady Hester Stanhope's lover, and it was the one dramatic hour of a useless, lazy life. Lavalette escaped, but his rescuers were thrown into jail, and when the news reached Hester she felt a momentary rekindling of her old love, though it was not so much love as the maternal instinct in her nature, which impelled her to write to Michael Bruce, offering to come herself to Paris, if she could be of any use to him. At the same time she sent a letter to Louis XVIII, whom she had often met in the days when he was a poor *emigré* living on the bounty of her Grenville cousins. She implored the King to forgive "ce jeune étourdi Mons. Bruce . . . ce jeune homme égaré par la sensibilité de son caractère qui s'est entamé dans une affaire aussi sérieuse que délicate." And she made a point of reminding him of his obligations to her family by sending the letter to England to be forwarded by the Marquess of Buckingham, the head of the Grenville family.

After a few months, Bruce was released and the exquisite young dandy became the hero of the Parisian drawing-rooms, where he sunned himself in the smiles of La Princesse Moskowa and La Duchesse de St. Leu. From now onwards he sank into mediocrity, and Lady Charlotte Bury said of him that she knew of no other young man to whom one could so well apply the Scottish proverb of "Great cry and little wool."

Michael Bruce's knight-errantry seemed very colourless in comparison with the bloodthirsty reprisals with which Hester Stanhope avenged the murder of a French officer. Colonel Boutin, one of the bravest soldiers and most talented engineers in Napoleon's armies, had landed in Egypt in 1810, where he had been engaged on a secret mission to make an exact survey of every place in Egypt and Syria. Lady Hester first met him at a dinner-party in Cairo, when she laughingly accused him of being one of Napoleon's spies. But they appreciated one another's qualities, and the fact that their countries were at war did not prevent them from becoming friends. When he passed through Sidon in 1814, they met again at the French Consulate, and for a few days he was her Ladyship's guest at Mars Elias. It was there that he told her that he was about to cross the unexplored Ansáry mountains, inhabited by dangerous religious fanatics, who allowed no Europeans to pry into the secrets of their faith. Hester dissuaded him from attempting this mad adventure, but he refused to listen either to her arguments or the prayers of Monsieur Guys, the French Consul at Tripoli, and he set out on his journey unaccompanied, save for an Egyptian groom.

There was no news of him for many months, then suspicions were aroused, when a watch identified to be his was sold in the bazaars of Damascus.

Hester Stanhope, who had nothing to do at the time except to amuse herself with certain experiments in medicine, proving the efficacy of the serpent or bezoar stones in curing venomous bites, roused herself to immediate action. Volpi, her Italian doctor, a fearless adventurer, who was a refreshing contrast to the phlegmatic Meryon, a hardy Druse muleteer, and the irrepressible Pierre were disguised as humble pedlars and sent off into the Ansáry mountains to investigate into the details of the murder.

Meanwhile, the French Consuls made no attempt to inquire into the disappearance of their countryman. It was useless for them to solicit the aid of the local governors, for none of them were going to embroil themselves with the villainous Ansárys in order to avenge a Christian's death. But Hester Stanhope had appointed herself as Ambassadress in Syria, and she was not only the English Ambassadress but the defender of the friendless and the oppressed. When Volpi returned from Latakia, giving her exact details of Boutin's murder, telling her the name of the village and that of the tribe who had committed the foul deed, she sent a message to the Pasha of Acre, asking him to send an army to avenge the Frenchman's assassination. Soliman, who was a mild and pacific man, had no intention of becoming involved in dangerous guerilla warfare, and because he lacked the courage to refuse her Ladyship point-blank, he informed her that during the winter months it was impossible for his men to fight in those high mountain regions.

The spring of 1816 came, and still Boutin's murder was unavenged. Hester was appalled by the slackness of the Consuls and the weakness of the governors. She arrayed herself in her most gorgeous apparel—the mantle of purple and gold which was only worn on a visit to a great pasha, and, accompanied by an imposing retinue of servants, she set out for Acre. Charming, obliging, Mr. Cattafago once more received her as his guest, but he felt somewhat uncomfortable when she told him that she had come to harangue the pasha. Soliman greeted her with polite embarrassment. He resorted to all the favourite methods of oriental diplomacy, loading her with presents and mollifying her with flattering words. But Hester was obdurate. She was Nemesis incarnate come to ask for Ansáry blood, and when he refused to comply with her wishes she threatened to make trouble with the Porte. The woman who but a year ago had travelled through Acre with a *Capidgi Bachi* in attendance, was not one to be trifled with, and in the end Soliman Pasha was forced to give way to her imperious demands.

The picked garrisons of Acre, commanded by Mustapha Berber, the governor of Tripoli, waited on her orders. More bloodthirsty than any Turk, she commanded them to kill, burn and pillage. Here was their chance to devastate the villages of the hated Ansárys, to probe the secret mysteries of their religion, which worked for the ruin of Islam. Mustapha Berber, a fanatical Moslem, was a suitable leader for such an expedition. Forgetting that he had to avenge a Christian's death, he set forth in the spirit of a religious crusade. The Ansárys were powerless against the combined garrisons of the pashalik, and fifty-two villages were razed to the ground and three hundred men killed before a messenger arrived from Stamboul, ordering all warfare to cease.

Colonel Boutin's death was amply revenged, and Hester Stanhope's pride was satisfied. What matter if three hundred innocent people had died, and as many more left homeless and destitute? She had shown the people of Syria that her word was law, and now she could afford to thank the Pasha of Acre very prettily for all his trouble. Doctor Meryon, who had returned from Egypt, and a few timid Consuls may have shuddered at a justice which was enforced in such a sanguinary way, but the Turks admired the Englishwoman's indomitable spirit and paid homage to her courage, and Burckhardt, who had never been one of her admirers, now wrote to her from Cairo: "It was an army that taught the Egyptians respect for the English character, your spirited and dignified conduct does impress the Syrians with the same notions, and while your Ladyship is thus providing for your own comfort, you are rendering, at the same time, the most effectual service to your country." But her proudest moment was when the French Foreign Office expressed their grateful thanks for her having avenged the death of their brave compatriot.

It must have been some perverse streak in her character which inspired her to go to Antioch in the autumn of 1816— Antioch, at the very foot of those mountains inhabited by the people whose husbands, brothers and sons had been killed and whose homes had been wrecked at her express commands. True, there was Mr. Barker, whom she had to see on an important business matter, but why had she chosen to meet Mr. Barker just there? Any other town in Syria would have served their purpose. The tiresome Princess of Wales, with her retinue of vulgar charlatans, was journeying through the Holy Land, and was at any moment liable to land at Sidon and expect a royal reception at Mars Elias. So it was preferable to escape from such an insufferable ordeal, leaving the doctor to await her Highness's arrival. Still, there was no reason why she should have decided to go to Antioch and to stay there unprotected except for a dragoman and a single servant. Even the townspeople wondered at her daring and even Mr. Barker was slightly apprehensive when he shared her meals, for the Ansárys were versed in the knowledge of subtle poisons.

Hester stressed her audacity still further; she went for solitary rides up into the mountains to those very villages whose scarred trees and blackened walls still bore the marks of Mustapha Berber's marauding armies. And because she was too proud to ride disguised through the territory of her enemies, she proclaimed that she was the *Sytt*, at whose orders their country had been invaded, their wives raped and their husbands murdered; that she had done all this in order to avenge the death of a man, who, though an enemy of her country, was entitled to be protected by the laws of hospitality, and every decent person was bound to condemn those who violated the laws by committing a foul and underhand murder. The Ansárys, who had never had a white woman in their midst, regarded her as a supernatural being. Her courage was born from a fatalism as great as their own. She disarmed them by showing them openly that she had nothing to fear from them, and they let her go in peace. Their power was gone, for the graves of their *Imans* had been desecrated through the will of a pale-faced woman. In the streets of Antioch the people pointed out the tall, striding figure with the wild blue eyes and the sudden charming smile, and they wondered what heavenly body watched over her to preserve her from Ansáry vengeance.

CHAPTER TWENTY-ONE

THE European wars were at an end. Napoleon languished on the rocks of St. Helena and the victorious allies danced and gambled in the precincts of the Tuileries. After an arduous life spent in the restricted quarters of military camps, young Englishmen were not slow in spending the golden guineas which their fathers had accumulated during their absence abroad. Discharged naval officers came pleasure-cruising to the Levant and many a smartly painted yacht sailed into the harbour of Sidon. From her windows at Mars Elias Lady Hester could see the high masts flying the British flag, and Beaudin would be ordered to gallop down into the town to ascertain the name and business of the new arrivals.

The first visitors knocked at the doors of Mars Elias in the spring of 1816. William Bankes, the future member for Cambridge University, arrived with a portfolio of sketches under his arm, a renegade Albanian soldier as his servant, and a gold fitted dressing-case laden with perfumes. He was the kind of conceited, self-opinionated young man with whom her Ladyship had very little patience, but he was made welcome for he brought her messages from her brother and news of her old friends. His luggage, which seemed to be somewhat excessive for one person, was explained by the fact that he had been travelling with a friend of his named James Silk Buckingham, who had decided to take a different route from Jerusalem, and he begged Lady Hester to be allowed to leave Mr. Buckingham's trunks in her custody, as the unfortunate creature was liable to appear at any moment with nothing to wear but the soiled Arab clothes in which he had been travelling for weeks. William Bankes was one of the enterprising young Englishmen who refused to leave the country without visiting Palmyra, and though Lady Hester did not show much enthusiasm over his plan, she offered to furnish him with credentials for the 'King of the desert' and proposed the faithful Pierre as a sure and trusted guide.

Mahanna had no mercy towards the Europeans who ventured into the desert without her protection, and the credentials which she gave her friends were divided into two categories. Those who were great men and whose word she could trust as her own were to be treated as princes. Mock fights were to be staged for their amusement and a camel killed and roasted in their honour. These credentials were marked with two seals; but for the ordinary English gentleman such as Mr. Bankes, all that was asked for was a safe convoy and these letters were only stamped with one seal. Unfortunately, in an unguarded moment, Lady Hester told her guest of this agreement between her and the Bedouin chief, and Mr. Bankes, who was a young man with a very good opinion of himself, took it for granted that his credentials would be marked with two seals. He was not particularly anxious to secure Lady Hester's intervention, preferring to rely on his own resources and his well-filled purse. He had not much faith in the protection of a half-crazed woman who solemnly told him that she was destined to reign as Queen of Jerusalem and to lead God's chosen people.

The prophecy foretold by Brothers and confirmed by Loustenau had already taken a firm hold on her senses, when among her servants she found an old man named Metta, who dabbled in astrology and the occult sciences, and who told her of the existence of a magic book which predicted that "a European woman would come and live on Mount Lebanon at a certain epoch, and build a house there and obtain power and influence greater than a Sultan's; that a boy without a father would join her and his destiny would be fulfilled under her wing; that the coming of the Mahdi would follow, but would be preceded by war, pestilence and other calamities; that the Mahdi would ride a horse born saddled and a woman would come from a far country to partake in the mission." A heavy bag of piastres enabled Lady Hester to see this magic book, but as she was by no means proficient in Arabic she had to rely on her servant's interpretation. By some strange coincidence the words of the Bedlam prophet, echoed by a crazy Frenchman, were found in an Arabic manuscript, and minds less credulous than Hester Stanhope's might have been tempted to believe in the truth of the prophecy.

Mr. Bankes smiled politely when her Ladyship told him of the great part she was to play in the world upheaval, and he humoured her as one humours those whose minds are slightly deranged. But when on departing from Mars Elias he opened the letter she had given him for the Bedouin chief and found that his credentials were only sealed with one seal, then there was no more question of humouring. His wounded vanity vented itself in rage and spite against the woman who had dismissed him as an ordinary traveller, with no claim to especial honours and attentions. He threw away the letter and sent back her servant, little realizing the difficulties it would lead him into. Relying on the protection of the Pasha of Damascus, he attempted the journey to Tadmor without paying tribute to the princes of the desert; and he had only reached the Belaz mountains when he was arrested by Naser and politely conducted back to Hamah. Nothing daunted, he set out once more, but this time he was wise enough to pay the heavy fine which Mahanna imposed on all those who wished to cross the Syrian desert. Even then his troubles were not at an end, for while he was staying at Palmyra he came across another son of Mahanna, who demanded an additional present and imprisoned him on his refusal. Finally he returned in safety to Hamah—a poorer and a wiser man—and one cannot blame him for regarding Lady Hester as the cause of his misfortunes and for spreading the report that she was bent on preventing her countrymen from travelling in safety to Palmyra.

On his return to England, William Bankes was responsible for circulating many libellous and ridiculous stories about the woman who had once given him hospitality. The unkind way in which he besmirched her reputation finally reached Lady Hester's ears and decided her to close her doors against her ungrateful countrymen. She very rarely relaxed this rigid rule.

During one of his brief visits to England, Stratford Canning met Mr. Bankes at the house of Mr. Frere, and was highly entertained by the young man's amusing anecdotes of Lady Hester Stanhope's madness. He was not surprised to hear that the woman who had planned to visit Napoleon in the bitterest days of war, should now dream of becoming Queen of Jerusalem. According to Mr. Bankes, the prophecy was limited to a certain date, "and she had already exceeded the probationary term by two years."

William Bankes had barely left Mars Elias when a man, looking like a Mahomedan sheik, rode up the steep hillside. He arrived "in a state of extreme illness and exhaustion," and proved to be none other than the unfortunate Buckingham, who had suffered many vicissitudes since he had departed from his friend. Hester insisted on his remaining with her till he had recovered his strength, and in his book of travels he gives a portrait of his kind and amiable hostess, which is interesting because it shows Hester Stanhope in a new light. He is the only man who ever described her as "having soft blue eyes and an expression of habitual pensiveness and tranquil resignation." And he writes: "If to be sincerely and generally beloved by those among whom we reside, to possess power and influence with those who govern, and to have abundant opportunities of exercising these for the weak and helpless, be sources of delight, it may be safely concluded that Lady Hester Stanhope is one of the happiest of human beings." From these lines one may assume that Mr. Buckingham had been fortunate enough to please her exacting Ladyship. He stayed nine days at Mars Elias, and was enthusiastic over the elegant simplicity of his surroundings, the excellent cuisine and the perfect horses in the stables. When he left on his way to India he bade a tender and grateful farewell to his hostess, who provided him with some useful letters of introduction.

This was one of the rare occasions on which her kindness was fully appreciated. People were all too ready to ignore her numerous acts of charity and to blazon her eccentricities to the world.

Elizabeth Williams, her late companion who had remained with her sister at Malta, now braved the ordeal of a long and perilous journey in order to share her exile. This timid little English girl, brought up within the sound of Bow bells, landed at Beyrout in the early spring, and was met by a veiled woman in strange oriental garments, whom she could hardly recognize to be her old friend Mrs. Fry. Anne had express orders from her Ladyship to instruct Elizabeth in all the niceties of Turkish etiquette and to see that she was properly veiled before she rode through the town of Beyrout.

Poor Anne Fry! At last she had a chance of pouring out her grievances to sympathetic ears. She had suffered six years of exile without a soul to confide in except the absent-minded doctor, who never listened to her complaints. Long before she reached Mars Elias, Elizabeth Williams must have wished that she had never left Malta, for Mrs. Fry lost no time in telling her of the black slaves who only obeyed when they felt the lash across their backs, and of the Syrian servants who could not utter one word of truth, and of the neighbouring Druses who devoured raw meat. Some of these tales were vaguely disquieting for Elizabeth. It was horrible to think that her poor, dear mistress, who used to be so kind and considerate towards her inferiors, now suffered from such black rages that she was capable of bastinadoing her servants for the most harmless offence. And though she knew that her Ladyship had adopted male apparel she did not realize that she had not only shaved her head, but had adopted oriental habits even to the length of smoking a long amber-mounted pipe.

Hester was very touched by her little companion's devotion, and for a few days it amused her to show her all the beauties of her new surroundings; but when she was no longer a novelty she was relegated to the post of a household drudge and burdened with all the complicated, domestic arrangements of an untrained, unruly staff.

The Princess Caroline never came to Sidon, but many another visitor rode through the mulberry orchards to the convent of Mars Elias—Russian scientists and wise old men of the East, famous astrologers and medicine men possessing the secrets of magic herbs. Lady Hester had turned to the study of the stars and the occult sciences. She learned how the destiny of a man could be determined by the star of his nativity, and the signs about the mouth and the eyes which showed the beneficial or malignant character of the heavenly bodies which ruled his life. She evoked the help of supernatural agencies to further her own schemes and to make her loved and feared by the superstitious peasants of the mountains. She was in correspondence with the philosophers and magicians of Baghdad and Damascus, and pilgrims from Mecca appeared at her gates, bearing her gifts of gold dust from the Arabian deserts and scented aloe from the mountains of El Kaf. The name of the English Princess was famous throughout the East. Her vengeance on the Ansáry tribes had won her the title of 'The Defender of the Oppressed,' and her power was such that even the Bedouin sheiks solicited her protection. When Naser's careless thieving of the granaries of Homs embroiled him with the Pasha of Damascus, Mahanna dispatched one of his chieftains to Mars Elias with a flowery letter begging the *Melika's* intervention.

Naval officers and French diplomats came to pay their respects to the acknowledged Queen of the Lebanon, and Firmin Didot, the son of the famous Parisian printer, has left an interesting account of his visit—interesting, but somewhat inaccurate, for it is hard to believe that Lady Hester chose to confide in a complete stranger about her love for General Moore. People have been fond of asserting that General Moore was her one real love, but it was a love born of illusions and hero-worship with no fundamental basis. It was a love which had known neither the joys of fulfilment nor the pangs of disappointment, and now that Michael Bruce had failed her, she may have deliberately reverted to an hysterical adoration for her heroic general. But surely her pride could never have allowed her to inform Monsieur Didot that "her grief at the loss of her brother and of General Moore, whom she was to have married, had inspired her with that profound disgust of the world, which had so long retained her in the solitude of Mount Lebanon."

The end of the year brought Georgiaki Dallegio back from England, where he had been so indulged and spoilt by Lady Hester's friends as to have become quite insufferable. He declared that he had danced with the Duchess of York and dined with the Marquess of Buckingham and that English royalty was mean and niggardly, for the Princess Charlotte had only presented him with a little silver chain when he brought her Lady Hester's generous gifts. This was an unpardonable offence in the eyes of an oriental, for it is the custom in the East to reward the bearer of a present with an offering two-thirds of its value. Lady Hester forgave him all his impertinences, when he told her that on his visit to Chevening he was shown the Gains-borough portrait of Lord Chatham and was immediately struck by the extraordinary resemblance she bore her famous grandfather.

The new doctor arrived by the same boat, and Meryon was free to return to England, but the eagerly awaited day of departure had now become a painful ordeal. Like Bruce, he found it hard to break the chains which bound him to a wilful and imperious woman. She had obtained complete ascendancy over his mind and spirit. At times she had tyrannized and bullied him till he almost hated her, and then she would win him over with that extraordinary charm, that infectious gaiety, which occasionally overcame her habitual gravity. Meryon was enslaved for life. He might serve other masters and love other women, but his first thoughts would always be of her, this strange, unaccountable creature with whom he had lived in the greatest intimacy, who had confessed to him every detail of her private life, who had raved and wept in front of him and yet had never condescended to take his arm—for only a member of the aristocracy could be honoured with that mark of favour.

Doctor Meryon departed, and Lady Hester saw him go without the slightest tremor of regret. She could not foresee that in a few years' time she would be writing pathetic letters begging him to return.

Shortly after the doctor's departure she heard the news of Lord Stanhope's death. Though Georgiaki had been allowed to visit Chevening, no communication had passed between her and her father since she had left her home in the early days of the century. The only notice she took of his death was to write a cruel and bitter letter to her eldest brother, who now succeeded to the title. After accusing him of ingratitude, "that abominable vice unknown even to wild beasts," she informed him that she wished him to place any sums coming to her from the estate into the hands of Mr. Coutts. Her father's death enabled her to touch the capital of the ten thousand pounds left her by Charles Stanhope, and for a short time her financial prospects looked brighter. But instead of using the additional income to pay back her loans, she immediately launched out in new extravagances. Georgiaki's visit to England was both unnecessary and expensive, and this was not the only occasion on which worthless young Levantines were dispatched at her bidding to London and Marseilles. Lady Hester did things in the grand manner, and combined English liberality and oriental magnificence.

She still kept up a correspondence with her younger brother. For a little time there was some talk of her meeting him in France, and she would toy with the idea of settling down in an old chateau in Provence; but to Paris she would not go, for she declared that "the sight of those odious ministers of ours running about to do mischief would be too disgusting." According to her, the great allied victory heralded "an age of terror and perfidy." She was horrified at the way in which the English had treated Napoleon, "the man who had enlightened human nature and who still caused half the known world to tremble." It was not only Bonaparte personally whom she admired, but the character of the French nation who had followed him with such energy and sacrifice and who were now humiliated by their conquerors. Pitt's niece had Napoleon's portrait hanging in her drawing-room, and Frenchmen were always welcome to Mars Elias.

No wonder her letters were not popular among her English kinsmen, and whenever James attempted a mild remonstration, she immediately railed against him as if he had been her cruellest enemy. No brother could have been more affectionate and more loyal, and when Michael Bruce returned to England, he sought his friendship and tried to atone for the harsh things he had said against his sister's lover. This reconciliation gave Hester great pleasure, and she wrote to her old friend, Mr. Coutts, "You will see Bruce and my brother in England, probably ere you receive this; they have made it up and now are, thank God, as great friends as ever. This takes one great weight off my mind, for the only thing I wish to avoid in the world is hurting the feelings of others and dividing friends; as to how I 'injure' myself that is no sort of consequence." In the same letter she describes Michael Bruce as a young man "who thought all business to be a bore and that to sit under a tree with 'Homer' in one's hand and to make visionary plans was infinitely more sensible."

Still, she excused him and condoned his faults; and well she might, for few young men would have behaved as generously as he did, and both Mr. Coutts and Mr. Murray had the tact not to tell James Stanhope of the large sums which his sister owed to the banking house of Crawford Bruce.

CHAPTER TWENTY-TWO

"AND the Messiah shall ride a horse born saddled," so ran the prophecy in Metta's magic book. In 1817, in the stables of Mars Elias, a beautiful mare gave birth to a foal with a deformed spine and hollow back, which formed a complete Turkish saddle. The mare had been the gift of the Emir Bechir. Her genealogy was preserved with religious care and was said to extend in an unbroken line to the parent stock in the stables of King Solomon. Hester regarded the birth of the foal as a miracle and announced the great event to the Emir, who laughed outright at the idea of a deformed animal being destined to bear the Messiah into Jerusalem.

In these days Hester was still on friendly terms with her formidable neighbour, and Princess Maria Teresa Asmar, an inmate of the Emir's harem and a Christian refugee from the religious persecutions of Baghdad, declares in her memoirs that the English lady was a constant guest both at Iptedin and in the great Druse houses of the neighbourhood. She describes how she first met Hester Stanhope, while visiting a famous *aakel*. "Reclining on the *mushud* by his side with crossed legs *à l'orientale*, smoking a long and elegantly mounted *narghileh*, was a tall and splendid figure dressed in a long, saffron-coloured robe with red stripes, an embroidered *sadrieh*, fastened at the throat by an aigrette of gold, whose appearance, though somewhat wan, was dignified and majestic. Although the figure was attired in all respects as a man, I at once discovered that it belonged to the other sex. Her right hand grasped the stem of her pipe . . . and in her left she held a long rosary of amber, the beads of which she let fall one by one in slow succession."

Princess Asmar's description of Hester's conversation shows that already, in 1817, she was obsessed by the occult sciences. As soon as she heard that the 'Babylonian princess' came from Chaldea, the land of the wise, she began to talk about astrology, of Solomon El Hakim, the famous soothsayer of Damascus and of the sorcerers who possessed the power of discovering the whereabouts of hidden treasure. All the child-like beliefs of the credulous Syrians were expounded by her in a calm, philosophic manner, and Maria Teresa Asmar, who in common with most Asiatic Christians tried to ape European manners and customs as much as possible, was somewhat disconcerted when this strange visitor informed her that Europe was the centre of vice and corruption, and that pure, disinterested motives were only to be found among the Arabs of the desert.

The chief sign of Hester Stanhope's growing abnormality lay in her hatred and disgust of Europe. The ingratitude of a few of her compatriots aroused her resentment against her country, and gradually she left off corresponding with her old friends, for she was too self-centred to take an interest in other people's lives unless she could be at hand to help and advise them. She was delighted when the governors and pashas came to consult her and she refused to admit that there were certain subjects about which she was profoundly ignorant. Mr. Barker had many amusing tales to recount of the Beys who solicited her advice when they were suffering from the result of excessive indulgence in early youth. On these occasions, Lady Hester would assume the expression of a mysterious Sibyl and trace the course of the star which ruled the destiny of the wretched man who could no longer enjoy the beauties of his harem. She still possessed an extraordinary sexual naïveté, and in the East, where sex plays such an all-important part, her complete disregard and seeming lack of it made her appear to be a mysterious and unattainable being.

"Les sentiments tendres n'ont rien d'analogue à ce qu'on eprouve à sa vue," so wrote Louis Damoiseau, the young French horse dealer, who in 1819 accompanied the Baron de Portes to Syria on a mission to buy Arab chargers for the French Government. Damoiseau was highly honoured when he received an invitation to visit the 'Queen of Palmyra'; but

there was a motive for Lady Hester's amiability, for one of her horses was ill and she had heard of his skill as a vet.

When he arrived at Mars Elias an Arab servant ushered him into a courtyard where he was kept waiting for half an hour. Then a pretty maid appeared dressed in a Greek costume, who clapped her hands and called out, "Milady, milady, it's the Frenchman." Dressed as a Bedouin sheik, Lady Hester advanced to greet him, and excused herself for having let him wait. From her summerhouse in the garden she could watch every stranger coming up the hill, and at first she had mistaken him for an Englishman, in which case all he would have been offered would have been a dinner in the ante-room. Mr. Bankes and his cruel jibes were not forgotten and Damoiseau was surprised, not only by the bitterness in which she spoke against her compatriots, but by the enthusiasm with which she mentioned Napoleon's name. Lady Hester must have been an embarrassing companion for a normal, healthy young man, who was primarily interested in horses. Her religion, a strange medley of Moslem, Jewish and Christian beliefs, was bewildering, and her interminable flow of conversation was quite impossible to keep pace with. Her new physician, Dr. Newbery, had proved himself unable to stand the strain of the long *tête-à-tête* evenings with his patient, and one night he had fainted from sheer exhaustion. Lady Hester had interrupted her impassioned monologue, and had rung for Miss Williams, telling her that the doctor had fainted out of commiseration for the sad state of European politics. There was no need for the visitors to Mars Elias to be good conversationalists but they had to be versed in the art of listening. Damoiseau was kept up all night, while, veiled in a cloud of tobacco smoke, his hostess evoked visions of transcendent glory. It was somewhat incongruous to hear legends and myths of the Arabian Nights interpreted by a Western mind and described in Lady Hester's stilted French—the formal, courteous French she had spoken with exiled princes in the drawing-rooms of Downing Street.

No wonder Damoiseau remarked that she was "*une créature*

à part qu' étonne mais ne peut charmer," fascinating, strange, but rather frightening, with those wide blue eyes which could probe into the minds of men.

It was a relief to find her so normal and businesslike the next morning, when she showed him round her stables and discussed the ailments of her horses.

He was greatly struck by the beauty of the horse which had been presented to her by the Emir Naser. She showed him a mare which she had intended sending to Napoleon, but which was eventually given to his chief, the Baron de Portes, who brought it back to France, where it became the pride of the stud of the Duchesse d'Angoulême.

Damoiseau noticed the curious deformity of the 'filly born saddled,' but he failed to appreciate its beauty, even when Lady Hester told him of an antique bas-relief she had once seen in Rome, which depicted its exact likeness. A hard-bitten horse dealer could hardly be expected to believe in the mythical stables of King Solomon.

It was about this time that another Frenchman came to visit her—the Vicomte de Marcellus, the young diplomat who won immortal fame through discovering the Venus de Milo during a tour of the Levant.

Marcellus was a product of the new romantic age, which had flowered out of the carnage of the Napoleonic wars, and he found all the mystery and glamour he was searching for in the person of Hester Stanhope. She received him, sitting on a bearskin rug in a jasmine-scented arbour. Her pale face and dreamy, far-away look struck him as beautiful. She appealed to him in the *rôle* of the religious mystic, who despised the empty strife and petty slanders of the world, and he was enthralled when she spoke to him of the poetry of Antar and of how she had once spent eight days in the grotto of a hermit of Mount Lebanon, who had initiated her into the profounder secrets of the Koran. She had created her own religion, and adored a God who was master of the world and who would reward her for doing good and punish her for committing evil. She said, "I am not Anglican, neither am I a Mahomedan, though sometimes I quote from the Koran. How can one choose a religion in these deserts where flourish a thousand sects?"

The freemasonry of the Druses appealed to her love of mystery. At Meshmushy she had lived only a few steps away from the sacred grottoes where they indulged in the nocturnal debauches which were part of their religious rites. "Did the Druses worship the Golden Calf?" was a favourite question of Hester Stanhope's visitors, but she never divulged the secrets of her strange neighbours.

The old pagan forces were still alive in the mountains, the legends of Baal and Astarte had never died, and the sun and the moon and the stars still ruled the destiny of the Syrian people.

Her own God was the jealous, watchful Jehovah of the Old Testament; she practised the divine art of charity as taught by Christ, and in her daily life she adopted the abstinence of a pious Moslem. Religious teachers of every sect came to Mars Elias in order to propound the doctrines of their faith. No wonder she confessed to Marcellus that at first she hardly dared to profess a cult for any especial god. But now her beliefs were fixed. *"Je veux mériter les bontés de ce dieu, seul et tout puissant, dont mon âme tout entière reconnait l'existence."*

Did Hester Stanhope ever really know what god she was worshipping and what dogmas she believed in?

For seven hours she talked and, as the evening wore on, they moved into the house, where they were served with sorbets and coffee in a large empty drawing-room with the walls hung with Arab weapons. There were only two pictures in the room—one depicted a horse braving a torrent, and the other was a portrait of Bonaparte.

Marcellus was invited to make a longer stay at Mars Elias, but he was pressed for time and forced to leave the next morning for Jerusalem. His hostess's last kind attention was to send two Arab horses to conduct him to the bottom of the mountain.

Thirteen years later, when Lamartine's eulogistic pen blazoned Hester Stanhope's name throughout the whole of Europe, Marcellus sent the poet an admiring tribute of the work, which had aroused so many vivid memories in his mind. "You have at the present awakened my recollections; and you alone shall judge whether some traits which I have preserved are worthy of being added to your glowing pictures. Lady Hester Stanhope, then more connected with Europe and its political existence, had not, at the time I had the honour of seeing her, forgotten the world, but she certainly despised it. . . . Disgusted with the religions of Europe, although but imperfectly acquainted with them; rejecting the various sects of the desert, whose mysteries she had solved, she had created a deism of her own and preserved nothing of the Christian religion but the practice of benevolence and the doctrine of charity. . . . 'Shall you ever re-visit England?' I asked her. 'No, never,' she energetically replied, 'your Europe is so insipid. Leave me my desert. Why should I return to Europe to behold nations worthy of their fetters and monarchs unworthy of their thrones? Very shortly your worn-out continent will be shaken to its base. You have seen Athens; you are going to see Tyre. Mark the remains of these noble republics, protectresses of the arts; of these monarchies, queens of commerce and the ocean! So will it be with Europe. She is going rapidly to decay. Her kings are no longer worthy of their descent; they fall, either by death or by means of their misrule, and degenerate in their successors. Her aristocracy, nearly exterminated, is superseded by a pitiful and effeminate commonalty without life or vigour. The people, and those of the labouring class alone, still preserve a character and some virtue. You may tremble, should they ever learn their strength. No, your Europe sickens me! I turn a deaf ear to all the reports which reach me from thence, and which quickly die away in this isolated region. Let us talk no more of Europe, I have done with her.' "

After thirteen years he remembered every one of Hester Stanhope's words and his letter ends, "I am thinking as I write of that sun which disappeared behind the mountains of Cyprus and cast its last tints on the peaks of Anti-Lebanon; I am thinking of that deep blue sea, the waves of which, expiring without foam, scarcely touched the beach of Sidon. You, better than anyone, will understand how strongly the imagination and the memory are arrested, how forcibly the heart beats when, in such an amphitheatre, an Englishwoman, whom the Arabs, forgetting her sex, have called Lord, veiled under the costume of a Bedouin, lets fall such words amidst the silence of the desert."

All these travellers who came to pay homage to Hester Stanhope played no part in her life. She was utterly friendless and alone. Even Dr. Newbery soon found that he was unable to stand the life at Mars Elias and he left, together with Anne Fry, whose bad state of health forced her to return to England. Elizabeth Williams, the refined little gentlewoman, with her sketching and her needlework and her thin, reed-like voice, was Hester's only companion during those long winter evenings when the storms raged in the mountains and the swollen torrents burst the bridges, so that messengers bearing letters from Beyrout and Acre had many a time to ford across the rivers.

It was not an enviable job to be in the service of Lady Hester Stanhope, for her messengers and dragomans never had a minute's peace. They were liable to be despatched in the middle of the night to the most distant parts of Syria, and no sympathy was ever shown for any misfortune which might befall them on the road. When Beaudin had his horse stolen from a wayside *khan* near Tyre and had to walk on foot through the rain to Acre, where he apprised her Ladyship of his loss, the only answer he got was a laconic note, saying, "If you have mislaid your horse, find her." But to be in her service was a useful stepping ladder for procuring a lucrative government appointment.

She was harsh and often cruel towards her servants. The

very memory of the spotless tiring maids at Chevening and
the elegant footmen of Downing Street was sufficient to send
her in a wild rage against the filthy wretches who scratched
themselves in front of her and pilfered her preserves. Then
she would write to Meryon in despair and beg him to find her
a decent Scotch housekeeper and sensible, good-tempered
maids, and the poor doctor, who was now in the employ of Sir
Gilbert Heathcote (that exquisite dandy who had flirted with
Lady Hester during her first season), was forced to run round in
search of serving-maids. The results were invariably disastrous.
Hester had adopted the oriental habit of corporal punishment,
and no superior English lady's maid or free-born Swiss was
going to stand having her face slapped, an art in which her
Ladyship was particularly proud of excelling. One by one
they fled back to their native country, where they circulated
reports of her madness, "of her absurd life and of the contempt
in which her family held her." And Hester declared that they
used her name in securing posts as governesses in rich merchant
families, where they could entertain their mistresses with
stories of her doings. The neglect of her family preyed on her
mind, and, owing to political differences, she even quarrelled
with her beloved James. She complained to Mr. Coutts that
"One of my greatest sorrows is to suppose him rather trifling,
his politics nonsense. I know but too well the characters,
opinions and principles, and also the capability of all the
leading politicians in England, and James cannot therefore
enlighten me." There was something definitely abnormal
about the woman who could let a political difference come
between her and her brother, who was so devoted to her that
in 1818 he paid off bills which she thought had been settled
by Michael Bruce. As soon as James Stanhope heard of the
large sums owing to Bruce, he wrote to his sister's banker:—

"My dear Sir,
    I have just written to Mr. Murray to take means to get the
mortgage paid in and I have had Lady Hester's instructions

about the mode of disposing of her money, except as to her exchequer bills, which I took on myself to direct. I will give Dr. Meryon the order, and have written to Mr. Bruce to take away his money, so I beg you not to tell Lady Hester it has not been drawn by him."

Perhaps if Hester had known of his generous gesture she might have spared them both a lot of unnecessary heartache.

The picture of Hester Stanhope, shouting at her servants, interfering in every domestic detail, mixing black doses for some unfortunate dependent, and spending long evenings with the faithful Williams in discussing her debts and loans, does not conform with the idealized, ethereal creature evoked in the memoirs of a French romantic.

At first she had no real love of the East, no feeling for its culture and traditions. There was a time when she thought of going to America, "the land of liberty, industry and liberality," and if either Metta or Loustenau had foretold that her glorious destiny were to be fulfilled in the West, she would have left Syria without a moment's hesitation. What a welcome Chatham's granddaughter would have received in the colony whose rights he had been the first to defend, and the last to renounce!

The *Mahdi* was to rise in the East, and she was to be the chosen bride, so she waited in her damp and gloomy convent for the glory of the second advent. Gradually the country took hold of her, sapping her vitality, draining her resources. The beliefs she had fostered in order to gain influence among the credulous Syrians and Arabs, were beginning to dominate her, and she was obsessed by the desire for power. It was true that her word was law in the mountain, but only as long as it pleased the Emir Bechir to humour her whims.

In 1818 the famous Spanish traveller and astronomer, Badia y Leblich, who had adopted the Moslem faith and the name of Ali Bey El Abbassi, was poisoned at Balka, a caravan halt about one hundred and twenty miles from Damascus. He had started out from Mecca in order to discover the whereabouts of Timbuctoo, and he was in the pay of the French Government, who employed him partly as a secret service agent, partly as a scientific expert to make certain astronomical experiments. The poison was administered in a dish of rhubarb, and when he was dying, he sent a letter addressed to the French Admiralty and a specimen of the rhubarb under cover to Lady Hester Stanhope, whom he had never met, but whom he regarded as the only influential European in the country. Travellers in distress never called on her in vain, and messengers on fleet-footed dromedaries were despatched to Mecca to inquire into the cause of his death; but they never returned, for they were overtaken in the desert by a band of Bedouin robbers. Some friendly Arabs brought Hester the news that Ali Bey's astronomical instruments and papers had been seized by a Moghreb chief of Damascus, and she was determined to retrieve his possessions and to present them to the French Government. She pictured a triumphal repetition of the 'Affaire Boutin,' but, alas! she was unsuccessful, and she had to be satisfied in handing Marcellus the packet of poisoned rhubarb and the letter to the French Admiralty.

It required a vast fortune to play the *rôle* of the protector of the distressed. Every month a procession of spies and messengers came to collect their wages at Mars Elias, and Hester had to borrow money at enormous interest. The Pasha of Damascus died, and there was confusion in the Pashalik. The money market was shut and prices soared, and Chatham's granddaughter signed drafts to usurers at Malta and Stamboul. In the cold winter of 1819 there was so much distress among the peasants, owing to the bad harvests of the preceding year, that free meals were supplied at Mars Elias. Then Lady Hester fell ill, and there was a return of her gasping, tearing cough. The news of her illness reached London, and the faithful Meryon decided to venture once more to Syria. This visit is veiled in mystery. It coincided with one of the strangest episodes in Lady Hester's life, an episode carefully omitted from the Duchess of Cleveland's tactful biography and never once referred to by Meryon, who merely commented on his visit: "I found that her Ladyship had in the meanwhile completely familiarized herself with the usages of the East, conducting her establishment entirely in the Turkish manner and adopting even much of their medical empiricism. Under these circumstances, and at her own suggestion, I again bade her adieu."

CHAPTER TWENTY-THREE

HESTER STANHOPE was forty-four. Love, affection, even friendship no longer played any part with her. Occasionally she was roused to a brief display of emotion by some memory of her former life, but her attitude, whether with Turks or Europeans, was completely detached. Her fantastic delusions saved her from realizing the barrenness of her life, a vivid, exciting life, which had given her very little satisfaction and very little happiness. There were certain desires, certain expectations, which refused to be stilled. She was growing old. The faint tracery of veins under the delicate white skin was darker, the skin itself had a slight waxen look. There were sharp lines round the charming mouth, and the Pitt nose stuck out thin and angular, contemptuous and assertive. Hester Stanhope looked down the high bridge of her aristocratic nose and men moved nervously away. So it had been all her life, and throughout her wild, restless career she had known only a few years of physical fulfilment.

Now that she had renounced the hopes and aspirations of a normal woman she was suddenly to give way to an unaccountable and uncontrolled physical obsession.

On the 15th January, 1820, a tall, well-built young man, an ex-officer of Napoleon's Imperial Guard, landed at Sidon. He had come to Syria in search of his father, General Loustenau, who was known to have been shipwrecked off the coast seven years before. It was not an arduous search, for every child throughout the country had heard of the mad prophet who lived on the bounty of the English princess, and before he was conducted to Mars Elias, the Captain heard many exaggerated tales of Lady Hester Stanhope's wealth. Old Loustenau received the news of his son's arrival with a stony calm, and when the young man rushed forward to embrace him he repulsed him, saying, "Why all this excitement, all this astonishment? Don't you know that everything is written? I waited for you, I was certain of seeing you again. Read your

Bible; it will enlighten you in every science; it will reconstruct the past and unveil the future"—which was hardly an enthusiastic reception for the son, who had been searching for him during the past four years.

The Captain refused to be discouraged; he had been quick to see his opportunities. God had given him good looks and an engaging manner, and it would be worth his while to ingratiate himself into her Ladyship's favour. Hester Stanhope granted him an audience and his future was assured, for the benevolent fates had cast his features in the mould of those of General Moore. He had his look, his voice, his walk, and when she cast his horoscope she discovered that his stars were favourable to her own. As the highest mark of honour she appointed him stud groom to her sacred mares, and in memory of General Moore she attempted to bind his destiny to her own. Loustenau was both mediocre and lazy, both an adventurer and a sponger, and the attitude he adopted to Pitt's niece was that of a handsome fellow hiring himself out to please the fantasy of a rich old woman.

The Consuls of Sidon murmured when Lady Hester went riding through the streets accompanied by her swaggering cavalier. They had been informed that the Captain was on his way to India, where he proposed to collect the remains of his paternal fortune, but now he seemed to be definitely settled at Mars Elias and his hostess declared that her guests were under no jurisdiction except her own.

Vulgar and comparatively uneducated, he obtained a complete domination over her mind. This strange infatuation was born out of hallucinations. Moore's untimely death at Corunna had robbed her of her one chance of happiness, and now she made a pathetic attempt to re-find it in this gross, ordinary young man who was quite incapable of appreciating the elegance and charm which was still her chief characteristic. Four years later, when Captain Yorke, afterwards Lord Hardwicke, visited her at Djoun, he wrote to his father, "I at once became delighted with her wit, her knowledge, and, I must say, her beauty, for she is still one of the finest specimens of a woman I ever saw." But how could a commonplace French officer understand the grandeur of the Pitt manner?

This was one of the saddest episodes of Lady Hester's life, and Meryon returned to Syria to find her in the toils of this extraordinary obsession. Even the mad old General seems to have resented his son's influence. Perhaps Lady Hester paid less attention to his prophecies, now that she was living so ardently in the present. However, the Captain's days were numbered; over-indulgence in the pleasures of the table forced him to take recourse to the purifying waters of Tiberias. It was too late. He succumbed to an acute gastritis, and died in the middle of August. The doctor must have been in Syria at the time of his death, but there is no mention of it in his memoirs.

Lady Hester, miserable and inconsolable, retired to the heights of Meshmushy, and at her own suggestion Meryon returned to England. She wrote to Mr. Coutts that she had sent her doctor back because she wanted no communication with her own country, and for his part Meryon was only too happy to resume his employment with Sir Gilbert Heathcote. Following the example of his noble patron, he launched out on an expensive and romantic *attachement* with a French ballet-girl, who had enjoyed a brief spell of notoriety as Lord Lowther's favourite mistress. After presenting her benefactor with a daughter she moved to Paris, where she met Meryon, and at the end of the year 1821 he was a proud but somewhat nervous father. It is amusing to note that this timid, despised little man, who submitted to all Hester Stanhope's moods and vagaries, was an object of passionate adoration to his French mistress, and even when he married, a year or two later, he never neglected her or his illegitimate son. Hester Stanhope was not interested in her doctor's private life. While he remained in Europe he was merely useful to her as a willing drudge to carry out all her complicated commissions. When she said good-bye to him in 1820, she was far too miserable over Loustenau's death to give him a single thought.

The unfortunate young Captain was buried in her garden, and when she moved to Djoun, his bones were transferred to her new abode. One of her last wishes was to be buried beside him, for the same stars presided over their destinies.

.   .   .   .   .

1820 and guns re-echoing in the mountains. Soliman Pasha had died, and his young nephew Abdallah reigned in his stead. Cruel, weak and avaricious, he had none of his uncle's noble qualities, and he was more occupied with his harem than with the affairs of state. Yet when it came to extorting money from his subjects he could show himself as hard as steel, and during the first year of his reign the Emir Bechir was forced to fly to the Hauran in order to evade paying the enormous taxes. Abdallah needed the support of the prince of the mountains, and six months later they joined forces against Darwish, the new Pasha of Damascus.

At the edge of the Pashalik of Acre, at the very borders of the Emir's territory, sat Hester Stanhope, and she was not one to turn a deaf ear to the rumours of rebellion. Rigid believer in the divine right of kings, she upraised the Sultan's standard and her wrath fell on those who dared to revolt against his appointed emissaries. Charitable and compassionate, her heart went out to the poor peasants whose homes were devastated and whose vineyards were burnt, while the pashas evoked the horrors of civil war. Mars Elias, the peaceful little convent overlooking the blue Mediterranean, was not large enough to harbour the refugees who came begging at her door, and in 1821 she moved to the ruined monastery of Djoun, overlooking a narrow mountain valley in the impregnable heart of the Lebanon. Doctor Meryon says that her removal to this isolated spot proceeded from her love of absolute power, which could not be so thoroughly gratified in the midst of a numerous population as in a lonely and isolated residence. He says that, "She chose to dwell apart and out of the immediate reach of that influence and restraint which neighbourhood and society necessarily exert upon us." At Djoun she could make her own

laws and mete out her own punishments. Her servants had
no alternatives but to obey. There could be no repetition of
the scene at Mars Elias, when all her negro slaves escaped in
the night after having submitted to one of her mad rages.
It was impossible to escape from Djoun. To reach either
Beyrout, Sidon or Deir El Kammar one had to cross a district
of perilous rocks abounding in wolves and jackals, and no
frightened negress or superstitious Syrian dared to face the
demon spirits of the mountains, which walked abroad at
night. It was better to bow to the tyranny of the English
princess whose harshness was tempered by generosity. At the
feast of *Bairam* every servant was dressed in a grand new suit of
clothes and presented with a bag of piastres, and when they
told their mistress some pathetic tale of their family's poverty
she was never known to refuse material help.

Hester Stanhope had the real love of giving. She would
pawn her pelisse in order to pour gold into the hands of her
unworthy dependents, and when Abdallah Pasha fell on evil
days and was taken in chains to Stamboul, it was to an Englishwoman that he came whining for part of his ransom. Bechir
and Abdallah had advanced in triumph against the regiments
of Darwish, till Mahmoud raised himself from his lethargy
and commanded the armies of five pashaliks to march upon the
rebels. Bechir fled to Egypt and sought the Viceroy's protection, who gave him a royal reception in his palace at Choubra,
for Mehemet Ali thought lovingly of the rich provinces of
Syria, and he saw Bechir as a useful ally when the time came
for him to wrest that country from the ineffectual grasp of the
Sublime Porte. If it had not been for him and his famous son, the
Wahabees would have over-run Arabia and the town of Mahomet
would have been in their hands. It was Ibrahim who, at the age
of sixteen, brought the keys of the gates of Mecca in triumph
to Stamboul; and the servant who was more powerful than
the master obtained Bechir's pardon from the Sublime Porte.

Abdallah was still in chains at Stamboul with a ransom of
three thousand purses on his head, and Hester Stanhope could

not refuse the demand of one who was not only the nephew of her old friend, but who had also married his favourite daughter. Though she had not a penny at Stamboul, she took a loan from Mr. Coutts's representative, Mr. Sarell, and trusted the Ambassador at the Porte to guarantee her draft. Her own financial affairs were in such a precarious state that she was forced to sell her reversion on the Burton Pynsent estate, and in 1823 she sent General Loustenau to Damascus to borrow money from her ex-dragoman, Monsieur Beaudin, who was now installed as French agent.

Abdallah returned to Acre, but was very dilatory in paying back the loan, and some of Hester Stanhope's most treasured possessions were to be found in the dirty pawnbroker shops of Beyrout. She pawned her furs and snuff-boxes, yet, at the same time, she installed a whole army of workmen at Djoun. Her new home was built on her own extravagant plans; walls within walls, with long, twisting corridors connecting a series of detached cottages; secret courts and gardens with winding staircases; stables and covered paddocks, and hidden spy-holes from whence could be watched every movement of an un-suspecting visitor; trap-doors leading to passages cut in the rocks, through which refugees from the Emir's tyranny might escape into the open country. What had been a small ruined monastery on the bare top of a table mountain now assumed the aspect of a warlike fortress. Once the gates were opened one entered into an enchanted paradise, scented gardens with marble statues overgrown with morning glory, splashing fountains beneath pergolas of jasmine and roses, periwinkles and clematis reflecting in clear pools of water. Memories of the formal eighteenth century gardens of her childhood, memories of the gardens of Therapia and Buyukdereh, the rose thickets of Brusa and the blossoming groves of Damascus were evoked by Hester Stanhope from the rocks of the Lebanon. In the heart of her private garden a marble urn marked the grave of the unfortunate young Frenchman whose destiny for a short while had run parallel to her own.

CHAPTER TWENTY-FOUR

THE mountain of Djoun rose out of a broad, deep valley surrounded on every side by bare hills of chalk and limestone, with cleft rocks and precipitous ravines. Shaken by earthquakes, blasted by lightning, corroded by rain, the very stones assumed a deathlike appearance. Eagles and vultures swooped round Lady Hester's mountain eyrie and jackals howled outside her gates. Her only neighbours were the peasants of Djoun, who tended their mulberry orchards and vineyards in the valley, and the Maronite monks of the monastery of Dahr Mkhallas. Far in the distance, through a gap in the mountains, could be seen the shores of Sidon, shimmering in the sunlight. In the old days, with her clear, piercing eyesight, Hester would have been able to distinguish every boat which came sailing into the harbour, but now her vision was blurred and faint. The merciless sun of the Syrian desert, the white glare of the limestone rocks, had permanently impaired her eyesight, and though she scornfully refused to wear the spectacles which the thoughtful Meryon was constantly sending from England, she was now forced to dictate her correspondence to Miss Williams. Old friends still came to visit her. The Chevalier Guys and Monsieur Regnault, the French Consuls of Beyrout and Tripoli, and the faithful Mr. Barker, who was beginning to have serious doubts of her sanity. Her *rôle* of a Delphic Sibyl was somewhat alarming to a man who was 'the best kind of John Bull,' and when she wrote begging him to remove his family from Aleppo, which, according to the predictions of General Loustenau, was going to be destroyed by a mighty earthquake, he paid no attention to the fantasy of a mad woman—but the prophecy was realized within a year, and in his despatches to Mr. Salt, the Consul-General at Alexandria, Mr. Barker noted that a certain General Loustenau, living on the bounty of Lady Hester Stanhope, had foretold the Aleppo earthquake of 1822.

All her strange dreams and fantasies were not as pathetic as her vanity, which forbade her to expose her ageing features to the light of the day. She never rose from her bed till the afternoon. No visitor was admitted to her presence till dusk. They were allowed one short interval for dinner and then were kept awake till dawn. Her room was in perpetual twilight. No man was ever allowed to see how thin and gaunt she had become, for she still treasured memories of herself as the tall, strapping girl with rosy cheeks, beside whom so many beauties had looked pallid and insignificant.

Swathed in her white robes, her chin veiled by the *keffiyah*, she even now gave the illusion of being a beautiful woman, and she still had the coquetry to expose her lovely hands as much as possible, those delicate, tapering fingers, which could put themselves to every task, from cooking and dressmaking to managing an unruly Arab steed. One of her greatest sorrows was when the bad state of her health forced her to give up riding.

After the doctor's departure, she had fallen into the hands of Arab charlatans and quack medicine-men, who submitted her to a treatment of continual bleedings, which weakened her whole system. At the same time she prescribed her own medicines and indulged excessively in Turkish baths. She believed that "every star had attached to it two aerial beings, two animals, two trees, two flowers, two minerals, etc., whose antipathies and sympathies became congenial with the being born under the same star. Where the particular tree, that was beneficial or pleasurable to him, flourished naturally, or the mineral was found, there the soil and air were salubrious to that individual." And by merely knowing her star, she fancied that she could divine the medicines most beneficial to her. She insisted on treating her illness as asthma, when it was really consumption, and her weakness was such that soon she was unable to stir more than a league from her own house. She lost much of her glamorous prestige when the peasants no longer saw her richly dressed figure galloping on horseback across the mountains, when the merchants no longer met her riding on her white ass through the bazaars of Beyrout and Damascus. At the same time she obtained a curious ascendancy over the minds of the people; chieftains and slaves alike regarded the cloistered prophetess of Mount Lebanon as a holy woman. Twelve Arab chargers still champed in her stables, not to count the two sacred mares, Laila and Loulou, who each had their own groom and private paddock. Laila was the 'horse born saddled' and Loulou was a milk-white mare, whose beauty entitled her to be ridden by the Messiah's bride. No one was suffered to mount them under penalty of being dismissed from her Ladyship's service, and if any servant or villager dared to look at them, he was severely beaten. Only a few favoured travellers were allowed to see these mares in their stable, and this permission was never granted until Hester had proved that their stars were favourable. Her world was dominated by superstitions, and the most ordinary domestic mishap was attributed to some supernatural influence.

The last eighteen years of her life were spent at Djoun, and though the bare chronicling of these latter years makes pathetic reading, one must remember that Hester Stanhope's material life was merely subsidiary to the mythical existence she had created in her own imagination.

One's heart goes out to Miss Williams when one pictures her alone in the solitude of Djoun with her eccentric mistress, who maintained that the elements were peopled with delicate aerial beings, "so that she never moved a foot without asking those guardian sylphs to watch over her, and never saw a blundering fellow knock his head against the top of a doorway, without thinking that he was breaking some of their delicate members." What could the little companion make of the mistress who quoted the Bible till it sounded almost like blasphemy, when she twisted round the Scriptures to suit her own ends, putting the words of John the Baptist into the mouth of .Christ and always referring back to the second Advent, when the living and dead would pay homage to the Messiah? Poor Miss Williams, clinging to the tenets of the Anglican faith and never even being allowed to see the missionaries who came knocking at the doors of Djoun! Her Ladyship had a horror of missionaries, whether Roman Catholic or Anglican, and the Abbè Demazurés and Mr. Way were treated in the same manner. The former was so persistent in his endeavour to see her, that in the end he was warned by his Consul not to molest her any more and, though Mr. Way was granted an interview, Hester exerted all her influence to prevent him propagating his faith in Syria, and she was so successful that he was forced to leave the country.

The most summary treatment of all was meted out to the Jewish convert, Dr. Joseph Wolff, who arrived from Malta, bringing Miss Williams a letter from her sister. He had the audacity to send the letter direct to Miss Williams, without mentioning Lady Hester's name. Her Ladyship looked upon this as an unpardonable affront, and she was undignified enough to write, "I am astonished that an apostate should dare to thrust himself into observation into my family. Had you been a learned Jew, you would never have abandoned a religion, rich in itself, though defective, nor would you have embraced the shadow of a one—I mean the Christian religion. Light travels faster than sound, therefore the supreme Being could not have allowed His creatures to live in darkness for nearly two thousand years, until paid, speculating wanderers deem it proper to raise their venial voices to enlighten them." And Dr. Wolff had the courage to reply, "Madam, I have just received a letter which bears your Ladyship's signature, but I doubt its being genuine, as I never had the honour of writing to you, or of mentioning your name in my letter to Miss Williams. With regard to my views and pursuits—they give me perfect rest and happiness, and they must be quite im-material to your Ladyship."

The messenger who brought this letter was kicked and beaten by Lady Hester's orders, and came back limping to his master, saying that he had been bastinadoed by the King of England's daughter.

It is doubtful whether Miss Williams ever received her sister's letter, for she was suffering from an acute attack of homesickness, and Lady Hester was continually intercepting her correspondence in order to prevent her making plans for returning to Malta. How she must have regretted the gay Maltese society, which she had abandoned for this prison life, for her Ladyship observed the laws of the harem as strictly as in a Turkish capital. At Mars Elias, Elizabeth Williams had been comparatively free, but now she was forced to lead a sequestered existence, and loyalty to her mistress could not keep her from resenting the fact that she was not even allowed to see the few English visitors who were received at Djoun. She was still young and pretty, and unconsciously Hester was jealous of her youth and delicate charm. Visitors to Mars Elias must have found her very sweet and restful, after their exuberant and exhausting hostess, and the good-looking Syrian dragomans, who followed one another in rapid succession, were not averse to flirting with Milady's English companion. Hanah Massad, a handsome young man from Beyrout and a great favourite with his mistress, was bolder than the rest, and he and Elizabeth indulged in a romantic liaison, till they were imprudent enough to confess their love to Lady Hester, who made herself as unpleasant as possible. Massad was dismissed from her service with a pecuniary compensation, and from that time Miss Williams's situation was not an enviable one. To teach Arab cooks to make English puddings, and Levantine butlers to polish silver; to keep the servants from pilfering the preserves and supervise the cleanliness of negro slaves were her principal occupations. She faded and wilted, gradually degenerating into a drab, mouse-like creature, drained of all vitality; a frail little shadow, drifting down the corridors of Djoun, and Hester never noticed that she was overtaxing the strength and resources of her faithful companion.

The rooms of Djoun were dark and gloomy, and the air was charged with secrecy and mystery. Strange people entered by the doors, but no one saw them go. These were her Ladyship's spies, who came and left in different disguises. Then there were the agents, who protected her interests with the natives. Youssef, the cringing tailor, and Girius Gemmal, the club-footed farmer, who was known to possess the evil eye and to be versed in the casting of charms. Occasionally there was a visit from the mad General, to whom Lady Hester had relegated her old home of Mars Elias, as his cantankerous temper made it impossible for her to keep him in her vicinity.

Hester Stanhope was now living in the heart of the Emir's territory, and Bechir was her bitterest enemy. On his return from Egypt he had found his country in a state of rebellion, for his chief minister, the Sheik Bechir, had raised his standards and proclaimed himself as sole sovereign of the Lebanon. All during the years of 1823 and 1824 there was bitter warfare in the narrow mountain valleys, and at times it looked as if the Sheik Bechir would win the day. Wounded Druses crept up the steep hill of Djoun begging for the *Sytt's* protection. With her own hands Lady Hester cut up blankets and mixed gruels for the two hundred people who found refuge within her walls.

Money fell through Lady Hester's fingers like water and many of the old sources had run dry. She had severed all connection with Michael Bruce when he announced his marriage to a middle-aged widow; General Oakes had left Malta, and the new Governor refused to guarantee her drafts, and in the year 1822 she had lost one of her best friends through the death of Mr. Coutts. In despair she borrowed from the merchants of Sidon and Beyrout, and the stories of the English-woman's fabulous wealth melted in thin air when fat grocers and Jewish usurers could claim to be her creditors.

Still the war raged on, till in 1824 Abdallah Pasha joined the Emir in his struggle with the Sheik. The cannons of the Pashalik of Acre were levelled against the rebels at the battle of Moukhtara, and the Sheik Bechir was borne in chains to Acre, where he was beheaded by order of the Pasha. Not content with the annihilation of his enemies, the Emir Bechir summoned his two young nephews who had been compromised in the rebellion, and burnt out their eyes with redhot irons. When the Sheik's widow took refuge in a mountain cave, Bechir put his bloodhounds on her track, and her child was cut into pieces before her very eyes. The mountains reechoed with the terrible tales of his cruelty until they reached Lady Hester's ears. The blood of her cousin, Lord Camelford, came to the surface. "The Emir would find that no real Pitt ever tolerated injustice." Racked with disease and crippled with debt, an Englishwoman dared to defy the tyrant of the Lebanon by giving shelter to his enemies. She had not even the support of the British agents on the coast, for she was at daggers drawn with Mr. Abbot, the English Consul at Beyrout, who had appointed a defrocked Armenian Bishop as his agent at Sidon. This Yacoub Aga was a man with a notorious reputation, who had been accused of poisoning his wife and children, and Lady Hester lost no time in letting Mr. Abbot know that she refused to have any dealings with him. The Armenian curried favour with the Emir by telling him that he could rid himself of the Englishwoman with impunity, as neither her family nor her friends would lift a hand to help her.

The first open quarrel between Lady Hester and Bechir arose in the late autumn of 1826, when her Ladyship's camels were pressed into service by the Emir's workmen in order to convey slabs of marble from Sidon to Iptedin. The camels halted for a short while at Djoun, and in the space of half an hour Lady Hester saw that every one of the marble slabs was broken to pieces. A few days later there was more trouble when an outlaw, who had taken refuge in the mountain under the Emir's protection, picked a quarrel with one of Lady Hester's water carriers, which resulted in a free fight between their supporters. The Emir had now only one wish—to rid himself of his impossible neighbour; and one evening at sunset, from the roofs of every village throughout his territory, his public crier denounced the *Sytt* and declared that all her servants were to leave her and to return to their homes upon pain of losing their property and lives.

Hester Stanhope was a prisoner on her mountain, but such was her ascendancy over the minds of her dependents that none of them obeyed the Emir's edict. She was cut off from all intercourse with the outside world. The few peasants who cared to risk their lives for a handsome compensation brought her water and provisions at dead of night, but not one of the people whom she had sheltered during the days of war came to her rescue; not even Abdallah Pasha, for whose sake she had pawned her robe of ceremony. She was at the mercy of a blood-thirsty tyrant, yet she never faltered for one moment. At night she went to bed with a dagger under her pillow, an Arab mace above her head and "she slept as sound as a top." Poor Miss Williams was terrified out of her senses and could not bear to be separated from her mistress for a moment. Men were killed at the very gates of Djoun in order to frighten Lady Hester into submission, and the Emir sent his officers with threatening messages to intimidate her into leaving the country. Hester Stanhope threw back her head and laughed: "Let them tell their master that she cared not a fig for his poisons and daggers, and if he sent her his son to make terms with her she would gladly kill him with her own hands."

News of her situation reached Constantinople. Lord Strangford, who had succeeded Liston as Ambassador to the Porte, had never taken any interest in her affairs. Her numerous letters of complaint had been neatly docketed in the chancery files, and his Lordship had thought it sufficient to soothe her grievances with a few formal words. Now Stratford Canning had returned to his old post, and loyalty to Pitt's memory, together with a half-hearted admiration for the eccentric woman who had shown such indomitable courage, made him insist on the Sultan redressing Lady Hester's wrongs. A secretary from the British Embassy landed at Sidon, and both the Pasha of Acre and the Emir Bechir were warned that the mad Englishwoman was still powerful enough to be entitled to the especial protection of the Grand Signior. Ill, worn and harassed by her debts, Lady Hester could still summon the spirit to write triumphantly to her doctor, "The Emir Bechir with all the art and meanness well known to him has now become abjectly humble . . . finding that he had made a false calculation and displeased the great and small in the country by his vile conduct, he is humble enough and repents having given me an opportunity of showing what I am. I am thus become more popular than ever, having shown an example of firmness and courage no one could calculate upon."

Nevertheless those years of 1823 to 1827 had been years of sorrow and disaster. The one happy event had been the visit of Captain Yorke, who had come to Sidon in 1824 and had been so enchanted with his hostess that he constituted himself as her knight-errant in protecting her interests at home. It was one of the rare occasions when Hester Stanhope was truly appreciated by a young man who came of the same class as herself, who had the same upbringing and the same moral code. Though she usually refused to receive her compatriots, she made an exception in his favour, for she had known many of the Yorkes in the old days, and she might well say of him that "he was the kindest-hearted man existing, a most manly, firm character." What matter if she spoke to him of marvels and plagues and pestilence, of predestination and supernatural agencies? What matter if at night she talked so wildly and strangely that it was pathetically clear that her mind was disordered? He could still see the brave, noble spirit which refused to give in to her misfortunes and ill-health; he could still admire the great lady who smilingly apologised for the simplicity of her table. The refugees who crowded her courtyard testified to her compassion, the Bedouin sheiks who waited at her gates testified to her power in the desert. What matter if the cushions of her divan were faded and torn and her dinner service of common earthenware? When the time came for Captain Yorke to return to his ship Lady Hester had gained a life-long friend, and he took it upon himself to write to Lord Chatham telling him of her poverty and distress and begging him to communicate the news to her brother James.

James Stanhope never heard of his sister's vicissitudes. In 1820 he had married a daughter of the Earl of Mansfield, and after four years of happiness, she died, leaving him two small children. Weak and unstable, he now allowed himself to give way to that melancholy streak which had always underlined his superficial gaiety. He was broken-hearted and life seemed unbearable. One spring day, his father-in-law found him hanging from a tree in the grounds of Ken Wood.

Through some freakish whim of her wounded vanity Hester had never written to him during the last years. She did not even write to him after his wife's death, though she shared his affliction. The news only reached her six months later. "To write—not to write—no proper conveyance—what to say— after a year perhaps to open the wounds of his heart without being able to pour in one drop of the balm of consolation. What she could say would be vain, for he considered her only as a sort of poor mad woman who had once loved him."

When the Lebanon flamed with revolt, she heard the tidings of his tragic end; the last human tie was severed, the last bond of family affection had broken down. Hester never recovered from her grief, and from that day she never stepped outside the gates of Djoun.

CHAPTER TWENTY-FIVE

AFTER her brother's death Lady Hester sought comfort in the study of medicine and astrology. "She read very few books and trusted to the stars for her sublime knowledge, and her nights were spent in communing with those heavenly teachers." She began to dabble in magic and necromancy, allowing herself to believe in the credulous legends reported by the ignorant Arabs.

The visitors who came to Dahr Djoun were at a loss what to make of her rambling, disconnected tales of human-headed serpents in the caves of Tarsus and magic sticks which led the way to secret treasure hoards. At times she would interrupt these strange tales of Eastern magic with shrewd, piercing remarks on the political situation in Europe, showing a critical insight into the characters of the leading statesmen of the day. For a brief flash her drawling voice and trenchant wit would recall the brilliant drawing-rooms of the eighteenth century. The blue eyes would sparkle and Hester Stanhope's rare, enchanting smile would cast a spell over her listener.

Dr. Madden, who was later to gain fame as the friend and biographer of the 'gorgeous' Lady Blessington, visited her in 1827 and described Djoun as an enchanted palace. The gates of the mountain fortress opened and he entered into a world of murmuring fountains and luxuriant gardens. In a *kiosque* of roses an excellent dinner with the choicest wines was served to him by mute black slaves. It might have been the background of a tale from the Arabian Nights, and at sunset he was introduced into the darkened chamber of his mysterious hostess. For seven hours they conversed on every subject connected with oriental learning, and the doctor records that "every observation of her Ladyship was couched in such eloquent and energetic language as to impress me with the idea that I was conversing with a woman of no ordinary intellect. The peculiarity of some of her opinions in no wise detracted from the general profundity of her reflections; and though I could not assent to many of her notions, regarding astral influence and astrological science, I had still no reason to alter my opinion of her exalted talents, though it might appear, they were unfortunately directed to very speculative studies. . . . I am quite sure that whatever may be the eccentricity of Lady Hester Stanhope, that few women can boast of more real genius, and none of more active benevolence."

Within the first two hours of their interview she acquainted him with "every peculiar lineament of his mind, with as much facility and correctness as if she had been tracing those of his countenance." Though she informed him that craniology and physiognomy were but secondary sciences, Madden considered that she drew her deductions far more from these sciences than from consulting the stars. At this time Lady Hester had no European doctor in her service, and Madden was invited to stay for several days in order to treat her bad eyes. Every night he was entertained to her interminable monologues. Canning and Castlereagh were amongst those who were submitted to her severe censure; faithful to her old affections, she paid a eulogistic tribute to the memory of the Duke of York, harking back to the golden days when she reigned at Downing Street. Dr. Madden was enthralled "by the society of a person, whose originality and eccentricity was a far less prominent feature in her character than her extensive information, her intrepidity of speech and her courteous manners."

Years later, when he sat in the garish luxury of Lady Blessington's overcrowded drawing-room, with all the *literati* and *illuminati* of intellectual London gathering round Bulwer Lytton, while he instructed his fair hostess in the new science of crystal-gazing, Madden must have thought back to the prophetess of Mount Lebanon, in her dark, smoke-laden room, telling him in her slow, deep voice "that the practice of such arts was unholy as well as vulgar and would be derogatory to her high rank in the heavenly kingdom."

Other travellers had not the slightest compunction in denouncing Lady Hester as mad. Count Léon Laborde, who accompanied his father to Djoun in 1827, looked upon her as a crazy old woman. The fortified castle, which was nothing more than a series of detached dwellings enclosed within high walls, gave him the impression of a lunatic asylum. The interior struck him as bourgeois, and his last illusion vanished when Miss Williams offered him a cup of tea in what he termed 'the accents of the Strand.' He and his father were admitted to their hostess at midnight, and the critical young Frenchman found fault with every detail of her appearance. He saw no beauty in the long, bony face, with the sunken eyes and sharp, aquiline nose, and he disapproved of her costume, which struck him as awkward and inappropriate. "But how could masculine apparel worn by a woman, and an Englishwoman at that, look otherwise? Even her majestic airs did not seem natural to her, while the furniture of her room, a mixture of the Oriental and the English, was in the worst of taste." Altogether the young man did not have one word to say in Lady Hester's favour, and when she began telling him quite seriously of the prophecies of Metta and of 'the boy without a father,' whom for some reason she believed to be the Duc de Reichstadt, he could hardly control his laughter. He finally dissolved into hysterics when she brought him a white egg plant, claiming that she had discovered the original Adam's Apple. Pleading a somewhat bald excuse, he took his leave and went to bed, shaking with helpless mirth.

Many visitors came to Djoun without ever seeing their hostess. Lord and Lady Belmore, those indefatigable travellers, who had often met Lady Hester during their peregrinations in the Holy Land, were merely treated to the attentions of her housekeeper; and at other times complete strangers were welcomed with the warmest hospitality.

The young Duc de Richelieu was honoured to the point that he was invited to dine *tête-à-tête* with his hostess, a mark of courtesy which was accorded to very few. And Hester's old love of quizzing asserted itself, when she told him plainly that he had nothing of a duke about him, for he neither looked like one nor talked like one. She went so far as to tease him about a *belle marquise* who, by a shrewd guess, she thought to be his *chère amie*, which showed that the Sibyl of the mountains could still take an interest in worldly topics.

The visitor who made the most impression on her was a Polish nobleman, Count Rewiczki, who, under the pseudonym of Deltophilus, had gained considerable distinction as a translator of Greek manuscripts. He had been in correspondence with Lady Hester long before they met, for he had allowed his mind to become completely obsessed by the occult sciences, and he was convinced that her star ruled his destiny. In different times of crisis she had appeared to him in his dreams, deciding him on what course of action to pursue, and he regarded her as a benignant influence in his life. During his short stay at Djoun, Hester's inordinate vanity and restless ambition were at peace, but, alas! these happy interludes were all too rare. She was beset on every side by creditors, and at times she talked of leaving her goods and chattels in their hands and of throwing herself on the charity of the nomad tribes. She pictured herself wandering out into the desert, leading the mare from the stable of Solomon and bearing a sheaf of the corn of Beni-Israel. This corn was a special kind of wheat with a fourfold ear, which she regarded as sacred.

James had left her an annuity of fifteen hundred pounds, but her debts and liabilities were so vast that only a considerable fortune could save her.

In 1826 she was the dupe of a wretched impostor, who said that he had been sent from England by His Royal Highness the Duke of Sussex and an influential company of Freemasons in order to inquire into the state of her finances and supply her with fresh funds. Poor Lady Hester was only too ready to believe in this fantastic story, and for months the adventurer lived at her expense without her ever seeing a farthing of the promised riches. The natives of Sidon and Beyrout, the merchants and usurers, and the poor whom she had befriended in their times of trouble, waited for the treasure ship which would relieve the distress of their beloved *Sytt*; for the simple people still loved and venerated her, and many a dun would knock at her gates and go away empty-handed, awed and abashed by her magnificent pride.

Finally Lady Hester discovered that she had been tricked and abused by a miserable set of swindlers, and Dr. Meryon was kept busy in England by tracing all the people who had been implicated in the fraud, but he never discovered the real instigator.

In her neatly kept ledger Miss Williams noted down that Milady's debts amounted to nearly ten thousand pounds, but a score of workmen were still employed in her house, which had now assumed the proportions of an enclosed village, far larger than the small hamlet which nestled in the valley.

When the news of the battle of Navarino re-echoed across the Mediterranean, fanning the flame of religious fanaticism in every Moslem breast, all the Christian merchants of Sidon fled from the town and sought refuge in the Englishwoman's castle. Hester had never had any sympathy with her co-religionists, for there was very little to be said in favour of the Syrian Christians, but the gates of Djoun were thrown open to all those in distress and the neighbouring peasants were commanded to yield part of their stores of grain, so as to feed the starving refugees. She spared neither her own nor her companion's strength in order to supply comforts for the people she despised, and by the time they returned to their own homes, both she and Elizabeth Williams were so weak and exhausted that they fell victims to an epidemic of yellow fever.

Left to the care of quack Arab doctors, with no white woman to nurse them, at the mercy of ignorant black slaves and thieving Syrian maids, they lay amidst crumpled blankets in dirty, untidy rooms. The store-rooms were rifled, the coffers were opened, the very hangings were torn down from the walls, and for the first time Lady Hester was powerless in the hands of her servants. Occasionally she would rouse herself sufficiently to send her companion some medicinal preparation. One morning she ordered her a dose of salts and senna, never stopping to question if the maid had mixed it in the right proportions. There can be little doubt that this black dose caused poor Miss Williams's death, for she was never free of its action until she expired the next morning. An old sewing woman from the village related how the body retained its natural heat for a whole day after the heart stopped beating, while the cheeks still kept their normal colour "and something kept bubbling inside her like boiling water." An Arab doctor was called in and opened a vein, and the blood spurted out as from a living person, but life never returned. These strange phenomenas terrified the superstitious servants, who fled from the house, leaving only two black slaves and a little Metoualy girl, eight years old, to attend on her Ladyship. Hester's affliction over her companion's death reduced her to a state of delirium and her screams re-echoed in the deserted corridors. There was no one to wash her or to give her food. Utterly neglected and surrounded by filth, Chatham's granddaughter was left alone to die. By chance a rich peasant happened to be passing through the village and heard of her sad plight. He rode up to the gates of Djoun and the little Metoualy girl admitted him to the empty courtyards and silent gardens. After traversing a hundred trellised passages he came to Lady Hester's chamber, and found her stiff and cold and dying of hunger. He summoned a village woman, and together they nursed her back to life. Her wonderful spirit helped her to combat her physical weakness and, though she grieved bitterly over Miss Williams's untimely end, in a few weeks she was to be found sitting up in bed entertaining Monsieur Beaudin with some particularly lively anecdotes of the famous Duke of Dorset. Hearing of her illness, her ex-dragoman had proved his devotion by coming all the way from Damascus with a substantial sum of money with which to pay her most pressing debts. There were still some men who were content to be her satellites.

The sycamore trees of the convent of Dahr El Mkhallas wept over Miss Williams's grave, and a rough hedge of cactus kept the jackals from scratching for her corpse. During her lifetime she had done her best to preserve an atmosphere of elegance and decorum in the gloomy rooms of Djoun. Gentle and retiring by nature, she had been forced to shoulder every domestic burden of an untrained, uncivilized household. Lady Hester had every reason to bewail the loss of her faithful companion. Maids came and went, each more inefficient than the last; secretaries were engaged to organize her correspondence and Italian major-domos to supervize the comforts of her guests, but everything went to rack and ruin. Packing-cases full of provisions and domestic utensils arrived from Marseilles and were left mouldering in damp granaries, because Lady Hester was too immersed in her sublime reflections to supervize the unpacking. When Dr. Meryon came back to Syria in the late autumn of 1830, he was horrified by the state of chaos which reigned at Djoun.

Meryon had gone through many vicissitudes in England. He had wasted the most valuable years of his youth in Lady Hester's service, and he was unable to make any headway in his profession. Mrs. Meryon was a delicate, well-born woman, who expected every kind of luxury and attention. Already in 1823, Lady Hester had written asking him to return to his old post, and she had been bitterly offended when he had excused himself on the grounds that he was bound by a previous professional engagement to Sir Gilbert Heathcote. However, in 1827 he was glad enough to avail himself of her offer, and she even went so far as to overrule her dislike of her own sex, by suggesting that she would build his family a cottage in the grounds of Djoun. But his journey was doomed to misfortune. The ship had already got as far as Cyprus when it was overtaken by some Greek privateers, so that all the passengers were forced to return to Leghorn. Mrs. Meryon's nerves were shattered, and for the next three years her husband was kept running between London, Leghorn and Marseilles before she could make up her mind to brave the perils of another voyage. Meanwhile, Lady Hester wrote anxious letters urging him not to delay his journey. These letters strike one as very pathetic coming from a haughty woman, who in sheer loneliness and despair now longed for the companionship of the doctor whom she had formally despised. She had no sympathy for Mrs. Meryon's fears and tears, and she said quite plainly that it would be wiser to leave her at home.

By the time they reached Beyrout, in the late autumn of 1830, Lady Hester had worked herself into a state of indignation and fury against the woman, who had not only been responsible for keeping her husband away from his employment, but who in the end had insisted on accompanying him, when it was quite clear that she was not wanted. Lady Hester's sarcastic tongue had always been particularly eloquent on the subject of henpecked husbands, and she resolved to ignore Mrs. Meryon's existence. There was no longer any question of finding them a lodging in the grounds of Djoun, and a cottage in the village was prepared for their reception.

In her note of welcome to the doctor she informed him "that his family must not expect any other attentions from her than such as would make them comfortable in their cottage; that they were not to take this ill on her part, as she had long before apprized him that she did not think English ladies could make themselves happy in Syria, and that therefore he who had brought them must take the consequences."

This was hardly an amicable beginning, and the doctor realized that his situation was going to be somewhat strained. Mrs. Meryon was left to the care of Milady's Levantine secretary and her husband proceeded to Djoun, where he was overwhelmed by the warmth of his reception. Gone were the days when he was treated with superior condescension; now he was honoured with every mark of attention. Lady Hester greeted him "with apparent pleasure, kissing him on both cheeks, ordering sorbets, the pipes, coffee and orange water, all of which civilities at meeting were regarded in the East as marks of the most cordial and distinguished regard." His astonishment was increased when she insisted on him sitting beside her on the sofa, a privilege which had always been denied him.

At first sight she looked very much the same as when he had seen her last. The years had dealt kindly with her. Her skin was still of an astonishing whiteness, and though she had finally been reduced to wearing spectacles, her blue eyes still retained their old fire, while her commanding figure had lost none of its grace and majesty, yet gradually he noticed that her ample draperies were cleverly arranged so as to conceal the excessive thinness of her body and the slight hunchback which had developed during her long illnesses. Her teeth were rotting and her nails were cracked, and in the hard light of day one could see that she was an old woman; but muffled in her *abah*, swathed in her cashmere shawls, sitting in a darkened room lit by a single candle, she was a figure which might have inspired the pencil of a Michael Angelo or a Guercino. When she spoke in her drawling, melodious voice, that voice that could subjugate and fascinate, Meryon was once more enthralled. He forgot his wife and child waiting for him in their new home; he forgot any claims and obligations they might lay on him, and for twelve hours he listened to Lady Hester recounting her various misfortunes and troubles, her far-reaching political schemes and sublime dreams. He dined with her in her shabby drawing-room, and in his honour she pulled out from under her sofa pillow the few remaining silver spoons and forks which she had been able to save from the rapacity of her servants. He was shocked by her poverty, shocked that she, the most fastidious of all great ladies, could be content to dine off broken china, serving herself with a bone-handled knife and drinking out of a cracked glass. As for her bedroom, it was hardly better than a common peasant's. Her bedstead was made of planks nailed together on low trestles, and a drab felt covered the ground. Everything was in confusion. Even the dirty red curtain was torn off its hinges, cobwebs covered her books and hundreds of odds and ends littered her tables, while scissors, spectacles, pipes and every kind of medicament were thrown pell-mell on the dusty shelves. An earthenware jug and a copper basin served for her toilet, and a walnut box draped with a piece of calico was her only wardrobe. A black slave slept on a cushion at the door of her room, and her one luxury was the adjoining Turkish bath. How far removed it all seemed from the cool Adam drawing-room of Montagu Square, where Lady Hester had received him for the first time.

It was past midnight when Meryon returned to his cottage, where he was met with tears and reproaches. Poor man! it must have been an impossible life, trying to conciliate both his patient and his wife. On the one occasion when Milady consented to receive Mrs. Meryon, the latter committed the unpardonable offence of refusing to accept the magnificent robe of ceremony with which Lady Hester invested her on her arrival. Nervous and bewildered by her surroundings, lending an eager ear to all the frightening stories of plagues and dangers, Mrs. Meryon found it impossible to acclimatize herself. Her husband, who had been so loving and considerate, was deaf to all her entreaties, and spent the best part of his day and night with an autocratic old virago who refused to treat her with common civility. He allowed himself to be bullied and commanded by a woman who was too poor to pay him a salary, but too proud to receive his wife. He appeased her creditors and organized her household. He acted as her secretary and read aloud to her at night the memoirs of Lady Charlotte Bury and Nathaniel Wraxall, books which he had brought from England as being those most likely to entertain her.

Mrs. Meryon was systematically neglected; the well-bred, educated Englishwoman was ostracized, while her Ladyship still maintained friendly relations with that perfidious Pasha of Acre, who had never lifted a finger to help her during her warfare with Bechir. She flattered herself that he listened to her political advice and took her scoldings in good part, and in the spring of 1831 she spent many hours in making designs for the new pleasure gardens, which he was destined never to enjoy. The nomads of the desert were always sure of a warm welcome at Djoun and any learned Jew was given hospitality, for Hester still dreamed of the day when she was to be crowned in the Temple of Jerusalem.

Mrs. Meryon raised her eyebrows in disapproval over some of her Ladyship's guests. There was Hamady, the hangman of Mount Lebanon, with his black, rolling eyes and nervous, jerky gait, who was a constant visitor at Djoun, and Mrs. Meryon declared that her Ladyship could not be so fastidious if she consented to receive a common Jack Ketch. Even the doctor could not hide his surprise when Lady Hester invited him to split a bottle of champagne with her strange friend, whose religious principles did not prevent him from taking spirits. Hamady was useful to her; his visit was sufficient to reduce her serving maids to a state of blind obedience, for his instruments of torture were unpleasant sights for an uneasy conscience. He was the friend and confidential adviser of the Emir Bechir, but this in no wise interfered in his relations with Lady Hester, and it was he who counselled his master to leave the intrepid Englishwoman in peace, telling him "You had better have nothing to do with her. Fair or foul means, it is all alike to her. She has been so flattered in her life that no praise can turn her head. Money she thinks no more of than dirt, and as for fear, she does not know what it is."

While Hamady drank Lady Hester's champagne, Mrs. Meryon sat in her lonely cottage waiting for her husband's return. No open quarrel arose between her and Lady Hester until the early spring, when there was a question of Meryon going to Damascus in order to attend a pasha who lay dangerously ill. This pasha was one of her Ladyship's oldest friends, and she not only commanded, she even begged her doctor to go to his assistance, but Mrs. Meryon was obdurate. She refused to be left alone in a strange country. The plague was raging at Damascus, and why should her husband run the risk of being contaminated for the sake of a wretched Turk? Lady Hester's vanity was at stake, and she used all the means in her power to persuade Mrs. Meryon to change her mind. She flattered and cajoled, she stormed and threatened; for the first time in twenty years someone dared to contradict her openly, to defy her wishes in her own domain. From now onwards Mrs. Meryon was treated as an enemy. She was subjugated to endless humiliations. Lady Hester's servants were sent to revile her within hearing of the whole village. When the peasants heard that she had incurred the anger of the *Sytt* they refused to supply her with provisions, for not one of them dared to risk losing the favour of the mistress of Dahr Djoun. Meryon soon found the situation intolerable, and in the summer of 1831 he suggested returning to England. At first Lady Hester refused to consent to his departure, and he knew that it would be impossible for him to leave without her permission. Every muleteer and camel driver in the neighbourhood was attached to her service; none of the Consuls on the coast dared to go against her orders, and both Abdallah and Bechir remembered too well the warnings of the Sublime Porte. The Meryons were prisoners till her Ladyship chose to relent. Once she had asserted her authority she was ready to be kind and reasonable, and she herself chartered a boat for their journey to Cyprus, and loaded them with presents on their departure.

Her last interview with the doctor was characteristic of her. She invited him to drink tea with her one evening, and in the middle of a conversation she sent him out of the room on a trifling message. When he returned, he found the door of her chamber locked and barred, and one of her maids brought him the message that her Ladyship would see him no more so as to save them both the pain of saying farewell.

CHAPTER TWENTY-SIX

THROUGH the Sultan's obstinacy the pride of Mehemet Ali's fleet had been destroyed at Navarino. In all the viceroy's domains, in the lush meadows of Upper Egypt, in the sands of the Sudan and the salt deserts of Arabia, there was no timber from which to rebuild his vanished ships, and once more his eyes turned towards Syria, to the waving pines of Fahkredin shadowing the orange sands of Beyrout, to the sacred cedars on the slopes of Lebanon. He was tired of being the Sultan's vassal, of enriching the treasuries of Stamboul through the conquests of his son, and in the late autumn of 1831 he sent a peremptory despatch to Acre, commanding Abdallah Pasha to deport the two hundred Egyptian fellahs whom he had taken under his protection. Abdallah refused, and in November, 1831, Acre was invaded by land and sea.

From his palace of Iptedin in the interior of the mountains Bechir waited for future developments. He offered no help to Abdallah but neither did he commit himself by siding openly with the Egyptians. He had to be certain of their victory before he ventured to declare himself as their ally; before he sold the independence of his people for the sake of Mehemet Ali's friendship.

How different was the attitude of Hester Stanhope. She had no quarrel with the Egyptian viceroy. Years ago he had received her with singular courtesy in the Usbekieh palace. She was an admirer of his reforms and she regarded his son Ibrahim as one of the greatest war heroes of his age. She had no real affection for Abdallah Pasha, who had never shown her any gratitude or consideration, but she had sworn to defend the Sultan's power against all usurpers and aggressors, and when Boghoz Bey, Mehemet Ali's favourite minister, wrote warning her not to interfere in political affairs, she answered him: "Sir, I once knew, when I was in Egypt, a Mr. Boghoz, a polite and accomplished gentleman, who left very agreeable impressions of himself in my memory. I hear now there is a Boghoz Bey, the minister of His Highness the Viceroy of Egypt, and that he has joined in a revolution with his master against his legitimate sovereign. If Boghoz Bey would listen to me, I would tell him that partial revolutions never succeed, and that I never thought well of them. The lot of those who rise against their lawful sovereign has always been unfortunate. Show me an example of a usurper who has not ended badly. . . . The column of power which Mehemet Ali has raised will melt away like snow before the sun, as soon as his good fortune has come to its zenith. I cannot change my opinion, and Boghoz Bey need not attempt to make me." And Ibrahim Pasha, the invincible, all-destroying conqueror, had no wish to make himself a laughing-stock by embroiling himself with the mad old Englishwoman.

Abdallah's Albanian mercenaries put up a brave front against the Egyptian armies. The town held out for seven months and even the unstable, lascivious pasha displayed heroic qualities. But all his valour was of no avail against the cannons of Mehemet Ali. At the feast of *Bairam* the Porte struck out the names of Mehemet Ali and Ibrahim from the list of the pashas of the Empire, but not a single ship was sent in aid of the desperate garrisons of Acre.

The town fell on the 7th May, 1832, and was given over to plunder. When Abdallah was taken prisoner, he said with pride, "I had walls, men and money with which to defend Acre; when Ibrahim took it, the walls had been destroyed; of my six thousand men, five thousand six hundred were dead, and of my treasures nothing remained but a few jewels," and he added bitterly that "the Porte had the honour of a dancing girl."

Ibrahim's triumphant armies marched upon Beyrout and Damascus, on Homs and Aleppo, and in despair the frightened Sultan of Stamboul solicited the aid of his old enemy the Czar.

From her fortress in the Lebanon, Hester Stanhope hurled defiance at the invaders. Mutilated soldiers and penniless widows, bearing naked children in their arms, wounded

mamelukes and helpless orphans came fleeing to the mountains, begging for the *Sytt's* protection, and once more Djoun
was crowded with the homeless and the destitute. For three
years seventy-five refugees were housed in the grounds, and the
last survivors of Abdallah's Albanian soldiers were converted
into her Ladyship's armed guard. When the prisoners of the
Sultan's defeated armies, taken after the battle of Homs, were
marched by Sidon, not a single Turk or Christian dared to
give them as much as a glass of water, and they would have
died of thirst and starvation if Lady Hester had not sent her
servants to feed them in the market place.

At first Ibrahim behaved with exemplary patience. There
was no point in offending the woman who had obtained such an
ascendancy over the people and who was the friend and ally of
the dangerous nomad tribes in the unknown wilderness of the
Syrian desert. But his polite emissaries were answered with
violence and his offers of friendship were rudely ignored. He
complained to his father, who lodged a formal protest with
Colonel Campbell, the British Consul-General at Alexandria,
requesting her Ladyship to produce a complete list of the people
to whom she had given protection. Colonel Campbell was
only too willing to comply with this very reasonable demand,
but Lady Hester returned him his letter unopened, and during
the first few years of the Egyptian occupation she remained
free and unmolested, holding despotic sway over her own small
territory and the neighbouring villages.

When Alphonse de Lamartine landed at Beyrout, in September, 1832, he found the town in the hands of an Egyptian
governor. Mehemet Ali had not yet enforced his hated monopolies, and Ibrahim was still regarded as a saviour by the people,
while Europeans were treated with a courtesy they had never
known under Turkish rule. Bechir, the prince of the Lebanon,
had proclaimed his alliance with the conqueror, and after the
battle of Konia the Sultan had been forced to leave the rich
pashaliks of Syria in the hands of his hated vassal. Lamartine
was both an idealist and a poet and he viewed the political

situation in Syria through a pair of very rosy spectacles. He had not been long in Beyrout before he heard tales of the 'wondrous white woman of the mountains' whom Monsieur Poujoulat once described as 'the most interesting ruin of the Lebanon.'

Lady Hester, who in these days opened her doors to very few travellers of note, was too vain to resist the entreaties of a stranger who wrote, "Milady, like you, I am a traveller and a stranger in the East; like you, I have only come in search of beauty, the beauty of nature, of ruins, and of the works of God. . . . I shall reckon as the most memorable day of my journey, the one in which I shall have met the woman, who is herself one of the marvels of the East."

Lamartine's name was famous throughout Europe, but it had no familiar sound for Lady Hester's ears. The ghosts of another century filled her world, and the woman who had sneered at Byron was not likely to have any interest in the verses of the French Romantics. Never for a moment did he suspect that she consented to receive him for no better reason than that his letter pleased her.

Lamartine's description of the evening he spent at Dahr Djoun is tinged with poetic licence. The fierce Albanians hanging round the courtyards; the squalling cats whom her Ladyship regarded as sacred animals; the dilapidation of the building and the shabbiness of the rooms were sublimely ignored. From the glaring sunlight of a September afternoon, Lamartine passed into the darkened cloister of the 'Circe of the deserts,' and he writes, "It was so extremely dark, that with difficulty I could distinguish her noble, grave, yet mild and majestic features. . . . The lady appears to be about fifty years of age but possesses those peculiar features which years cannot alter: freshness, colour and grace depart with youth; but when beauty resides in the form itself, in purity of expression, in dignity, in majesty, in a thoughtful countenance, whether in man or woman, beauty may change with the different periods of life, but it does not pass away; such is the person of Lady Hester Stanhope."

At the time of the poet's visit Lady Hester's fortunes were at their lowest ebb. Every article of value she possessed was in the hands of her creditors; and all her jewels had been lost in the shipwreck twenty years before. She gloried in her rags. When her doctor had visited her in 1830, she had said to him, "After all, what is dress? Look at my ragged doublet, it is not worth sixpence; do you suppose that affects my value? I warrant you Sultan Mahmoud would not look at that if he saw me." But Lamartine could not resist dressing her in a tunic of Persian brocade fastened by a clasp of pearls.

She talked to him of the stars, of the future and of the coming of the Messiah. She expounded her strange religious *credo*, which he was bold enough to question, though, like her, he hoped for the coming of one who would redress the social, political and religious abuses of his age. From his eyes and his brow she knew him to be a poet, while Mercury was his guiding star; and she told him quite bluntly that she had never heard his name, which could hardly have pleased anyone as famous and as self-centred as Lamartine. Hester, who read so clearly into the minds of men, realized that she had offended the vanity of a poet, and she proceeded to flatter him by saying that also the sun had an influence over his destiny and that, because of the affinity in their stars, they were destined to meet again. As a mark of her especial favour she showed him the holy mares and she kept him talking late into the night.

Lamartine little knew that "that tender smile, that radiant look, which had something almost divine," was not above noticing and criticizing his smallest defects and mannerisms. Lonely and starved for company, Hester was grateful for an audience. She was willing to hold forth on her heavenly visions to any willing listener, but her mocking spirit and wonderful gift of mimicry had not deserted her, and how could she resist making fun of a man who affected dandyism to the point of carrying a pet lap dog under his arm on whom he showered every term of endearment? She considered him very humorous, "with his straight body and straight fingers and self-conscious airs and graces"; it amused her to see how he flushed with pleasure when she told him that, like her, he had the foot of the East, the Arabian foot, and though she enjoyed his company, he was grievously mistaken if he thought to have made a great effect. She gave him a letter of introduction to Abu Ghosh, the chieftain of Judæa, and was quite frankly annoyed when she heard that he had tried to pass himself off as a great man in Europe, for, barring herself, there was no room in Syria for any other great Europeans.

In his 'Souvenirs de l'Orient' Lamartine paid a gracious and beautiful tribute to Lady Hester Stanhope's memory. He evoked the glamour of her name for a new generation who had never heard of her existence. The most fervid of all romantics recaptured the spirit of an eighteenth-century eccentric. "The elegant versifier, the man who behaved like a humbler kind of dandy," brought the name of Hester Stanhope into the full blaze of publicity and he was one of the few who acknowledged openly that, had she wanted it, she could have secured herself an enormous material position in the East. He not only paid a tribute to her brilliant talents, but he defended her sanity. "Lady Hester is not mad: madness, which is written so strongly in the eyes, is not expressed in her beautiful and amiable look; folly, which always betrays itself in conversation, interrupting the sequence by irregular, eccentric and sudden departures from the subject, is in no wise to be perceived in the elevated, mystic and cloudy, but well-sustained and connected conversation of her Ladyship. If I were to pronounce, I should rather say that it is a studied, a voluntary madness, conscious of itself and acting from peculiar motives. The strong admiration which her genius has kindled, and still attracts among the Arab population surrounding the mountains, sufficiently proves that this affected madness is but a policy. The men inhabiting this country of prodigies—those men of rocks and deserts—whose imagination is higher coloured and yet more cloudy than the horizon of their sands and their seas, act according to the word of Mahomet and Lady Hester Stanhope. They require a commerce with the stars, with prophecies, miracles and the second sight of genius: Lady Hester understood this, first by the exalted views of her truly superior intelligence, and in the sequel, perhaps like all beings endowed with powerful intellectual faculties, she deceives herself as well as others, and is become a convert to that faith she creates in them."

Lamartine and Kinglake, who both visited her during the last years of her life, agree that Hester Stanhope was in full possession of her faculties. She was normal on every subject except that of metaphysics, and when, following the publication of Lamartine's book, a strange Englishwoman, calling herself the Baroness de Feriat, wrote to her from America, announcing her intention of coming to Syria in order to pass the rest of her life with her, she was ready to believe that another part of Metta's prophecy was about to be fulfilled by "a woman coming from a far country to help in her mission." Whether this Baroness de Feriat was a mad woman or an impostor has never been ascertained. She wrote that she had once had a glimpse of Lady Hester thirty-eight years before and that she had never been able to forget her. Lamartine's book describing her courageous conduct and mode of life had decided her to sell her estates in America and to settle in Syria, so as to be near the woman she so ardently admired. It is amusing to think that Lady Hester, whose dislike of her own sex had increased with age, should have been quite willing to accept this strange woman in her house and that she even went so far as to spend a vast amount of money on building her a cottage in her garden, furnished with every luxury, while her own rooms were tumbling to rack and ruin.

While one defends Lady Hester's sanity, one cannot help admitting that at certain times she overstepped the borders, in which eccentricity becomes madness. Following Lord Camelford's example, she ordered a whole herd of goats to be killed, because the goatherd had been swindling her over the milk. If any of her servants were found to be riding her horses, the poor animals were immediately shot, though not before the bailiff had whispered in their ears a tender farewell from their mistress. She had adopted certain Metoualy customs and followed their example in never allowing anyone else to eat off her dishes. Her own kitchen was quite apart from that of her visitors, and the most honoured guest was not allowed to wipe his mouth with one of her napkins or to drink out of her glass, even if it was but an old chipped cup. Her week was divided into lucky and unlucky days—Wednesday was a day doomed to misfortune, and for twenty-four hours she would shut herself up in her room, refusing to have any business dealings or to see any of her servants. No wonder the neighbouring villagers looked upon her as mad, while the servants professed a kind of cult for her. In the East mad people are venerated as holy, and Lady Hester was allowed to indulge in her whims without losing any of her prestige.

In 1833, an English naval officer named Welstead was camping with some Bedouin tribesmen near Mount Sinai, when he overheard them discussing the sanity of Lady Hester Stanhope. "One party strenuously maintained that it was impossible that a lady so charitable, so munificent, could be otherwise than in full possession of her faculties. Their opponents alleged that her assuming herself to be the Virgin Mary, her anticipated entry with our Saviour into Jerusalem, and other vagaries attributed to her, were proofs to the contrary. An old man with a white beard called for silence (a call from the aged amidst the Arabs is seldom made in vain). 'She is mad,' said he and, lowering his voice to a whisper, as if fearful that such an outrage against established custom should spread beyond his circle, he added, 'for she puts sugar in her coffee.' This was conclusive."

So spread the ridiculous legends regarding Lady Hester's madness, but many a young man who came to Djoun went to bed "puzzled with all the various, curious, incoherent tales of magic" he had been told by his hostess, who had solemnly informed him that the Scots and Irish were descended from wandering Arab tribes, and that the Duke of Leinster's motto

'Crom-a-boo' alluded to the most learned of all Arab works. She always insisted that she herself was descended from the Koreish, a famous nomad tribe, whom for many years she had referred to as her family. Ignoring etymology, she based her deductions on the similarity of sounds in the pronunciation of names and words, and she even wrote a long letter on this subject to Sir Gore Ouseley, the well-known orientalist.

According to Joseph Bonhommie, a French archæologist who visited her in 1833, she kept up an active correspondence with the St. Simonians, that strange sect named after the Comte de St. Simon, whom many claim to have been the founder of modern socialism. Their present leader, Le Père Enfantin, had been imprisoned in Paris for his subversive doctrines and had now settled in Egypt, where he was still in search of the 'Mystic Mother,' who was destined to be the Messiah's bride. He had sent a delegation to Djoun, as well as a handsome present, which her Ladyship declined to accept. In her eyes Enfantin was a charlatan, who dared to pose as the Messiah; his morals were lax and he was said to be searching for his 'bride' among the courtesans of Cairo. "The sect might be destined to make great progress in Europe among the unlearned in Astrology, for Enfantin was in possession of a Kabalistic word, which he had shrewdness enough to turn to his advantage, but sooner or later it would be overthrown."

She again referred to the St. Simonians in a conversation with Alexander Kinglake, who came to Djoun in the late autumn of 1835, bringing her memories of the old days at Burton Pynsent when in her 'condescending kindness' she had sought the friendship of his mother's family.

Of all the diaries, memoirs and books of travel containing descriptions of Hester Stanhope in her Eastern home, none is more enthralling than *Eothen*. Kinglake was both a poet and a humorist. At twenty-six he had all the enthusiasm of youth combined with the tolerance of age, and the flowering phrases of Lamartine wilt beside the purple passages of *Eothen*. It was not without trepidation that he wrote to her

Ladyship from Beyrout, mentioning his mother's maiden name, and saying that if she had any wish to hear of her old Somersetshire acquaintance, he would make a point of visiting her. He had very little hope of being received, for the current gossip of Beyrout was that her Ladyship had shut her doors against all Europeans, especially her own compatriots, but Hester remembered 'the sweet, lovely girl' who, over thirty years ago, had accompanied her on her rides across Sedgemoor, and for Mrs. Kinglake's sake she consented to receive her son.

It was a dark, rainy night, when Kinglake was ushered into Lady Hester's presence. After being served with an excellent dinner and the choicest wines, he was led through wet court-yards and draughty corridors to the small chamber, where sat the lady prophetess. For "the woman before him had exactly the person of a prophetess—not indeed of the divine Sibyl imagined by Domenichino, so sweetly distracted between love and mystery, but of a good, businesslike, practical prophetess, long used to the exercise of her sacred calling." He was struck by the resemblance she bore her famous grandfather, and she somewhat intimidated him when, after a few perfunctory inquiries respecting his mother and her marriage, "she shuffled away the subject of poor, dear Somersetshire and bounded onward in loftier spheres of thought."

At Cambridge, Kinglake had occasionally dabbled in the occult sciences and he was able to bear a part, "though of course a very humble one" in the conversation. He asked her the very questions she delighted in answering and "she went so far as to say she would adopt him as her *élève* in occult science."

He was not really interested in her tales of sorcery and magic —in her rambling talk on religion and the stars; and only the fragrant fumes of the pipes, which were refilled every quarter of an hour, enabled him to keep up the attitude of a patient disciple.

"For hours and hours this wondrous white woman poured forth her speech; but every now and then she would stay her lofty flight and swoop down upon the world again; whenever this happened I was interested in her conversation."

It was thrilling to hear of her journeys in the desert, of the power she had once possessed over the Arab tribes, but which had now diminished through poverty and old age, and he admired the steadfast courage with which she defied the might of Mehemet Ali. Her curious obsessions and firm belief in her heavenly rank did not prevent her from being a magnificent survival of a dying aristocracy. When she descended from her high topics to more worldly chat then "she was no longer the prophetess, but the sort of woman that you sometimes see, I am told, in London drawing-rooms—cool, decisive in manner, unsparing of enemies, full of audacious fun, and saying the downright things that the sheepish society around her is afraid to utter. I am told that Lady Hester was, in her youth, a capital mimic; and she showed me that not all the queenly dulness to which she had condemned herself—not all the fasting and solitude had destroyed this terrible power."

To amuse her young visitor, Hester Stanhope gave some first-class imitations. After twenty-five years she recalled every one of Lord Byron's affectations and mannerisms, yet one feels that she might have had the gratitude not to ridicule and mimic Alphonse de Lamartine, who had championed her so nobly in his memoirs.

Kinglake spent two nights at Dahr Djoun and when he left he could say that, "in truth this half-ruined convent, guarded by the proud heart of an English gentlewoman, was the only spot throughout all Syria and Palestine in which the will of Mehemet Ali and his fierce lieutenant was not the law. . . . and so long as Chatham's granddaughter breathed a breath of life, there was always one hillock, and that too in the midst of a most populous district, which stood out and kept its freedom."

The Egyptian conqueror now held Syria in an iron grasp. He had seized the monopolies of the silk and tobacco trade and had enforced conscription with unparalleled brutality. White-bearded fathers were beaten with the *korbash* till they delivered over their sons, and able-bodied young men were seized in the market-place and shipped off to Egypt or marched to the Hedjaz. Under Turkish rule the soldiers had been hired mercenaries and the horrors of conscription were unknown in Syria. There was no definite term of service, for once a man had joined Ibrahim's army, he was a soldier until death or desertion broke the chain. The European Consuls abused their rights by selling protection to the sons of rich merchants, and the foreign *khans* were crowded with honorary dragomans and clerks, who had managed to evade conscription. Lady Hester still protected her Albanians, and when Ibrahim Pasha commanded her to deliver them up to him, she answered disdainfully that he was at liberty to come and take them by force, yet not one of his soldiers ever crossed her threshold.

Her old debts were steadily accumulating and she had incurred fresh ones by borrowing at enormous interest, in order to satisfy her most pressing creditors. Many visitors came to Djoun and were turned away, either because she was too ill to receive them or too poor to entertain them. They little realized how she had to exert herself in order to give them hospitality; there was not one servant on whom she could rely. If they asked for a lemonade, it was she who had to mix it with her own hands, and she had to supervise every detail of their dinner, from the ordering of the food to the setting of the table.

As soon as she received her quarterly allowance she would launch out in fresh extravagances. Cases of champagne and of every kind of delicacy were despatched from France to be distributed among her Syrian friends and protégées. Old Loustenau, who was still living at Mars Elias, was fed and clothed at her expense, and the irrepressible Pierre, who had saved enough money in her service to set himself up as an innkeeper at Deir El Kammar, was a continual recipient of her bounty, for not only was he a great favourite, but he was useful to her as a spy in the Emir's territory. She had secret agents scattered throughout the country, and in her mountain solitudes she was informed of the latest developments of the political situation. Hassan El Logmagi, the captain of the boat which had conveyed the Meryons to Cyprus, was now in her service. He had fought for Abdallah during the siege of Acre and his bravery and shrewdness had gained him her patronage. Maybe his good looks and jovial manner helped to influence her in his favour and she appointed him her purveyor, steward, emissary and general factotum in all transactions with the people of the country. He could always be relied upon to recount the kind of news which Lady Hester enjoyed hearing, and she some-times sent him on devious errands as far as Smyrna and Con-stantinople, from which he invariably returned with a fund of stories of how he had heard men speak of her greatness in the bazaars of Stamboul and of how her name was known in the most distant parts of the Empire. Logmagi was well paid for his services and his new house in Sidon was built at Lady Hester's expense.

Meanwhile her health went from bad to worse. Her Italian physician was a doctor only in name, for he was an ex-servant of her banker at Leghorn, who had recommended him as useful and dependable, and, because he was devoted to his mistress, he was allowed to style himself as doctor and to practise his profession in the neighbouring villages. Worn and emaciated, racked by a continual cough, vomiting blood, and in continual pain, Lady Hester's magnificent spirits never deserted her. She still cherished bright hopes of the future, and in 1836 she was under the delusion that a large property in Ireland was coming to her, which would help her to pay her debts.

Years before, a Colonel Needham had made a will, leaving his estates to Pitt out of gratitude for his public services. Un-fortunately Pitt predeceased him and the Colonel's property reverted to Lord Kilmorey, his rightful heir. Lady Hester was idealistic enough to imagine that Lord Kilmorey would leave her his estates, for no better reason than that she was Pitt's niece; and after his death she wrote to Captain Yorke, who had now become Lord Hardwicke, begging him to inquire into the disposal of the Kilmorey property. Lord Hardwicke informed her that her hopes were vain, but she persisted in her optimism, and, breaking a silence of many years, she wrote to her childhood's friend, Sir Francis Burdett, asking him to assist her in the claiming of the estate. At the same time, she wrote to Dr. Meryon, requesting him to return to Syria and to help her in the settling of her debts, for she was in daily expectation of a large legacy.

The doctor and his family were eking out a penurious existence at Nice, and this time even Mrs. Meryon raised no objection to a post which would at least entail free living. The doctor was delighted to accept the offer. He had amassed no riches in Lady Hester's service, but he had memorized a fund of stories; he had kept detailed diaries, recording her habits and conversation, and he had hopes of collecting enough material with which to fill a volume of memoirs. He had witnessed the interest that her name had aroused in recent publications, and by returning to Djoun he would have an invaluable opportunity of encouraging her Ladyship to recount those anecdotes which would be most interesting to his readers. In July, 1837, the Meryon family landed at Beyrout.

CHAPTER TWENTY-SEVEN

"WHAT, didn't those dogs of Druses have a single bullet for us?" cried Ibrahim Pasha within full hearing of his *Divan*, when they brought him the news that the Lebanon had been subdued without a single shot being fired.

It was not until 1836 that the Egyptians attempted the subjugation of the mountain, and then the perfidious Emir betrayed his people with that consummate hypocrisy which had kept him on his perilous throne for over fifty years. In the summer, while the Druses were busy with their harvest, Egyptian armies were marched in secret from Damascus and Tripoli, from Acre and Beyrout, till they surrounded the mountains on every side, penetrating into the heart of the capital, Deir El Kammar. When the regiments marched into the courtyard of the Emir's palace, he feigned such trepidation and alarm that his household were persuaded that he had been the dupe of Ibrahim's ambitious schemes. The hardy mountaineers, taken by surprise at their work, without arms with which to defend themselves, were forced to surrender, and the fastnesses of the Lebanon, the inaccessible villages and Crusader castles were in the hands of the Egyptian usurpers. This gigantic hoax had already been planned many months before by Mehemet Ali and the Emir Bechir, and now Ibrahim dealt the cruellest blow of all, by forcing the people to disarm. Those who resisted were beaten or put to death, but many managed to secrete their guns in the hidden mountain caves and it was not long before they realized that they had been sold by their own sovereign.

Druses, Maronites and Metoualys, the bravest people of Syria, had been conquered without bloodshed. Even Ibrahim was surprised, and his scathing words, overheard by Lady Hester's spies, served as the kindling torch to the Druse rebellion. Whenever a Druse sheik visited Dahr Djoun he was greeted by his hostess with the phrase, "Dog of a Druse, why hadn't you a single bullet for Ibrahim Pasha?" She made it a byword among her servants; in every quarter, through every channel, echoed the Pasha's words rousing the spirit of vengeance. When Ibrahim tried to enforce conscription, it was she who spread the seeds of revolt in the breasts of the independent mountaineers, so that thousands fled to the Hauran rather than submit to the foreign yoke. In these stony desert wastes they joined forces with the Bedouin Arabs and the winter of 1837 saw the outbreak of the Druse rebellion. Well could Mehemet Ali say that "the Englishwoman had given him more trouble than all the insurgent people of Syria and Palestine."

On his next return to Djoun, Dr. Meryon found his patient in a deplorable state of health. This time he had the sense to leave his family in Sidon, where he lodged them together with the mad general in the dilapidated convent of Mars Elias. He himself was getting old and blind and he was utterly incapable of disentangling Hester Stanhope's complicated affairs. His painstaking efforts were rewarded by querulous scoldings and bitter mockery. At one time Lady Hester would cajole and flatter him, the next minute she would treat him like the lowest servant, hurling rude Arabic epithets in his face, so that even her black slaves should be aware of his humiliation. Her nerves were frayed and she was so weak that she was unable to sit upright on the gentle mule on whom she would amble round the garden. Her flowers were now her only joy and, even when she was forced to stay in bed, she would sometimes stagger out at night into the moonlight, where for a moment she would find peace among the myrtle walks and scented arbours, overhung with a thousand roses. For days she was so weak that she could not even speak, and in such pain that she could not lift her head without feeling that she was going to suffocate, yet still she forced herself to eat what she considered to be invigorating foods, and the doctor was horrified to see her trying to stuff herself with spiced meat balls and indigestible sweetmeats in order to keep up the strength of her great frame.

She would lie in bed, suffering and irritable, always waiting for the letter from Sir Francis Burdett, which never came, and her bell would keep clanging through the house, for at no hour of the day or night could she let one of her servants rest in peace. She would call them all ungrateful, thieving wretches, but when Meryon suggested her getting rid of some of them, she invariably gave him the same answer: "Doctor, think of my rank." "She had a munificence that would have required the revenue of a kingdom to satisfy." Carpenters and masons would be sent at her order to build some poor man's house; clothes, furniture and bales of wheat would be given to anyone who kissed the hem of her garment and called her 'Queen'; yet at the same time she had adopted the methods of an Eastern despot and she thought nothing of sending her fierce Albanians to commandeer her provisions from the neighbouring villages.

Meanwhile the duns beset her house, and her debts were the chief topics in the bazaars of Sidon and Beyrout. Through the friendship of the French Consul, Monsieur Guys, she was still able to raise ready money with which to pay her servants and household expenses, but bankruptcy stared her in the face. English subjects were under the jurisdiction of their Consuls, however much Lady Hester might declare that they had no rights over the nobility but only over merchants. For many years her life certificate had been signed by Monsieur Guys and she had remained firm in her resolution not to have any dealings with the British agents at Beyrout. But now her creditors were waxing impatient and already in 1834 a usurer named Homsy had applied to the Consul, Mr. Moore, for the payment of his money. Mr. Moore, having no inclination for a passage at arms with the irascible lady, had declined to interfere in the matter, so Homsy had been forced to apply to higher quarters and had sent his petition direct to Mehemet Ali, who had demanded Colonel Campbell, the British Consul-General at Alexandria, to obtain payment of the debt.

For three years the unfortunate Consul-General was in correspondence with the Foreign Office on the subject of

Lady Hester's creditors, but as long as the Duke of Wellington remained in power no drastic action was taken. The Consul's letters to Lady Hester remained unanswered and in 1837 Homsy's debt was still unpaid. Mehemet Ali reminded Colonel Campbell politely "that whenever claims were brought forward by British merchants against Turks the most ready attention was paid to them, and therefore British subjects should be equally obliged to pay their just debts to the natives of the country."

This time Colonel Campbell's complaints were addressed to Lord Palmerston, the Secretary of State for Foreign Affairs of Her Majesty Queen Victoria. His Lordship was a politician of the new school and, unlike the Duke, he had never known Hester Stanhope in her brilliant youth. As a boy of nineteen he had once waited in Pitt's anteroom, too young and too obscure to be honoured by an invitation to dinner, and now he had no scruples in dictating the cruel sentence that her Ladyship's pension should be confiscated until she had paid off her debts.

A year ago the news had transpired in the bazaars that the Viceroy of Egypt had complained to the King of England on the subject of her debts, but Hester Stanhope had laughed at the idea of a 'dirty' Consul setting himself the task of controlling her affairs. She still held hopes of her Irish property, though her optimism waned as the months passed without bringing her any news. The rainy season set in and the water poured through the roof of her bedroom. The doctor had moved his family to the village of Djoun, but Lady Hester remained obstinate in refusing to receive either his daughter or his wife. They might have done much to relieve her discomfort, for her servants left everything in such a state of filth that now and then she would be forced to drag herself out of her bed, while the doctor supervised the cleaning of her room.

During a long, dreary winter Hester Stanhope lay in bed, occupying her restless fingers by cutting out paper patterns for her servants' clothes, ordering, lecturing, scolding and finally sobbing when she realized how little her lectures and scoldings were taken into account. Occasionally she would rouse her spirits when spies brought her the latest news of the Druse revolt, and her blue eyes would flash fire when she heard that Ibrahim's armies had been defeated in the Hauran. But Mehemet Ali had now a weapon in his hand with which to fight the invincible Englishwoman.

One winter night when the wind howled in the mountains and the rain beat against the rocks, a dervish knocked at the gates of Djoun. He was served with food, for no stranger was suffered to go away hungry from Lady Hester's doors, but, owing to her illness and her poverty, he was given neither alms nor a night's lodging. Clothed in nothing but a bearskin, with his tangled beard falling on his naked breast, with his raven locks and wild, rolling eyes, he must have been a frightening figure as he stood cursing the inmates of the house, who refused to give him *baksheesh*. Taking a horn from his side, he blew three blasts invoking the anger of God on the English *Sytt*. Even Meryon felt nervous and uneasy as he turned him away from the gates, while the servants crept down the gloomy corridors, fearful and apprehensive.

Only a few days later, the English Consul at Sidon came trudging up the hill bearing Colonel Campbell's fateful letter. The Consul-General emphasized that it was with reluctance and pain that he felt himself imperatively called upon to address her Ladyship on the subject of her debts. He reminded her of the previous letters, which she had never answered, and he informed her that, following the instructions of Lord Palmerston, he would be forced to take measures to prevent the French or any other foreign Consul from signing her life certificate which enabled her to draw her pension. Hester Stanhope was faced with penury. Charles's legacy and her mother's small inheritance had already been squandered many years ago. She still had her annuity from James, but what was fifteen hundred pounds to anyone with Pitt blood in her veins? She read the letter with a stony calm. The woman who stormed and raged when the gardener planted a field with lettuce instead of potatoes, who beat her servants if they ever dared to question one of her orders, was now quiet, almost gentle, as she read of the cruel slight which the ministers of the young Queen had dared to inflict on her. She, whose grandfather and uncle had been responsible for keeping the house of Brunswick on the throne, was to be deprived of her pension in a foreign country, where, for all they cared, she might starve to death. Where would the Queen be now if her brother Charles had not defended the Duke of Kent during the mutiny at Gibraltar—the Queen who dared to treat her as a common debtor and whose own mother had been dunned by creditors?

She was so calm that it was almost frightening, as she lay back in bed with the letter spread out before her, musing on the past, recollecting the words of the old King when he said "that she should have the greatest pension that could be granted to a woman," recollecting memories of Windsor Castle, of the Royal Dukes and of a vanished aristocracy whose very whims were laws. The young Queen was probably a good-natured German girl, helpless in the hands of her ministers. She remembered once seeing Lord Melbourne at a party sitting at the top of the stairs with his delicate little wife, an odd elf-like creature, daughter of her old rival Henrietta Bessborough. Lord Palmerston—was he the young Irishman just come down from college, who was always hanging about waiting to be introduced to her uncle?

It was her pride which now helped her to control her fury, so that even the doctor should not realize how deeply she was wounded. Did they think she would let them deprive her of her pension? No; she would resign it of her own free-will, and with it the name of a British subject. Let her debts be made public in the newspapers, so that English people should see how she had been treated by her family and their magnificent Queen. She replied to Colonel Campbell that she had no sort of an answer for his letter till she had seen a copy of her Majesty's commands or an official order from the Secretary of State for Foreign affairs.

Sitting up in bed, supported by pillows, her bones protruding through her skin, her lungs choked with phlegm, Hester Stanhope dictated a letter to the Queen.

"Madam. Your Majesty must allow me to say that few things are more disgraceful and inimical to royalty than giving commands without examining all their different bearings and to cast aspersion upon the integrity of any branch of a family who has faithfully served their country and the House of Hanover.

"As no inquiries have been made of what circumstances induced me to incur the debts alluded to by your Majesty's Secretary of State for Foreign Affairs, I deem it unnecessary to enter into any details or explanations upon the subject. But I shall not allow the pension, given me by your Royal Grandfather, to be stopped by force. I shall resign it for the payment of my debts, and with it the name of an English subject and the slavery at present annexed to it. And as your Majesty has given publicity to this business, by your Majesty's orders to Consular agents, I surely cannot be blamed for following your royal example."

It was the coldest, proudest letter that was ever written to a queen. Two copies were dispatched; one was enclosed in a letter to Lord Palmerston and one was sent under cover to the Duke of Wellington, to whom Lady Hester wrote at the same time, explaining her conduct. During the next few months she dictated letters to many of her old friends, to the Speaker, James Abercrombie, Sir Edward Sugden, to Lord Ebrington and Lord Hardwicke, who had both written, offering to do everything in their power to help her. She had only one wish, to make her correspondence public; she did not realize that another generation had grown up, who had no interest in Pitt's niece, for whom Chatham was but a name veiled in the mists of history and who would consider her claims to greatness as the crazy pretensions of a mad woman.

Spring came, her health improved, and by the end of March she was convalescent and able to sun herself in one of her garden alcoves. "A sofa covered with maroon coloured cloth, with flowered chintz cushions ran across the back of the alcove. On this she was leaning and, being dressed in her white *abah* with its large folds, she looked exactly like the statue of an antique Roman matron. Half-way up the avenue stood an attendant in a handsome *Nizam* dress, which is exceedingly becoming to youth, waiting her call. As I advanced towards her between two hedges—the one of double jessamine in full bud and the other of the bright green periwinkle with its blue flowers forming an azure band from one end to the other— I was struck with the magical illusion, which she contrived to throw around herself in the commonest circumstances of life." So wrote the doctor who was still under her spell.

Lady Hester was expecting a visitor. For the first time in many months she was opening her doors to a stranger who had made up his mind not to leave Syria before he had seen and spoken with her; who had bombarded her with flattering and enthusiastic letters, arousing her interest by his knowledge of astrology and the singularity of his pursuits. Pückler-Muskau, audacious German princeling, inveterate fortune-hunter and incorrigible reprobate, dare-devil rogue with a streak of genius and a strong philosophic bent, possessed all the qualities most likely to attract the mistress of Dahr Djoun. At first Lady Hester insisted that she was far too ill to receive any guests; even a business visit from her old friend Monsieur Guys had reduced her to a state of exhaustion and she needed every ounce of her strength to fight against her enemies. Then there was the question of expense. How could she afford to entertain a gentleman of his rank who was sure to travel with a numerous suite? And yet what a pleasure to talk once more to an educated man, to exchange ideas with someone of her own class, who in his letters assured her that he shared her views on many subjects. He was not only writing a book, but he also published articles in newspapers, and perhaps he would champion her troubles. Lady Hester weakened and the Prince was received at Djoun. The crumbling court-yards, shaken by the earthquake of the preceding year, once more re-echoed to the trampling of horses and the cries of Tartars.

Hermann Pückler-Muskau was a handsome man, whose fifty odd years sat lightly on his shoulders, and who still affected the airs of a dandy. "An immense Leghorn hat, lined under the brim with green taffetas, shaded his very fair complexion. An Arab *Keffiyah* was thrown over his shoulders in the shape of a scarf and a pair of blue pantaloons of ample dimensions marked the approach towards the Turkish *sherwals*, those indescribable brogues, which from their immense width take yards of cloth to make them, and his boots were Parisian in cut." But, unlike Lamartine with his lap-dog, he had the sense to leave his pet chameleon behind on his visits to her Ladyship, and the costume of a fop was counteracted by the bearing of a Prussian officer. His appearance delighted his hostess and she received him as a woman of the world "with an elegance and grace of manner not of everyday occurrence among Englishwomen, which, combined with the oriental dignity and repose of her bearing, gave her a peculiar charm." For many years Lady Hester had saluted her guests in the Eastern way, by laying her hand on her heart, and it is significant that she allowed the Prince to kiss that withered but still beautifully formed and aristocratic hand. Her vanity was not dead and in the doctor's memoirs one finds her pathetically asking him to interest the prince "not to write anything about her person, either as to her looks, figure, face or appearance, for what could anybody say of a person who had been ill for six months and in bed nearly four, that could be very pleasing to read?"

Pückler-Muskau respected her age and poverty and in his *Briefe eines Verstorbenen* he only dwells on the romantic qualities of 'the Queen of Palmyra.' Favoured by his hostess, he allowed himself certain liberties which few would have permitted themselves. He introduced an Abyssinian slave into her presence, a girl whom he treated quite officially as his mistress, and she condescended to cast her horoscope. Her Ladyship was singularly tolerant over the Prince's morals, for she also showed

great amiability to a handsome young Count, who occupied
a somewhat ambigious position in his household. At first she
found it hard to refuse anything to a man who was not only
learned in the occult sciences, but who sympathized with all
her troubles and she was confirmed in her high opinion of his
merits when, during a visit to her sacred mares, 'the horse born
saddled' stooped to lick his hand. These pampered animals
had long since grown too fat and they behaved 'like two old
princesses, obliged to grant an audience that bored them to
death.' Poor brutes! At Lady Hester's death they were sold to a
merchant of Beyrout, where the unaccustomed roughness of
their treatment caused them to pine away in a few months.

Prince Pückler put off his departure from day to day. The
Emir Bechir was awaiting him at Iptedin and, in order to
mortify her old enemy, Lady Hester took extra pleasure in
persuading him to prolong his visit. She amused, fascinated
and tyrannized him in turn; she forced him to swallow doses of
Epsom salts, to write at her dictation for interminable hours,
and when he tired her with his questions she thought nothing
of giving him a piece of her mind. The doctor, her faithful
companion of winter evenings, her only friend and confidant,
was treated with an icy coldness, so that even his patience was
exhausted and he had only one wish, to return to England.
When he told the Prince that he hoped to go home in the
summer Pückler replied, "You will surely not leave my lady
while she is so ill?" Meryon was far too loyal to pour out his
complaints to a stranger.

After a few days, Lady Hester found that her health could
not stand the strain of the Prince's visit and once more she
confided in her doctor. "He kills me by those long conversations, and he is so tiresome asking for this explanation and that
explanation." One evening, he had even asked her if a certain
Arab sheik had been her lover and it was on this occasion that
she made her famous reply—"the Arabs have never regarded me
either as a man or woman but as *un être à part*."

Prince Pückler took his leave with beautiful speeches and a

great display of emotion and as a parting gift he presented Lady Hester with a little black slave. His flamboyant *cortège* disappeared among the mulberry trees in the valley and once more the ruined courtyards of Djoun were wrapped in obscurity and silence. His exuberant presence and absurd fantasies had helped to enliven Hester's gloomy spirits, while his charming manners had reconciled her to the world, so that for a few days the doctor was entranced to find her in the best of humours and willing to entertain him with lively anecdotes of her youth. But soon her old querulousness returned and Meryon "was fairly worn off his legs by late hours, multiplied occupations and fruitless endeavours to soothe an irritated and neglected, although a high-born and gifted creature—the victim of fallen greatness, false hopes and superhuman efforts to effect vast projects of philanthropy and political combinations on small means and ruined resources." No wonder he longed for a peaceful old age; he had collected enough material for his memoirs and he had proved his devotion by giving the best years of his life to a woman who seemed determined not to appreciate his services. His health was shattered and he was on the verge of a nervous break-down.

In the year 1838 the Levant abounded with German noblemen and, towards the end of May, Lady Hester heard that a party of pilgrims, who had lost two of their number from the plague, had been placed in quarantine outside the town of Sidon. The kind monks of Dahr Mkhallas were willing to receive them but the Egyptian officers of health refused permission and they were forced to remain in tents by the seashore. They were said to be poor Germans and, in spite of all her worries, Hester's first thought was to provide for their comfort. Baskets of household remedies, of fruits and cooling syrups, were dispatched to the camp as "a humble offering from Lady Hester Stanhope to the sick Germans, with her request that they would make known their wants to her, whether for medicines or for whatever they might need." The first intimation that they were people of rank was when a letter arrived, signed by the Baron Buseck, requesting her to be kind enough to send her doctor as one of their party was ill. Her Ladyship commanded Meryon to attend on the invalid, but by now he had learnt how to refuse her arbitrary commands and, in spite of all her scoldings, he was determined not to run the risk of being contaminated by the plague. However, his fears and objections were overruled when a second letter arrived signed 'Maximilian, Duke of Bavaria.' Then he was only too anxious to saddle his horse and be off to Sidon, so as to pay his respects to a Prince of the blood royal. The illness of His Highness's black Mameluke proved to be typhus, so the party were released from quarantine and the Duke and his suite proposed to pay a visit to Djoun in order to thank Lady Hester for having lent them her doctor and supplied them with every comfort. Once more there was a bustle and flurry in the courtyards, the servants were decked out in their finery, the cracked china was sorted and re-sorted, the silver spoons were taken out of their hiding place. But on the day of the Duke's arrival, Lady Hester fell ill with a high fever and her guests were forced to turn back to Sidon, where they took the first boat for Europe.

Meanwhile rebellion had broken out all over Syria. The successful wars in the Hauran had given courage to the people of the mountains, and Maronites and Metoualys had united with the Druses to throw off the Egyptian yoke. The country swarmed with marauders and deserters; farms were pillaged and vineyards were trampled; the monks packed up their valuables; the peasants left their homes and in his palace of Iptedin, the Emir Bechir feared the vengeance of his people. Stricken with a mortal disease, without either money or resources, Hester Stanhope remained calm and unmoved. As soon as her fever abated she received the notables of the village, telling them to remain in their homes and that she herself would guarantee their safety. The Druses were her friends and if the wildest rebels were outside her gates, she would throw them open, knowing that not one of them would dare to touch her.

Her sanguine disposition, which had borne her through all these years of misery and hardship, now received two crushing blows. A cold, terse note from Lord Palmerston acknowledged her letter to the Queen and a diffuse, apologetic letter from Sir Francis Burdett dissipated every hope of her Irish inheritance. She had always been convinced that in the end her affairs would be righted and that her magnificent star which had led her through so many vicissitudes would rise once more in splendour. Pückler-Muskau had taken charge of duplicate copies of her correspondence, which he had promised to publish in the papers, but nothing had been heard. She did not know that the Prince was far too anxious to secure an English heiress to embroil himself with Her Majesty's Government.

Now the die was cast; this was the end of her ambitious schemes, her dreams of greatness. Her reaction to her poverty makes one realize that, in spite of all her speculations on sublime subjects, Lady Hester remained a materialist to the last. Her hopes were chained to the world she had suffered in; her glories were to be witnessed by her fellow-creatures, and her Messiah was a man of flesh and blood with a blazing sword in his hand. She, who had been deprived of everything she held most dear, now condemned herself to solitude and confinement. The doctor must leave and, with a few servants and Logmagi to assist her, she would remain immured till it pleased God to relieve her troubles. She would wall up her gates, leaving only an opening large enough to admit a cow or a beast of burden, and "if anyone tried to force her retirement, they would be received by her as Lord Camelford would have received them." She doomed herself to this living death and her doctor had no choice but to obey. He could do little to help her at Djoun and in England he could still carry out her cherished plan of publishing her correspondence. Alas! her grievances aroused nothing but ridicule and derision; the Press was hostile and her only champion was her old friend, Sir William Napier, who, in a letter to *The Times*, gave a noble vindication of her character and reputation, for no other reason than that "in early life he was an inmate of Mr. Pitt's house, when Lady Hester was the mistress of it and when those who now insulted her would have been too happy to lick the dust from her shoes."

On the 6th August the doctor departed with many tears and self-reproaches. He has incurred the censure of generations for having left his patient in these circumstances. Lady Hester's niece, the Duchess of Cleveland, is particularly severe on the subject of his desertion and she does not pay the slightest tribute of gratitude to a man who for over thirty years allowed himself to be the selfless and willing drudge of a woman who never gave him a sign of genuine affection. In one of her last letters to Lord Hardwicke, dated after Meryon's departure, Lady Hester writes: "Should you see the doctor in England, recollect that his *only* good quality in my sight is, I believe, being very honest in money matters; no other do I grant him; without judgment, without heart he goes through the world, like many others, blundering his way; and often from his want of accuracy doing mischief every time he opens his mouth." Surely these are the cruellest words she ever wrote.

Even when Meryon was back in England, he still spent his time in carrying out her instructions and commissions. She wrote to him once a month giving him the trifling details of her dreary hermit life and she often spoke of her approaching end, for she was persuaded that she would not die in her bed, but that she would be killed fighting. A dramatic, spectacular death was the last hope of Chatham's granddaughter.

Her proud, lonely spirit refused to give in, and in the last fortnight of her life, with failing eyesight and trembling hands, she wrote to Lord Hardwicke: "Do not be unhappy about my future fate. I have done what I believe my duty, the duty of everyone of *every* religion. I have no reproaches to make myself, but that I went rather too far; but such is my nature and a happy nature too, which can make up its mind to everything but *insult*. I have been treated like a vile criminal, but God is great!"

EPILOGUE
(1839)

ON a hot, breathless day in June, when the peasants were harvesting in the valleys and the bulbuls sang in the hedges, when the crests of Mount Lebanon floated pale and insubstantial in the thin, clear air and the roses in Lady Hester's gardens dripped their last store of dew on the gravel paths, a murmur rose in the cornfields and echoed across the mountains, passing from mouth to mouth, from village to village – the news that the *Sytt* was dead. Gaining in volume and significance, it echoed throughout the bazaars of Sidon, where even her duns and creditors paid tribute to her greatness; echoing across the orange sands of Beyrout, by the waving pines of Fakhredin to the white doors of the British Consulate.

She was buried by night in her garden by one of the Consuls whom she hated and one of the missionaries whom she despised, and, though she had renounced her rights as a British subject, they wrapped her in the English flag. Her servants bore her coffin to the arbour of jessamine and roses, where they laid her to rest at the side of the young French captain whose stars had been in affinity with her own. And only the peasants of Mount Lebanon paid homage to the memory of Lady Hester Stanhope, the last of the eighteenth-century eccentrics, the first of the nineteenth-century pioneers.

GENEALOGICAL TABLES

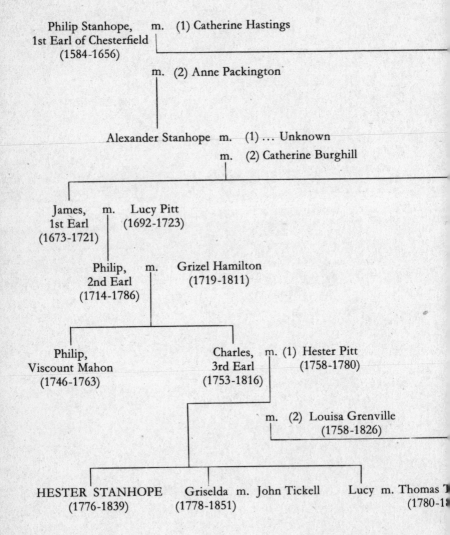

Philip Stanhope,   m.   (1) Catherine Hastings
1st Earl of Chesterfield
(1584-1656)

m.   (2) Anne Packington

Alexander Stanhope   m.   (1) ... Unknown
m.   (2) Catherine Burghill

James,   m.   Lucy Pitt
1st Earl   (1692-1723)
(1673-1721)

Philip,   m.   Grizel Hamilton
2nd Earl   (1719-1811)
(1714-1786)

Philip,   Charles,   m. (1) Hester Pitt
Viscount Mahon   3rd Earl   (1758-1780)
(1746-1763)   (1753-1816)

m.   (2) Louisa Grenville
(1758-1826)

HESTER STANHOPE   Griselda m. John Tickell   Lucy m. Thomas T
(1776-1839)   (1778-1851)   (1780-1

THE STANHOPES OF CHEVENING

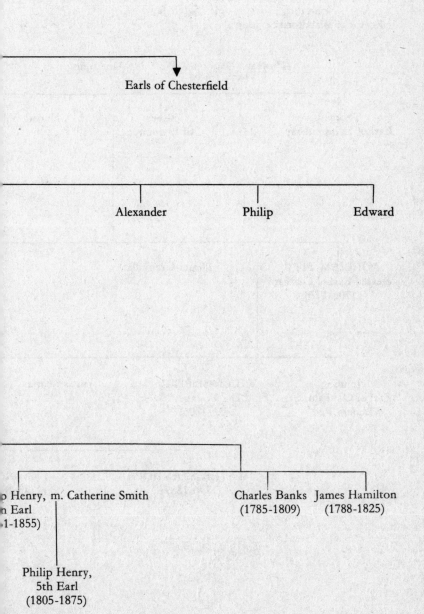

Earls of Chesterfield

Alexander   Philip   Edward

p Henry, m. Catherine Smith
n Earl
1-1855)

Philip Henry,
5th Earl
(1805-1875)

Charles Banks   James Hamilton
(1785-1809)   (1788-1825)

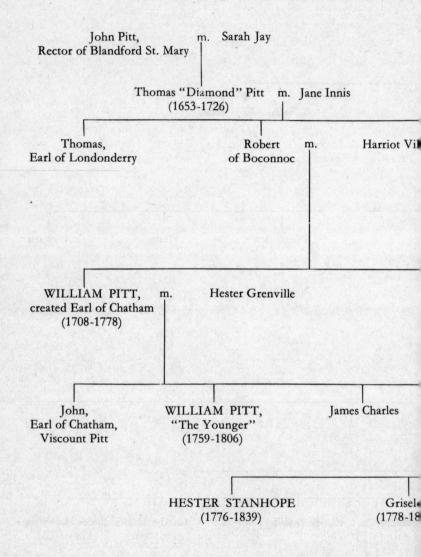

John Pitt,
Rector of Blandford St. Mary   m.   Sarah Jay

Thomas "Diamond" Pitt   m.   Jane Innis
(1653-1726)

Thomas,
Earl of Londonderry

Robert   m.   Harriot Vil
of Boconnoc

WILLIAM PITT,   m.   Hester Grenville
created Earl of Chatham
(1708-1778)

John,
Earl of Chatham,
Viscount Pitt

WILLIAM PITT,
"The Younger"
(1759-1806)

James Charles

HESTER STANHOPE
(1776-1839)

Grisel
(1778-18

THE FAMILY OF "PITT OF THE DOWN"

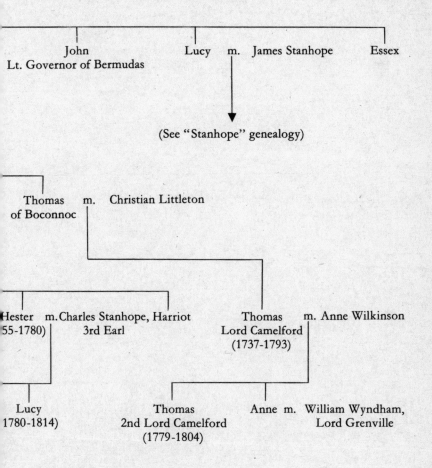

John
Lt. Governor of Bermudas
Lucy m. James Stanhope
Essex

(See "Stanhope" genealogy)

Thomas m. Christian Littleton
of Boconnoc

Hester m. Charles Stanhope, Harriot
55-1780)   3rd Earl

Thomas m. Anne Wilkinson
Lord Camelford
(1737-1793)

Lucy
1780-1814)

Thomas
2nd Lord Camelford
(1779-1804)

Anne m. William Wyndham,
Lord Grenville

GLOSSARY OF EASTERN TERMS

Aakel	A Druse Priest.
Abah	A Bedouin cloak.
Ansary Mountains	A mountainous region in the north of Syria.
Bairam	A Mahomedan festival which takes place twice yearly.
Baksheesh	Gratuity, alms.
Bostangi	An advance-guard in the Sultan's procession.
Capidgi Bachi or Zaym	A confidential officer of the Sultan.
Dahr	House, couvent.
Dahr El Sytt	The house of the princess.
Druse	A member of the secret religious sect of Mohamedan origin, inhabiting Mount Lebanon.
Firman	A passport from the Sultan entitling the holder to especial honours.
Keffiyah	Bedouin Arab's kerchief used as head-dress.
Korbash	A knotted whip.
Kyrios	One Greek name for Lord.
Maronite	A sect of Syrian Christians dwelling in the Lebanon.
Melika	Queen.
Metoualy	A religious sect following the tenets of the Levitical Code.
Nizam	Member of the Turkish regular army, dress of.
Ramadan	Ninth month in the Mahomedan year, a time of rigid fasting.
Sytt	Princess, lady.
Tacterwan	A litter drawn by mules.
Vails	Tips to servants.

Yataghan	Mahomedan sword without guard or cross-piece.
Mahmoud	Sultan at the time of Lady Hester's residence in the East.
Mehemet Ali	Viceroy of Egypt appointed by the Sultan. Declared his independence in 1832.
Ibrahim, his son	Conqueror of Syria and Asia Minor.